G·R·E·A·T EXPECTATIONS

The
Essential Guide to Breastfeeding

Marianne Neifert, MD

STERLING

New York / London
www.sterlingpublishing.com

Library of Congress Cataloging-in-Publication Data

Neifert, Marianne R.
  Great expectations : the essential guide to breastfeeding /
Marianne Neifert.
    p. cm.
  Includes index.
  ISBN 978-1-4027-5817-1 (pbk. with flaps)
  1. Breastfeeding--Popular works. I. Title.
  RJ216.N435 2009
  649'.33--dc22

                        2009005248

        2 4 6 8 10 9 7 5 3 1

Published by Sterling Publishing Co., Inc.
387 Park Avenue South, New York, NY 10016
Text © 2009 by Marianne Neifert, M.D.
Illustrations © 2009 by Laura Hartman-Maestro
Distributed in Canada by Sterling Publishing
C/o Canadian Manda Group, 165 Dufferin Street
Toronto, Ontario, Canada M6K 3H6
Distributed in the United Kingdom by GMC Distribution Services
Castle Place, 166 High Street, Lewes, East Sussex, England BN7 1XU
Distributed in Australia by Capricorn Link (Australia) Pty. Ltd.
P.O. Box 704, Windsor, NSW 2756, Australia

Sterling ISBN 978-1-4027-5817-1

For information about custom editions, special sales, premium and
corporate purchases, please contact Sterling Special Sales
Department at 800-805-5489 or
specialsales@sterlingpublishing.com.

DEDICATION & ACKNOWLEDGMENTS

This book is dedicated to those selfless breastfeeding champions in every community who tirelessly assist new parents in giving their babies the best possible start in life through successful breastfeeding.

No task as daunting as authoring a book can be undertaken without benefit of sustained sources of information, inspiration, expertise, and emotional support. I want to gratefully acknowledge those many individuals who have educated, emboldened, or encouraged me in this labor of love and through other life challenges:

My much adored children and bonus in-law children (in parentheses): Peter (Courtney) Neifert; Paige Neifert; Tricie Neifert; Heather (Phil) de Maine; Mark (Becky) Neifert—together with my treasured grandchildren—Brandon, Lindsey, Avery, Trey, Joey, and Mason—for being my anchors and the greatest joys in my life.

My cherished parents, the late Mary Annabel and the late Andrew M. Egeland, Sr., for nurturing me with an endless sense of possibility.

My beloved brothers and sisters and in-law siblings (in parentheses): Andrew M. Egeland, Jr. (Marie); Marcella A. Poncelow (Chuck); Aleta E. Boylan; Thomas A. Egeland (Charlene), for sustaining me with a lifetime of love and encouragement.

The countless breastfeeding mothers who have sought my help to overcome their lactation challenges, for continually inspiring me by the depth of their commitment to succeed at breastfeeding.

Joy Seacat, PhD, PA, RN, for co-founding The Lactation Program with me in 1985 and for all we learned, discerned, and contributed together to the field of breastfeeding medicine.

The numerous clinicians and support staff who have worked at The Lactation Program since its inception, for their essential contributions.

The current extraordinary staff at The Lactation Program: Amy Lutz, RN, IBCLC, Program Director; Marianne Kmak, RN, BSN, IBCLC, and Cathy Heise, RN, IBCLC, LCCE; Lenna Gregory, CLE, and Jenny Chockley, for their untiring dedication and unsurpassed expert and compassionate care of breastfeeding mother-baby pairs and for reviewing the book and providing valuable feedback;

The Colorado Health Foundation for their generous support in sponsoring The Lactation Program since 1998 and for their leadership in acknowledging the critical role of successful breastfeeding in promoting optimal maternal-child health and well-being.

My much admired Colorado colleagues and steadfast friends who regularly attend the Lactation Journal Club—hosted by The Lactation

Program for over 20 years—for renewing and invigorating me at each monthly gathering.

My knowledgeable and esteemed colleagues in the American Academy of Pediatrics Section on Breastfeeding, the Academy of Breastfeeding Medicine, and the International Lactation Consultant Association for consistently enlightening and challenging me.

Jennifer Dellaport, RD, MPH, Betty Heerman, RN, CLE, Lisbeth Gabrielski, RN, BSN, IBCLC, and Maya Bunik, MD, MSPH, FABM, for their inspiring example, empowering support, and enduring friendship.

The tens of thousands of health professionals who have attended my breastfeeding presentations nationwide over more than three decades, for energizing me with their enthusiasm and for their commitment to promote, support, and manage breastfeeding.

La Leche League International—most especially founding member, Mary Ann Kerwin, JD—for indelibly influencing my mothering and my professional career.

Faith Hamlin, my long-time literary agent and faithful advocate, for her unwavering support and for being the catalyst for this project.

Jennifer Williams, my extraordinary editor at Sterling Publishing, for laboring unstintingly to make this manuscript so "mom-friendly" and for serving as a skilled midwife in birthing the book.

Hannah Reich, project editor at Sterling Publishing, and Melanie Gold, copyeditor, for expert fine-tuning.

Fritz Metsch, art director at Sterling Publishing, and Laura Hartman Maestro, who produced the superb illustrations, for making the book so visually appealing.

My heartfelt appreciation is also extended to the countless unnamed individuals who have collectively taught me about the art, the science, and the heart of breastfeeding.

Contents

Introduction

I like to think that I have been preparing to write this book for the past forty years. It has been that long since I ventured to breastfeed my own first baby as a young premedical student at the University of Hawaii, thousands of miles from my extended family. Despite my youth and inexperience, few sources of support, no breastfeeding role models, and the challenge of attending school full time, breastfeeding my baby proved to be an immensely rewarding and worthwhile experience. Over the next seven years, I gave birth to four more children, each arriving during progressive phases of my medical training. While I savored the privilege of breastfeeding each of my first four children, I also experienced a profound sense of loss and disappointment when breastfeeding ended before I had wanted and sooner than my babies deserved. At the time I was breastfeeding and attending school or completing my pediatric residency training, today's convenient double electric breast pumps had not yet been invented and handling a "bodily fluid" at the workplace was unthinkable. Inevitably, the frequency of my breastfeeding diminished and my milk supply declined during long separations from my babies.

When my fifth child was born on the final day of my pediatric training, I was determined to change my priorities and restructure my life to accommodate unrestricted breastfeeding. I took an adequate maternity leave, read voraciously about breastfeeding, sought mother-to-mother support through La Leche League, and worked only part-time for the first year of my baby's life. Getting breastfeeding right and being able to nurse my last baby for as long as we both desired was one of the greatest gifts I gave to both of us.

My career in counseling women on breastfeeding and managing lactation difficulties began early in my medical training. As a young female intern and resident having and nursing my own babies—when there were still few women in medicine—new mothers sought me out for help and support for their breastfeeding challenges. As U.S. breastfeeding rates began to rise, the number of nursing mothers seeking my advice steadily grew, and I became increasingly more knowledgeable about the successful management of breastfeeding, the benefits of human milk, the physiology of lactation, and how to troubleshoot breastfeeding problems. In 1985, I co-founded The Lactation Program in Denver—one of the very first breastfeeding centers in the nation—to enable women to overcome common and complex breastfeeding difficulties and to educate health professionals about lactation management. I have conducted breastfeeding research and played a key role in introducing many of the interventions used in breastfeeding medicine today, including double pumping, pumping after feedings to increase milk production, and weighing babies before and after nursing to measure their milk consumption during breastfeeding. My work has been instrumental in identifying lactation risk factors in mothers and recognizing infants at risk for inadequate breastfeeding. In looking back over my lengthy career, I have found it enormously gratifying to witness the dramatic rise in national breastfeeding rates, the emergence of the role of lactation consultants, an explosion in breastfeeding technology, the enactment of breastfeeding legislation, an increase in workplace accommodations for nursing mothers, numerous national breastfeeding initiatives, and much more breastfeeding education for health professionals. Yet, each year in the U.S., more than 4 million new mothers need to rediscover the benefits and learn the basics of breastfeeding. Because today's mothers represent a wide diversity of lifestyles, support systems, priorities, circumstances, and ease of breastfeeding, there is no single recipe for a successful breastfeeding experience. Some women consider breastfeeding to be an integral part of their parenting style and nurse their babies for several years. Others may not relish breastfeeding, yet they make the commitment to nurse their babies for a time in order to provide them superior nutrition and immune benefits. A few mothers opt out of direct breastfeeding, choosing instead to pump their milk and feed it by bottle. Those who face significant challenges may be unable to breastfeed fully, through no fault of their own. Each new nursing mother ultimately makes her breastfeeding experience uniquely hers, based on her own reality.

My purpose in writing this book is to help you reach your personal breastfeeding goals and to help make your breastfeeding experience a thoroughly enjoyable one. I have offered realistic, practical, and empowering information gleaned from decades of experience to help give you the best possible start to nursing your baby. Using this information, you may be able to prevent common lactation problems and get breastfeeding back on track whenever difficulties arise. Because your baby will never be easier to care for than during your pregnancy, I urge you to read at least the first seven chapters before you give birth. You will want to refer again to Chapters 3, 4, and 5—covering your hospital experience, breastfeeding techniques, expected norms, common early problems, and new-parent concerns—when you begin breastfeeding. If you plan to express your milk, whether for convenience or necessity, review Chapter 6 for an in-depth discussion of pumping, storing, and handling expressed breastmilk. Once you get settled into your breastfeeding routines, look over Chapter 7 again, dealing with daily life as a breastfeeding mom. You can refer to Chapter 8 for solutions to specific breastfeeding problems as they arise. If you anticipate working outside the home, you will want to read Chapter 9 during your pregnancy and review it at least one month before going back to work. Chapter 10 is devoted to special circumstances, such as breastfeeding a hospitalized sick or premature newborn, nursing twins, and the impact of breast surgery on breastfeeding.

Because breastfeeding involves both art and science, and because every woman's experience is unique, breastfeeding advice sometimes varies among lactation experts. I acknowledge that there often is more than one approach to a problem and I trust you to tailor differing advice to your individual circumstances. Few memories are as precious to me as the recollection of breastfeeding my five babies, and few experiences now are more treasured than seeing my children's children successfully breastfeeding. I wrote this book—condensing my knowledge, experience, and abundant concern for parents and children—to offer a new generation of mothers a roadmap and trusted guide to experiencing the immeasurable joy and fulfillment of breastfeeding.

G·R·E·A·T
EXPECTATIONS

The
Essential
Guide to
Breastfeeding

Why
Breastfeed?

1

Congratulations! If you are reading this book, you are thinking about or have decided to breastfeed your baby. No material item you ever can buy will be as precious to your baby as this gift of yourself. As you prepare for your journey into parenthood, remember that only a mother can give her baby the priceless gifts of superior nutrition, improved health, optimal development, and unique intimacy through breastfeeding. No wonder more than three out of four new mothers in the United States breastfeed their babies. This book was written to guide you in achieving a thoroughly enjoyable and successful breastfeeding experience.

The advantages of breastfeeding over feeding with formula are numerous, diverse, and compelling. These benefits affect not only babies, they extend to mothers, families, and society, too. No doubt, you want to breastfeed because you already know that your milk is best for your baby. You may be more interested in the how-to of breastfeeding than the litany of advantages. Yet, learning more about the benefits of breastfeeding and human milk can strengthen your commitment to continue nursing your baby during those tough times when you wonder whether breastfeeding is worth the effort. For millions of mothers, the answer is a resounding "yes!"

The Health Benefits of Breastfeeding Your Baby

Most expectant parents are aware that human milk is better for their babies than infant formula in terms of nutritional quality, immune benefits, and the intimacy of the breastfeeding relationship. While there are many factors that may influence your decision to nurse your baby, most women choose to breastfeed because they know they are giving their babies countless health benefits each time they nurse.

HUMAN MILK IS MEANT FOR HUMAN BABIES!

One of the strongest arguments that your milk is the ideal food for your baby comes from scientific evidence that each species of mammals (and there are more than four thousand!) makes milk that is uniquely designed to meet the specific growth needs of its young. Not only does milk composition differ widely among mammals, the frequency of feedings and the number of nipples varies according to the special needs of each species. For example, aquatic and cold-weather mammals, like whales and polar bears, produce milk with an extremely high fat content to maintain an essential layer of insulating blubber.

Because human milk is so dilute, newborns nurse very frequently—every few hours, around the clock. This frequent feeding pattern provides an additional benefit. As you cuddle your baby at your breast to nurse him, the distance between his eyes and your face is ideal for his focusing on you. Thus, an intimate bond is forged between the two of you each time you nourish your baby.

WHAT MAKES YOUR MILK SO GREAT?

While infant formulas have been widely used in the United States for more than eighty years, no formula will ever be able to exactly duplicate your own milk. Cow's milk–based formulas and soy formulas will always represent a *distant* second choice. Not only is it impossible to change the milk of one mammal into that of another, all the ingredients in human milk have not yet been identified. Scientists continually discover new properties in human milk that are absent in formulas or gain new understandings about the function of a previously known component of human milk. Many ingredients in breastmilk, including most of the immune properties, simply cannot be incorporated into infant formulas.

Manufacturers are able to produce infant formulas containing approximately the same *percentage* of protein, fat, and carbohydrate as human milk, but the *quality* of each of these major nutrients differs significantly from the composition of breastmilk. Even minor differences between human milk and infant formula could have important consequences, since a newborn is totally dependent on a single food during the early months of critical growth and development. While quality infant formulas are essential for those infants whose mothers cannot or choose not to breastfeed, your own milk is uniquely superior to any breastmilk substitute.

A Healthy Trend

Many factors contribute to the steady increase in breastfeeding in recent decades, including intense breastfeeding promotion, especially by the Special Supplemental Nutrition Program for Women, Infants, and Children (WIC). In addition, there are greater numbers of lactation consultants; increased availability of specialized lactation services and electric breast pumps; more work-site support for employed breastfeeding women; more information and support for women delivering high-risk infants; increased breastfeeding education for health professionals; and additional research confirming the health benefits of breastfeeding.

IDEAL FOOD FOR YOUR BABY

All infant feeding experts agree that human milk is nature's perfect food for babies and that mother's milk is uniquely suited to promote optimal infant growth and development. Human milk contains more than two hundred ingredients—proteins, fats, carbohydrates, vitamins, minerals, trace metals, growth factors, hormones, enzymes, antibodies, white blood cells, and more—each in ideal proportion to the others. This precise symphony of ingredients cannot possibly be duplicated artificially. The unique components in human milk are far more than essential nutrients, since many play multiple roles in promoting the health and development of babies. For example, some nutrients also enhance the immune system, while others promote optimal brain development.

Protein. The *proteins* in human milk not only provide necessary building blocks for growth, they also perform other vital functions, including helping to protect babies from illness. The proportion of whey in human milk (70 percent) and casein (30 percent) differs markedly from cow's milk (18 percent whey, 82 percent casein). Whey proteins are more easily digested and include disease-fighting antibodies and other important immune properties. Human milk has less protein than infant formulas, but the protein it does contain is used more efficiently by babies. During digestion, proteins break down into amino acids. The composition of the amino acids in human milk is different from cow's milk or infant formulas and perfectly meets the unique metabolic requirements of infants. Human milk protein also forms a softer curd in your baby's stomach and is more easily digested than formula curd. Because their stomachs empty sooner, breastfed babies eat more often than formula-fed infants.

Fat. The *fats* in human milk provide its major source of calories and are essential for the optimal development of your infant's brain and nervous system. Your breastmilk conveniently contains the enzyme lipase, which helps your baby digest fat. Human milk is rich in long-chained polyunsaturated fatty acids, including docosahexaenoic acid (DHA), an essential omega-3 fatty acid, and arachidonic acid (ARA). ARA and DHA are present in your baby's rapidly developing brain and eye tissue and are associated with improved vision and development. This finding has spurred manufacturers to add DHA and ARA to infant formulas.

Carbohydrate. The predominant *carbohydrate* found in milk is *lactose*, also known as milk sugar because it is found only in milk. In addition to being an important source of calories and energy, lactose improves the absorption of certain minerals, including calcium. Lactose also promotes the growth of harmless gut bacteria in your breastfed baby's intestine. These benign bowel germs create an acid environment that helps protect babies from infant diarrhea by keeping harmful bacteria in check. *Probiotics* (beneficial bacteria) are being added to some infant formulas to try to replicate this health benefit of human milk.

PROTECTION AGAINST INFECTIOUS DISEASES

Breastmilk contains many substances that boost your baby's immune system, including a special type of antibody, known as secretory IgA, enzymes, white blood cells, and other immune components. Within a few days of being exposed to a germ, specific antibodies appear in your milk to help protect your baby against the same germs you encounter.

OTHER BENEFITS OF BREASTFEEDING FOR YOUR BABY

Some studies show that breastfeeding reduces the risk of sudden infant death syndrome (SIDS) and may reduce the risk of diabetes in childhood. Breastfeeding also has been linked with a reduced risk of childhood leukemia. Evidence suggests that breastfeeding provides significant protection against inflammatory bowel disease (including Crohn's disease and ulcerative colitis). These chronic digestive disorders can cause diarrhea, fever, poor growth, and other symptoms. In addition, breastfeeding has been shown to reduce the risk of childhood obesity. The longer

the duration of breastfeeding, the greater the protective effect against childhood weight problems. Although breastfed babies have a lower risk of developing eczema (atopic dermatitis) and allergy to cow's milk, research is inconclusive concerning whether breastfeeding helps protect against other allergic diseases, including asthma and other food allergies.

YOUR BABY'S BRAIN DEVELOPMENT

Many of the hormones and growth factors in human milk only recently have been identified, and their importance to babies is not yet fully understood. These precisely regulated hormones may influence the timing of certain developmental events. We know so little about the various hormones and growth factors in human milk, it is impossible to try to duplicate them in formulas. Meanwhile, no one knows if a baby's diet in early life will later affect his well-being as a senior citizen.

Whether early infant nutrition has a long-term impact on brain development remains controversial. However, several studies involving both full-term and preterm infants have found a link between breastfeeding and later cognitive performance. Children who were breastfed as infants achieved significantly higher scores on a variety of intelligence tests compared to those who had been fed formula. The differences attributed to breastfeeding were distinct from other factors known to influence intelligence, such

Nature's Perfect Food

Unlike infant formula, human milk is a dynamic fluid that varies in composition, depending on the stage of lactation, your diet, the time of day, and the duration of the feeding.

- *Colostrum*, the thick yellowish first milk your breasts produce, is easily digested by your newborn baby. Although colostrum is supplied in small quantities compared to mature milk, it is high in protein and rich in antibodies and other immunities, making it baby's first immunization.

- Approximately two to three days after your baby is born, abundant milk production begins with *transitional milk* that rapidly increases in quantity and gradually changes to *mature milk* within about ten days.

- Mature milk is lower in protein than colostrum and higher in lactose and fat. Although thinner in appearance, mature milk provides ideal nutrition for your baby.

- The fat content of your milk is low at the beginning of a feeding when your breast is full, then increases throughout the feeding as your breast is drained.

- Your diet affects the flavor of your milk. This early exposure to a variety of tastes will help increase your baby's acceptance of solid foods later on.

Super Milk

- In both developing countries and industrialized nations, breastfeeding helps protect babies from infectious diseases, including diarrhea, ear infections, lower respiratory infections, spinal meningitis, bloodstream infections, and urinary tract infections. It has been estimated that more than 1 million infant lives worldwide could be saved if all babies were breastfed.

- Premature babies are particularly susceptible to a serious, potentially life-threatening bowel infection known as necrotizing enterocolitis, commonly referred to as NEC. Premature infants who are fed human milk are less likely to develop NEC (and if they do, their cases will tend to be less severe) than premature babies who are fed infant formula.

- Breastfed babies are less likely to suffer severe bouts of diarrhea and vomiting than formula-fed infants, and continued breastfeeding is well tolerated during intestinal illnesses. The protective effect of human milk against diarrhea is greatest while a baby is exclusively breastfed.

- Ear infections are the most common childhood illness for which parents seek medical attention. Breastfed babies who nurse exclusively for four to six months experience only half as many ear infections as formula-fed babies.

as education and socioeconomic status of the parents.

SECURITY AND COMFORT

The breastfeeding relationship involves unique giving and receiving between you and your baby. Your baby has a regular and vital need for your milk and for physical closeness, and your full breasts regularly need to be relieved and drained. Breastfeeding assures that you and your baby remain intimately connected through the making and taking of milk. This reciprocal interaction can deepen the bond between you and your baby and will continue long after breastmilk ceases to be the sole source of his nutrition.

SOCIAL INTERACTION

Your breastfed baby has the privilege of being held for every nursing, and enjoys opportunities for frequent social interaction during feedings. On the other hand, the formula-fed infant who learns to hold his bottle—or worse yet, has it propped for him—may

Breastfeeding provides compelling health benefits for you and your baby.

be required to take his feeding alone, without the presence of an attentive caretaker—like you—with whom to socialize. As he feeds from alternate breasts, your nursing baby receives bilateral visual stimulation as well, in contrast to a bottle-fed baby who typically is held the same way for all feedings.

The Benefits for You

In addition to all the health benefits of breastfeeding for your baby, there are many ways that nursing improves your own health and well-being.

SHRINKING YOUR UTERUS AND REDUCING BLOOD LOSS

During the first few days after delivery, you may notice some abdominal cramps when you nurse your baby. This sensation is due to uterine contractions and is triggered by the release of oxytocin during breastfeeding. Oxytocin not only plays a key role in releasing milk from your breasts to make it readily available to your baby (see Chapter 4, page 80), it also helps shrink your uterus back to its normal size after delivery and reduces blood loss. In developing countries, where access to medical care may be limited, routine breastfeeding immediately after delivery helps protect against postpartum hemorrhage.

DELAYED MENSTRUAL PERIODS

If you breastfeed exclusively without giving your baby formula supplements, the return of your menstrual periods may be postponed for many months to a year or more. Amenorrhea (lack of menstrual periods) conserves iron stores and helps your body replenish the iron lost during pregnancy, childbirth, and postpartum bleeding. The suppression of your menstrual cycle during exclusive breastfeeding also offers a temporary contraceptive effect after the birth of your baby, although this effect declines over time. (See Chapter 7, pages 169–170.)

REDUCED RISK OF BREAST AND OVARIAN CANCER

A number of studies have found that breastfeeding has a significant protective effect against breast cancer, particularly if you are pre-menopausal. Many risk factors for breast cancer are beyond your control, such as heredity, family history, when you started menstruating, when you delivered your first baby, and your age at menopause. Research has also shown that the longer you breastfeed, over the course of your lifetime, the greater the protection against breast cancer. It is also believed that if you were breastfed yourself, you may have a lowered risk of breast cancer, and several studies have shown that breastfeeding may have a protective effect against ovarian cancer.

WEIGHT LOSS AFTER BIRTH

Producing milk for your baby uses about five hundred additional calories each day from your stores of body fat. While you are breastfeeding, you may lose about two pounds a month—especially from your lower body—for the first six months. Nursing your baby may help you return to your pre-pregnancy weight sooner than if you feed infant formula.

CONVENIENCE

When you breastfeed, you can easily take your baby anywhere, confident that your milk will be ready for him whenever he is hungry. Despite power outages, snowstorms, hurricanes, or other natural disasters, and in the absence of drinkable water, you can always feed your hungry baby. Breastfeeding in the middle of the night is more convenient than going to the kitchen to mix and warm a bottle of formula—and traveling or camping with a nursing baby is far easier than bringing formula on every outing.

CALMING BREAKS

The hormones prolactin and oxytocin, which are released during breastfeeding, have been called "mothering" hormones because they produce a peaceful, nurturing sensation. Taking a break during your busy day to nurse your baby actually has a calming effect. You and your baby each benefit and feel satisfaction as a result of this mutual giving and receiving.

SAVINGS

This is not to say that breastfeeding is completely free, but you will spend a lot less if you nurse than

---

More Benefits for You

For women without a history of gestational diabetes, breastfeeding has been found to reduce the risk of later developing type 2 diabetes. A recent study found that midlife women who had breastfed were less likely to develop metabolic syndrome and that a longer duration of breastfeeding provided even greater protection. Metabolic syndrome is a clustering of health risks—high blood pressure, obesity, abnormal cholesterol and triglyceride levels, and a reduced response to insulin—that increase your chances of developing heart disease, stroke, and diabetes. Some studies show that breastfeeding helps reduce the risk of osteoporosis and hip fracture after menopause, and a recent one found that breastfeeding for more than a year reduced women's risk of developing rheumatoid arthritis.

you would on infant formula (approximately $1,500 a year). However, a chunk of the money you save by breastfeeding may be spent on renting or buying an effective breast pump or paying a lactation consultant if you're having breastfeeding problems. Consider this money well spent to give your baby the best start in life.

A SPECIAL WAY TO BE A MOM

Breastfeeding is a style of mothering and nurturing as much as it is an act of nourishing your baby. Nursing serves not only as a source of life-sustaining food, but also as a way to provide warmth, comfort, and security for your baby. Whether your newborn is crying for food or human contact, his needs will be met by nursing. And whether your toddler just bumped his head or received a booster shot, nursing instantly calms and comforts life's woes.

How Your Partner Can Benefit

You might not have considered the many ways your baby's father can benefit from being part of a breastfeeding family. Although fathers often worry that they will feel left out of the breastfeeding experience, they are also influenced positively when their babies are breastfed.

A HEALTHIER PARTNER AND BABY

A father naturally wants to ensure the welfare of his partner and his baby. His support, encouragement, and direct help can be the decisive factors in your breastfeeding success. (See Chapter 5, pages 127–128, for more tips on how fathers can help support breastfeeding.) When his baby is breastfed, a father is proud and confident, knowing that he has contributed to the healthiest outcome for his baby and partner. Fewer infant illnesses mean less disruption of family life and less expense, while the long-term health benefits for you can have a positive impact on your quality of life.

EASE

When you breastfeed, middle-of-the night nursings are minimally disruptive because no one has to get up and shuffle into the kitchen to prepare a bottle. Your breastfed baby can be fed anywhere without any preparation or fuss, and he can be consoled in virtually any setting, simply by nursing.

ANOTHER WAY TO APPRECIATE YOUR BODY

Breastfeeding offers an entirely new way for your partner to perceive and appreciate your body. Your breasts, which give and receive so much pleasure to you and your partner as lovers, literally give life and nurturance to the baby you have created together.

Changing the Way Children Think About Breastfeeding

Today's children are bombarded with images of bottle-feeding babies. Dolls come with bottles, and formula feeding is highly visible in our society. Because public breastfeeding is uncommon, few children gain exposure to the functional role of the breast. When children see breastfeeding as a routine part of family life, they grow up assuming it is the natural way to feed a baby. As a little girl lifts her shirt and simulates breastfeeding her doll or stuffed animal, she is empowered to nurse her own babies someday.

Gains for Society

The decision to breastfeed affects more than just you, your baby, and your own family. It has a powerful impact on our society by affecting the health of millions of mothers and babies, the economy, and the environment.

HEALTHIER CITIZENS

The babies being born today will be our country's leaders tomorrow. The nutrition they receive in infancy will serve as the cornerstone of their optimal growth and development. When our nation's children are given every chance to reach their full potential, all of us stand to benefit. Conversely, when babies face health disadvantages because of their early diet, we all pay the price.

GREENER LIFESTYLE

Artificial formula eats up resources and creates enormous waste. And while it is true that women who breastfeed are using an increasing number of breast pumps, bottles, nipples, and storage bags, the environmental impact of breastfeeding is low compared to the resources used and industrial waste generated by feeding a baby formula for a year.

What Keeps Some Women from Breastfeeding?

Despite everything we know about the significant benefits of breastfeeding, there are still a number of social and personal barriers that prevent some women from beginning and continuing to nurse their babies:

- **Health professionals' attitudes and lack of knowledge.** Although some health providers are virtual breastfeeding champions, many have little knowledge about the practical management of breastfeeding problems and confess to feeling unprepared to assist breastfeeding mothers. Fortunately, a growing number of physician-training programs are implementing innovative curricula to teach breastfeeding, and many female practitioners have nursed their own babies.

- **The hospital experience and early discharge.** While almost every hospital in the United States has adopted some family-centered maternity care practices that support breastfeeding, many facilities continue practices that can undermine breastfeeding success. Although the American Academy of Pediatrics (AAP) recommends a follow-up infant visit within forty-eight hours of discharge, early follow-up is far from universal. Many women who encounter early breastfeeding difficulties do not receive the extra help they require.

- **Generations of bottle-feeding grandmothers.** In societies where breastfeeding is traditional, the art is passed from mother to daughter. While today's grandmothers have more firsthand breastfeeding knowledge than the preceding generation, very few have experienced the full course of breastfeeding for a year or more. Many contemporary grandmothers are unable to offer practical advice or direct assistance to their daughters or daughters-in-law.

- **Early return to work or school.** More than half of all new mothers return to work or become employed during their baby's first year. Regularly being separated from your baby due to work or school poses a major obstacle to continued breastfeeding. While many women are able to express their milk at work, women in entry-level and service positions often lack corporate support, adequate facilities, and effective pumps to allow them to maintain their milk supply or provide expressed milk for their baby's feedings.

- **Lack of services and lack of insurance reimbursement.** Hospital-based lactation consultants may have little time to offer follow-up breastfeeding help after new mothers are discharged, and few medical insurance companies reimburse for visits to a lactation consultant. More women who begin breastfeeding could continue long-term if they had convenient access to affordable, specialized lactation services to enable them to overcome breastfeeding problems.

- **Personal barriers.** You may not know anyone who has breastfed, or your baby's father or your own mother may be unsupportive. You may have been the victim of sexual abuse or you may suffer from a negative body image and find that you're not comfortable with direct breastfeeding. Or perhaps you've have had a previous unfavorable breastfeeding experience and you are reluctant to try nursing another baby. No matter what your experience has been, it is important to weigh the benefits of breastfeeding—not only for your baby but for you, too. Fortunately, many sources of help and support are available to reduce the barriers that may be preventing you from beginning or continuing to breastfeed.

Current Feeding Recommendations

The American Academy of Pediatrics and numerous other organizations of health professionals and governmental agencies recognize breastfeeding as the ideal method of feeding and nurturing babies. The AAP breastfeeding policy statement strongly recommends human milk as the preferred feeding for infants and acknowledges the critical role of breastfeeding in achieving optimal infant and child health, growth, and development.

It's Always Your Choice

If you are at all ambivalent about how to feed your baby, it makes good sense to begin breastfeeding. You can always stop breastfeeding and switch to formula later if you prefer. If you opt not to breastfeed, however, you might later wonder whether you would have enjoyed the chance to nurse your baby. Why close the door too soon on an experience you might cherish if you simply gave it a try?

AAP Infant Feeding Recommendations

- The AAP recommends exclusive breastfeeding for approximately the first six months of life.

- Iron-enriched solid foods should be added to the infant's diet beginning around six months.

- Continued breastfeeding is recommended for at least the first year of life, and as long beyond a year as mother and baby desire.

A Brief History of Breastfeeding

From the beginning of human history, successful breastfeeding has been essential to the survival of our species, just as it has been for all mammals. The search for a breastmilk substitute—for orphans and infants whose mothers couldn't breastfeed, or who chose not to—dates back to ancient times. However, the practice of feeding babies breastmilk substitutes has occurred on a large scale for only about eighty years. This radical departure in feeding practices has been relatively short in terms of the history of humankind, and the long-term consequences of this biological experiment are still unknown.

Although the widespread decline of breastfeeding began in the twentieth century, attempts to escape the biological necessity to breastfeed are not new. Historical reports show that in ancient Rome breastfeeding women sold their milk to other mothers at the marketplace; and throughout the ages, wet nurses were commonly employed by affluent women who could afford their services and thus opt out of breastfeeding. During the seventeenth and eighteenth centuries, abandoned or orphaned infants in foundling hospitals commonly were fed various kinds of animal milk or non-milk mixtures of *pap* or *panada*—a mix of flour, rice, and barley or biscuits combined with water and butter. Not surprisingly, few infants survived these non-nutritive concoctions and animal milks. Wet-nursing also resulted in high infant mortality due to corrupt practices, such as taking on too many babies and sedating them so they wouldn't demand to be fed. After the Industrial Revolution, around 1850, artificial feeding of babies became more commonplace as more women joined the workforce.

Breastfeeding declined dramatically once artificial formulas became reasonably safe and economically feasible. By 1920, numerous scientific advances contributed to the promotion of artificial feeding, including the development of glass bottles and rubber nipples, the availability of evaporated milk that could be stored on a shelf, sanitary water supplies and pasteurization, ice box refrigeration, and

(continued)

vitamin supplementation (e.g., vitamin C to prevent scurvy and cod liver oil to prevent rickets).

With the widespread employment of women in industry during World War II, breastfeeding became even less common. And it declined even more drastically in the decades that followed. By 1966, fewer than one in five newborns (18 percent) in the United States were breastfed exclusively at hospital discharge, as formula feeding became a new social norm. While higher-income, better-educated women led the departure away from breastfeeding, the same population is now spurring the trend back to breastfeeding.

In the 1970s, breastfeeding rates began to climb in the United States. The return to breastfeeding was part of a broader movement to "normalize" the childbirth experience. Breastfeeding was promoted along with more family-centered maternity care practices, including less medication during childbirth, the presence of partners during labor and delivery, rooming-in of infants and mothers, and informed consent for circumcision. From 1971 to 1982, in-hospital breastfeeding rates increased dramatically from 25 percent to 62 percent. By the early 1980s, breastfeeding was again the "community norm" for the first time in more than four decades.

Between 1982 and 1990, however, in-hospital breastfeeding fell to 52 percent. Possible explanations for this unexpected decline in breastfeeding include shorter hospital stays and inconsistent early follow-up after discharge, more employed mothers of infants, and lack of expert help for breastfeeding women who encountered problems. Perhaps there was a backlash when breastfeeding was enthusiastically promoted without ensuring sufficient support for women who needed extra help Fortunately, beginning in the 1990s, in-hospital breastfeeding rates—and greater support for nursing mothers—have increased steadily, and breastfeeding is a very popular choice once again. Today the percentage of U.S. mothers who begin breastfeeding their newborns is higher than it is has been in more than seventy years!

Getting Ready for Breastfeeding

Many expectant moms mistakenly believe that breastfeeding is completely natural and requires no preparation. After all, new mothers have been nursing babies since the human race began. Although your baby is born with natural reflexes that will help her breastfeed successfully, nursing her may not come as naturally or as easily as you might think. Breastfeeding is a learned art, but don't be discouraged. The more informed and prepared you are, the more successful and satisfying your breastfeeding experience is likely to be. Fortunately, there are many sources of prenatal breastfeeding information and support within your reach.

Prenatal Breastfeeding Classes

Whether you give birth in a hospital or birthing center, your postpartum stay will be relatively short, making it totally unrealistic to expect to learn everything you need to know about breastfeeding before you are discharged. Fortunately, prenatal breastfeeding classes are readily available—either through your hospital, your obstetrician's office, or through community-based programs— to help you prepare for a positive breastfeeding experience. You will have more time to read or attend a breastfeeding class during your pregnancy than during the early weeks with your newborn. Choose a class that is taught by an International Board Certified Lactation Consultant (IBCLC)

or a breastfeeding specialist with other credentials, such as a Certified Breastfeeding Educator (CBE) or a Certified Lactation Educator (CLE). Arriving at the hospital with empowering knowledge will raise your confidence and increase your chances of getting breastfeeding off to a good start.

LA LECHE LEAGUE INTERNATIONAL

In 1956, at the height of the U.S. bottle-feeding era, seven young mothers in a Chicago suburb were brought together by their mutual belief in the importance of breastfeeding—and their concern that the health-care system and greater society lacked adequate support for breastfeeding. These dedicated women began meeting together regularly for mutual support and to provide information and encouragement for other breastfeeding mothers. Out of these early informal gatherings grew an enduring, international mother-to-mother breastfeeding support group, known all over the world as La Leche League International (LLLI).

LLLI influences breastfeeding mothers through meetings, telephone counseling, publications, conferences, and the Internet. (See Resources.) In addition to participating in the informal discussion at La Leche League (LLL) meetings, expectant and new mothers learn invaluable parenting skills by observing the nurturing styles of other mothers in the group. These meetings are held in members' homes or at convenient public locations. Ten or more breastfeeding moms and their nursing babies, ranging in age from newborns to preschoolers, may be present. To attend an LLL meeting is to be immersed in a breastfeeding culture that models the LLL motto, "good mothering through breastfeeding." La Leche League also offers telephone advice, publications, conferences, breastfeeding supplies, professional education, and more. To find a group in your area, look in the white pages or online at www.llli.org.

THE WIC PROGRAM

The WIC Program (Special Supplemental Nutrition Program for Women, Infants, and Children) is a federal program, operated by the U.S. Department of Agriculture in partnership with state and local agencies. WIC provides breastfeeding and nutrition education, extra food, and health-care referrals for eligible women, and for infants and children up to age five. Eligibility is based on income guidelines and a nutritional need for WIC foods. Many working families qualify for WIC benefits, and nearly 50 percent of U.S. newborns participate in the WIC program. WIC strongly promotes breastfeeding and offers a variety of breastfeeding support services. WIC clients may receive one-on-one prenatal breastfeeding education, breastfeeding classes, and routine postpartum follow-up and counseling. Many WIC clinics have breastfeeding peer counselors, and virtually all have pump-loan programs for nursing mothers who require the use of a breast pump. Some WIC programs provide personal-use electric pumps for breastfeeding mothers who must

Labor and Postpartum Doulas

You may want to use the services of a professional labor doula, a woman who is trained to provide emotional and physical support during your labor and delivery, and to help you have a positive and empowering birthing experience. Similarly, a postpartum doula can work with you and your family to provide breastfeeding support and practical help after the birth of your baby. In helping you feel nurtured and cared for, a postpartum doula can ease the transition to your new parenting responsibilities. To find a doula in your area, contact www.dona.org.

return to work or school and are highly motivated to continue breastfeeding. Call your local WIC program to find out if you are eligible for WIC services. (See Resources.)

GETTING SUPPORT FROM FAMILY AND FRIENDS

With today's high breastfeeding rates, chances are good that you have a friend or relative who has breastfed. Ask her to tell you about her breastfeeding experience. If you never have seen a baby nurse from her mother, and you know someone who is currently breastfeeding, ask to watch her feed her baby. In many cultures, it is natural for girls to grow up observing breastfeeding in their own families. The more exposure you have to the art of breastfeeding, the more confident you will be. If you plan to have someone help you after you deliver, choose a close relative with whom you have a good relationship and who successfully breastfed her own children—or at least who is supportive of your commitment

to breastfeed. The services of a professional *doula* might also be a good choice for you.

Breastfeeding Supplies

While it certainly is possible to breastfeed successfully without any special equipment or supplies, a wide array of breastfeeding aids—just like other baby gear—can make your life easier. You may want to acquire some of the following items during your last trimester, based on your budget and personal preferences.

- **Nursing Bras.** You will need several comfortable maternity bras to support your breasts during pregnancy. You also will want to purchase at least two nursing bras during your seventh or eighth month. Lactating breasts are heavier than normal and usually feel more comfortable when properly supported. In addition, adequate support may help prevent later breast sagging, although breastfeeding probably has less

A Note to Expectant Dads

Your support is critical to your partner's choice and commitment to breastfeed and to her ongoing success. Rather than feeling left out of the intimate nursing relationship, please know that you are an essential part of the breastfeeding family. Plan to take paternity leave to help and support your partner after delivery and to bond with and learn to care for your new baby. Use your vacation time or sick days, and ask your company's human resources department whether or not you are entitled to unpaid family leave under the Family Medical Leave Act (FMLA). FMLA allows employees to take up to twelve weeks of unpaid leave to care for a newborn.

effect on sagging than pregnancy and inherited tendencies. Toward the end of the second week after the birth of your baby, when breast engorgement has subsided, you can buy several more nursing bras. The saleswomen at breastfeeding boutiques and many lactation consultants, who rent breast pumps or sell breastfeeding supplies, are certified to fit nursing bras correctly. Hard-to-fit sizes can be custom-made (see Resources) or purchased from lingerie and maternity stores.

Your nursing bra should fit comfortably, both in the cup area and around the rib cage. Nursing bras have a clasp in the front that allows the cup flaps to be pulled down to expose the breasts for nursing. Choose a bra with a clasp that is easy to maneuver with one hand, so you can release the bra flap while holding your baby.

- **Lanolin.** Many women, particularly those who live in dry climates, use ultra-pure, medical-grade lanolin (USP modified lanolin) as an emollient or lubricant for their nipples before their babies are born and during breastfeeding. Lanolin provides a soothing skin barrier to help prevent nipple damage and promote healing of sore nipples. (See Chapter 8, pages 195–203.)

- **Breast Pads.** Breast pads are worn inside your nursing bra to absorb leaking milk. Some women leak a great deal, while others do not. Without absorbent breast pads in place, leaking milk can soak through your bra onto your clothing. Convenient, disposable varieties are readily available. Reusable breast pads made of washable cotton are more cost-effective, or you can sew your own breast pads out of 100 percent cotton. Still another option is a special non-absorbent, reusable silicone nursing pad that prevents leaking by adhering tightly to your breast. (See Resources.)

- **Breast Pumps.** There are occasions when every breastfeeding mother needs to remove milk from overfull breasts or leave a supply of milk if she is unable to be at home to nurse her baby. If you learn the technique of hand expression (see Chapter 6, pages 137–138), you will always be able to express your milk, whether or not you have a breast pump. Breast pumps range from occasional use, inexpensive, manual or battery-operated versions to daily use, hospital-grade, electric rental models that drain both breasts at once. Talk with a lactation consultant about your anticipated pumping needs before purchasing a breast pump. Additional information about breast pumps is available from pump manufacturers, lactation consultants, hospital maternity wards, breastfeeding boutiques, baby superstores, some pharmacies, LLL, and WIC clinics. (See Resources.) Pumping, storing, and handling expressed breastmilk are all discussed in detail in Chapter 6.

- **Nursing Slings and Carriers.**
Nursing occurs more frequently
and breastfeeding is most
successful when mothers and
babies remain close to one
another so moms can read their
babies' cues. Infants love being
in slings, where they can feel the
rhythm of their mother's body
and the security of her presence.
Baby slings free up your arms
for other activities and allow you
to nurse your infant discreetly
while she is cradled in a comfy
nest. Many different styles of
cloth baby carriers are available,
each with unique features.

- **Nursing Pillows.** Learning to
position your baby correctly
to nurse can be awkward at
first. (See Chapter 3, pages
48–51.) Some women arrange
bed pillows to help position
their babies to nurse, while
others find it easier to use a
custom-made nursing pillow.
These handy pillows, which
are available in various shapes,
sizes, and designs, decrease the
distance from your lap to your
breast and provide support for
your arm at the elbow, making it
more comfortable to breastfeed.
Some nursing pillows can be
used for other purposes as your
baby gets older. (See Resources.)

- **Footstool.** You may spend many
hours each day nursing your
baby. If you are hunched over
you may develop a backache.
A nursing footstool is a sloped
footrest that raises your upper
legs and brings your baby
closer to your chest during
nursing. By keeping your back

straighter, breastfeeding is
more comfortable. After you've
weaned your baby, these
footstools make ideal footrests,
especially when you are working
at a computer station or doing
desk work for any length of time.

- **Nursing Clothing.** No
special clothing is required
to breastfeed, but if you're
interested in expanding your
wardrobe, nursing fashions
ranging from simple blouses to
evening gowns can be purchased
at maternity shops or through
specialty catalogs and cottage
industries. (See Resources.) But
you don't need couture clothing
to nurse discreetly in public.
If you unbutton your blouse
from the bottom, for example,
or simply lift the bottom of a
pullover shirt, you can nurse
your baby without anyone
noticing. (It helps to have a
good nursing bra that opens
easily with one hand.) You can
also drape a nursing cover or
shawl or a light baby blanket
over your shoulder for a little
privacy while you nurse. After
a while these simple methods
become automatic, and you will
be surprised by how easy it is to
nurse you baby no matter where
you are, and without anyone
noticing.

- **Rocker.** Many new moms enjoy
using a rocker or glider, but
before you buy one, make sure
it is comfortable, with adequate
back and arm support, and that
it is the right height for you. The
motion of the rocker may not be
ideal for learning to nurse, but

once things are going smoothly, a comfortable rocker can be a blessing.

- **Bassinet.** New studies confirm that the risk of SIDS (sudden infant death syndrome) is significantly reduced when babies sleep in the same room—but not in the same bed—as their mothers. (See Chapter 5, pages 113–114.) Even though expectant parents love to prepare a separate space for their baby's nursery, it is actually preferable *not* to have your baby sleep there. Besides, it is certainly more convenient to keep your newborn in a bassinet at your bedside at night than to trudge down the hall to the nursery several times before dawn while you are half-asleep.

Tip

Certainly breastfeeding is cheaper than buying formula, but you should not expect to feed your baby for free. Just as you spend money on your baby's nursery and layette, budget some funds to help you succeed at breastfeeding. Whether you purchase supplies, such as a special nursing pillow, rent an electric breast pump, or pay for a breastfeeding consultation, consider it money well spent.

When your baby outgrows her bassinet, you can let her sleep in a crib in your room until she is about six months old.

How Your Body Prepares for Breastfeeding

Beginning in early pregnancy, your breasts are getting ready for lactation, whether or not you plan to breastfeed. In fact, breast swelling and tenderness are one of the earliest signs of pregnancy.

MILK GLANDS AND DUCTS

The pregnancy hormones estrogen and progesterone cause tremendous growth in the number and size of the milk-producing glands in the breasts and the system of ducts that carry milk to the nipple openings. This remarkable prenatal breast development results in significant enlargement and varying degrees of breast tenderness within the first few months of pregnancy. In fact, the preparation of the breasts for breastfeeding is so effective that full milk production can occur even when an infant is born very early.

NIPPLE AND AREOLA

The nipple and areola (the dark circular area around the nipple) become larger and more pigmented during pregnancy. This darkening serves as a visual marker for the infant, who must grasp both the nipple and a significant portion of surrounding areola to nurse correctly.

Women's nipples vary greatly in size and shape. Most women's nipples protrude outward from the areola. When a newborn nuzzles and licks her mother's nipple as she is learning to nurse, this causes the nipple to become more erect and easier to grasp. The areola also comes in a variety of sizes and shapes. It can be so small that the baby easily takes it all into her mouth while nursing. Or, it can be up to four to five inches in diameter, so that only a small amount fits into her mouth. The areola usually is round, but it can be elliptical in shape. It contains hair follicles, and many women have some hairs on their areola.

Numerous small raised bumps, arranged in a ring around the

Internal Breast Structures

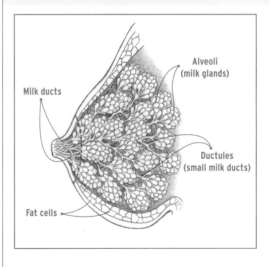

Internally, your breasts are composed of four main types of tissue: *milk glands* that produce milk, *milk ducts* that carry milk, *supporting tissue* that gives shape to your beasts, and *protective fat*. Variations in breast size are largely due to the amount of fatty tissue. Almost all women have sufficient glands to produce enough milk for their babies.

The *blood supply* to the breasts provides the nutritional components for making milk. During breastfeeding, *nerves* on the nipple and areola carry a message to your brain, which causes the release of pituitary hormones that trigger the making and ejecting of milk. (See Chapter 4, pages 79-81). Milk is produced in grape-like clusters of milk glands, known as *alveoli*. Tiny, band-like muscle cells surrounding the alveoli squeeze the glands to expel milk into small ductules. Ductules draining all areas of the breast merge to form multiple larger milk ducts that open at the nipple.

areola, are known as Montgomery glands. These bumps become more prominent during pregnancy and secrete an oily substance that naturally lubricates and cleanses the nipple and helps keep the areolar tissues healthy and soft. Montgomery glands also act as a scent organ and help a newborn find the nipple and attach to the breast. The nipple becomes more sensitive during pregnancy, the blood supply to the breasts greatly increases, and the branching veins on the surface of the breasts become much more prominent.

LEAKING COLOSTRUM

In the last few months of pregnancy, many women notice that their breasts leak a small amount of early milk, known as colostrum. You might see a few clear or yellow drops at the nipple openings when you compress your nipple between your thumb and forefinger or you might notice yellowish stains on your maternity bra. Some women don't notice any breast secretions until they start breastfeeding.

Conditioning Your Nipples

In the past, various techniques were recommended to prepare a woman's nipples for breastfeeding. All too often, however, these manipulations only damaged nipple skin and contributed to soreness once breastfeeding

began. Today we understand that Mother Nature does not need any help with nipple preparation. Some breastfeeding counselors advise women to bathe without using soap—which can have a drying effect on their nipples during the latter months of pregnancy— especially in low-humidity climates. Others recommend daily use of a cleanser or mild soap for proper hygiene.

Purified, USP modified lanolin (medical grade) makes an excellent emollient or moisturizer for the nipples, both before and after your baby is born. Beginning in the last trimester, try applying a thin coating of ultra-pure, anhydrous lanolin (Lansinoh or PureLan) each day to reduce dryness and help keep your nipples supple and elastic. (See Resources.) Although lanolin comes from sheep, you won't necessarily have a reaction to it if you are allergic to wool (allergy to lanolin is extremely rare), but if you are concerned, apply a small amount to the inside of your forearm as a test.

Breast Variations That Can Affect Breastfeeding

Contrary to idealized media portrayals, women's breasts come in a wide variety of sizes and shapes, ranging from tiny to very large, pert to pendulous, and rounded to bullet-shaped or tubular. Most women's breasts are not a matched pair. Rather, slight differences in size and appearance are quite common between the two breasts. Some women have marked differences in breast size or other significant variations in appearance between their two breasts that could affect breastfeeding.

Your obstetrical care provider should perform a prenatal breast evaluation, not only to screen for suspicious lumps but to detect possible breastfeeding risk factors as well. The purpose of screening for potential breastfeeding risk factors is not to be pessimistic, but rather to give the best possible advice to increase your chances for a positive breastfeeding experience. If you do have a breast variation that might impact breastfeeding, you can get extra help from a lactation consultant and make sure that your baby's weight is monitored closely after delivery.

- **Breast Size**
  Conventional wisdom says that breast size is unrelated to breastfeeding ability. Certainly, breast size *prior* to pregnancy is a poor predictor of breastfeeding success, since even very small breasts may enlarge dramatically as the milk glands and ducts rapidly develop during pregnancy. However, a woman whose breasts remain very small at the end of her pregnancy may be at increased risk for producing insufficient milk. While most women with small breasts can produce a normal supply of milk, small breast size may limit how much milk a

woman can store in her breasts and make it necessary for her to feed her baby more often than a woman with larger breasts. (See Chapter 6, pages 144 and 149.)

On the other hand, bigger isn't always better. Extremely large breasts can sometimes make breastfeeding more difficult. Large breasts don't necessarily have more functioning glands than average-size breasts, and they may, in fact, have fewer. Very large, pendulous breasts can make it awkward to position the baby to nurse. In addition, the weight of excessively large breasts may stretch and flatten the nipples, making them more difficult for an infant to grasp correctly.

- **Breast Enlargement During Pregnancy**
  Most women's breasts enlarge considerably during their pregnancy, due to the tremendous development of milk glands and ducts. Women with little or no breast enlargement should be followed closely after delivery to be sure they establish an adequate milk supply and that their babies gain weight as expected.

- **Breast Shape**
  Breast shape, or contour, can signal a potential breastfeeding problem. Tubular-shaped breasts, which are somewhat elongated and narrow, may have a limited number of milk glands compared to fuller, rounder breasts. The milk glands are concentrated under the areola, making it look

disproportionately large in comparison to the rest of the breast. Some women with this type of underdeveloped breasts have limited milk production, while others may produce an ample supply.

• **Breast Symmetry**
Nearly half of all women have a slight difference in the size of their breasts. This minor breast asymmetry is normal. However, moderate or marked differences in breast size may be linked with decreased milk production. Sometimes one breast (usually the larger) produces a normal amount of milk, while the other produces less. This is especially likely when one breast enlarges during pregnancy while the other grows very little. Although variations in breast appearance do not necessarily mean that a woman will have problems with breastfeeding, such differences should always be evaluated.

• **Previous Breast Surgery**
Cosmetic and diagnostic breast surgeries are commonly performed on women of childbearing age and may have a negative impact on subsequent breastfeeding. (See Chapter 10, pages 283-286.) Surgical incisions around the margin of the areola may cut milk ducts, which can interfere with proper milk drainage. Breastfeeding after augmentation often is successful, while reduction procedures are likely to reduce your milk supply. If you have had any type of breast or

nipple surgery, do not jump to conclusions. Inform both your obstetrical and pediatric health-care providers about your operation. You may need to use an electric breast pump after feedings for the first two weeks to maximize your milk production. It is important that your baby be followed very closely after hospital discharge to make sure that she is able to get enough milk by breastfeeding. Even if supplemental milk is required, partial breastfeeding still is possible and worthwhile.

• **Breast Radiation Therapy**
Whole breast radiation to treat breast cancer damages milk glands and ducts and prevents normal milk production from the treated breast. However, breastfeeding is still possible with the other breast. (See Chapter 10, page 287.)

• **Pierced Nipples**
Women with pierced nipples are usually able to breastfeed successfully, although piercing may cause scarring in milk ducts and increase your risk of a breast infection. To prevent your baby from choking on a nipple ring, the best solution is to remove it as soon as you know you are pregnant and reinsert it only after your baby has been weaned.

• **Extra Nipples**
Extra nipples occur in 1 percent to 2 percent of the general population and are usually found along the "milk line," from the

armpit to the groin. An extra nipple is typically smaller and less developed than a normal nipple and is often mistaken for a mole.

• **Nipple Protuberance**
While most women's nipples protrude from the areola, some are slightly flattened, and others barely stand out from the surrounding areola at all. It can be challenging for an infant to learn to nurse when her mother has flat nipples that do not easily become erect with stimulation. Flat nipples are also prone to skin injury during breastfeeding because they are more difficult to grasp correctly. A few women have extremely long nipples that may be difficult for a small baby to grasp. Nipple width can range from very narrow to extremely wide or bulbous. While some nipple types pose a greater challenge than others, a baby can learn to nurse successfully from almost any nipple.

• **Inverted Nipples**
A small percentage of women have inverted nipples that pull inward—instead of protruding outward—when they are compressed. Inverted nipples can range from those that retract only when they are compressed to loosely dimpled nipples or those that are so deeply inverted that the tip of the nipple cannot be seen. Since nipples tend to protrude more as pregnancy progresses, an inverted nipple may improve somewhat without any special treatment. A nipple that remains inverted

can pose several obstacles to successful breastfeeding: (1) Your baby may have difficulty latching on to your breast correctly. (2) Inverted nipples are prone to skin damage during breastfeeding. While normal nipples are pliable, supple, and stretch easily, inverted nipples can be tightly pulled inward and are less elastic. (3) Finally, a few inverted nipples are so deeply retracted that they block milk flow, preventing the infant from taking enough milk.

Detecting an inverted nipple. To test for an inverted nipple, use your thumb and index finger to gently compress the areola about an inch behind the base of your nipple. A normal nipple will protrude with this maneuver. If your nipple pulls inward, it is inverted. Also ask your obstetrical care provider to examine your nipples. Wearing breast shells during the last month of pregnancy may help pull your nipples out.

Wearing breast shells. A breast shell is a dome-shaped hard plastic device with two parts—an inner ring and an attached overlying dome. The breast shell is worn over an inverted nipple and is held in place by a maternity bra. (A bra with a larger cup size may be needed.) The central opening in the inner ring is placed over the inverted nipple, causing gentle, steady pressure around the base of the nipple that directs it forward into the central opening. The overlying dome keeps your bra from touching the nipple. Breast shells are usually prescribed during the last month of pregnancy. You can begin wearing them a few hours each day and progressively increase the time, based on your comfort level. After a few weeks of use, an inverted nipple may protrude normally. If necessary, you can continue to wear breast shells between feedings after your baby is born and can begin pumping to help your nipples protrude more. The milk you express can be fed to your baby while she is learning to nurse effectively. (See Chapter 3, page 63.)

- **Blood-Tinged Colostrum**
  On rare occasions, colostrum may contain blood, which can range from bright red to a brownish, rusty color. While any bloody nipple discharge is alarming and raises fears

of cancer, the cause is usually benign when the bleeding (1) occurs from both breasts late in pregnancy or during the first two weeks after the birth of your baby, and (2) does not persist. It is believed that temporary blood-tinged colostrum is related to the tremendous increase in blood vessels within the breast during pregnancy and the rapid development of milk ducts and glands. Typically the blood gradually clears as milk production increases after delivery, usually resolving completely by one to two weeks postpartum. This pattern of "clearing" as milk flow increases has led to the name *rusty-pipe syndrome*. Of course, you should notify your doctor whenever you notice an abnormal discoloration

A breast shell worn over an inverted nipple is held in place by a maternity bra.

Tip

Before wearing breast shells, consult your obstetrical care provider. Because nipple stimulation can trigger contractions of the uterus, the shells are not recommended for mothers at risk for premature labor. Breast shells are available from lactation consultants, hospitals, breastfeeding boutiques, La Leche League, breast pump manufacturers (including Ameda and Medela), and some WIC programs. (See Resources.)

of your colostrum or milk or any evidence of blood. Never dismiss such a symptom as normal without first being evaluated by your doctor.

• **Breast Lumps or Masses** Although regular breast examinations should continue throughout pregnancy and while you are breastfeeding, detecting breast lumps may be more difficult—new breast lumps are easily overlooked or mistakenly attributed to milk glands, clogged ducts, or other lactation-related explanations. Although mammograms are harder to interpret when performed on dense lactating breasts, the diagnosis of a suspicious lump does not have to be delayed. Ultrasound is an excellent way to distinguish solid tumors from fluid-filled cysts, even during pregnancy and breastfeeding. Biopsy of any suspicious lump should *not* be postponed. Modern breast biopsy no longer requires surgery. Ultrasound-guided breast biopsy is a special type of needle biopsy that accurately obtains a tissue sample without surgery. If you detect a breast lump, notify your doctor immediately and have it checked. If your doctor dismisses it without an ultrasound, biopsy, or close follow-up, *get a second opinion.*

Does Breastfeeding Cause Sagging?

Some women may be reluctant to breastfeed because of the unfounded myth that lactation causes a woman's breasts to lose shape and sag. However, a recent study by plastic surgeons has found that breastfeeding is not related to losing breast shape after pregnancy. Rather, the degree of breast sagging was found to be related to other factors, including a woman's body mass index (BMI), how many times she has been pregnant, having a larger pre-pregnant bra size, smoking, and age. Probably the greatest influence on how much a woman's breasts will sag over time is the type of breast-supporting tissues she inherits. In addition, rounded, wide-based breasts may be less prone to sagging than narrow and elongated breasts.

Because breasts look larger and firmer during lactation, they naturally seem smaller and somewhat saggy after weaning. In reality, the breasts might have changed very little from their original appearance, now long forgotten. Generally, flat-chested women prefer their breast size during lactation, while some large-busted women prefer the appearance of their breasts when they are no longer nursing. Women who are comfortable with their body image before becoming pregnant are more likely to remain satisfied with their physical appearance after giving birth and nursing their baby. No matter how your breasts look later, you can take pride in knowing that your body carried and provided ideal nourishment for your precious child and that your breasts were an immeasurable source of security and comfort.

Prenatal Planning for Special Circumstances

Many breastfeeding problems can be anticipated before you have your baby. Knowledge about the following challenges, for example, will help you use the prenatal period to prepare for unique circumstances well before your baby arrives.

- **Premature Delivery**
  Approximately 12 percent of babies are born prematurely, before thirty-seven weeks' gestation. Your pregnancy may be considered high-risk for premature delivery if you have gestational diabetes, an abnormality of the placenta or uterus, high blood pressure, poor growth of the fetus, or if you are carrying multiple babies. You can prepare for breastfeeding by talking with the lactation consultant at the hospital where you will deliver. Your lactation consultant can help you obtain a hospital-grade double electric breast pump after you give birth and show you how to begin breastfeeding when your baby is ready. (See Chapter 10, page 259–268.)

- **Multiple Births**
  The number of multiple births is at an all-time high, and breastfeeding twins and greater multiples pose a unique challenge. You will want to arrange for extra help after delivery and learn specific strategies for nursing multiple babies. (See Chapter 10, pages 268–272.) Your babies may arrive weeks to months before their due date and be smaller than average. You may want to join a Mother of Twins Club (see Resources) and talk with other women who have successfully nursed multiples. Specialized baby equipment designed for multiples, ranging from twin strollers to twin nursing pillows, can make caring for twins far easier (see Resources).

- **Birth Defects**
  The routine use of prenatal ultrasound and other diagnostic screening tests allows for the early recognition of various infant defects that, in the past, were not identified until after birth. Knowing in advance that your baby has a heart defect, cleft palate, Down syndrome, or other medical problem will enable you to begin planning for any special requirements concerning your baby's care and feeding, instead of surprising you at delivery. If the particular problem is likely to affect your baby's ability to breastfeed, you can arrange to meet with a lactation consultant and your baby's doctor before delivery to discuss anticipated feeding difficulties. You can join a support group for parents of babies with the same problem, interview surgeons or other specialists who will be

involved in your baby's care, and read at length about your baby's anticipated problem.

• **Medications**
Lack of information about medications you may be taking often results in delayed or interrupted breastfeeding. If you take regular medications— to treat asthma, high blood pressure, seizures, anxiety, or depression, for example—you can use the prenatal period to find out whether your medications are safe for breastfeeding. (See Chapter 8, pages 215–218.) Discuss the issue with your obstetrical and pediatric care providers before you deliver to avoid any unnecessary delays in nursing your baby after delivery. Fortunately, most drugs that are safe during pregnancy are also compatible with breastfeeding, since your baby's exposure to a drug is often significantly higher in utero than after birth through breastmilk.

• **Medical Conditions**
Many women wonder whether a medical condition, such as diabetes or multiple sclerosis, can affect their ability to breastfeed. If you have a chronic medical problem, talk to your specialist, as well as your obstetrical care provider and your baby's doctor, about your breastfeeding plans. Chances are good that you will be able to breastfeed, although your physician may want to monitor you more closely.

• **Employment or School**
If you plan to go back to work or school while you are still nursing your baby, you will benefit greatly by attending a prenatal class on breastfeeding and working. You can rent a hospital-grade double electric pump from a local pump-rental station, such as a breastfeeding boutique or pharmacy, or purchase a daily use, double electric pump. (See Resources.) Because high-quality retail breast pumps can be costly ($300 or more), you might want to register for one as a baby shower gift and encourage your friends and relatives to help you obtain one, or request gift certificates toward the purchase. It is never too early to begin talking with your employer about ways to accommodate breastfeeding when you return to work. Chapter 6 includes a detailed discussion of pumping, storing, and using expressed breastmilk. Chapter 9 covers various other aspects of breastfeeding after returning to work.

Tip

Begin your search for quality child care while you're still pregnant, making certain that the person you select shares your commitment to breastfeeding.

• **Previous Breastfeeding Difficulties**
If your previous breastfeeding experiences were less than

The Ten Steps to Successful Breastfeeding

The following ten steps summarize the recommended practice standards for all facilities that provide maternity services and care for newborn infants. These ideal practices should help you know what to ask for at your own hospital to assure the best possible start with breastfeeding.

1. **Have a written breastfeeding policy that is routinely communicated to all health-care staff.** The written policy should address all ten steps, prohibit the promotion of formula, be available to all staff, and be evaluated for its effectiveness.

2. **Train all health-care staff in skills necessary to implement this policy.** All staff should be trained in the advantages of breastfeeding and the basics of practical management. Selected staff members should receive specialized training to allow them to serve as resource people.

3. **Inform all pregnant women about the benefits and management of breastfeeding.** Pregnant women attending prenatal services at the hospital should be informed about the benefits and practical aspects of breastfeeding.

4. **Help mothers initiate breastfeeding within one hour of birth.** Healthy babies should be given to their mothers to be held skin-to-skin within thirty minutes of delivery and allowed to remain with their mothers for at least an hour. Mothers who have had cesarean deliveries should be given their babies to hold skin-to-skin within a half hour after they are able to respond to their babies.

5. **Show mothers how to breastfeed and how to maintain lactation, even if they are separated from their infants.** Nursing staff should offer all mothers further assistance with breastfeeding and verify that mothers can demonstrate correct breastfeeding technique. Mothers of babies in special-care nurseries should be shown how to express their milk frequently to maintain lactation.

6. **Give newborn infants no food or drink other than breastmilk, unless medically indicated.** Staff should know the valid medical reasons for offering supplements to breastfed infants. Formula used in hospitals should be purchased by the facility and not accepted for free or promoted in any way.

7. **Practice rooming-in—allow mothers and infants to remain together twenty-four hours a day.** Rooming-in should start within an hour of a normal birth or within an hour of when a cesarean mother can respond to her baby. Separations should occur only for necessary hospital procedures or medical indications.

8. **Encourage unrestricted breastfeeding.** Mothers should be advised to breastfeed whenever their babies show signs of hunger. No restrictions should be placed on the frequency or length of feedings.

9. **Give no pacifiers or artificial nipples to breastfeeding infants.** Mothers should be taught to avoid pacifiers and bottle feeds because they can interfere with breastfeeding.

10. **Foster the establishment of breastfeeding support groups and refer mothers to them on discharge from the hospital or clinic.** Key family members should be taught how to support the breastfeeding mother at home. Hospitals should have a system of follow-up for breastfeeding mothers after discharge, such as early prenatal visits, home visits, or telephone calls.

ideal and you're anxious or fearful of similar problems, you may be reluctant to try breastfeeding again. Rest assured that it is still possible to have a thoroughly enjoyable breastfeeding experience. Schedule a prenatal visit with a lactation consultant who can review your previous breastfeeding history and suggest ways to help you be successful this time around. While you can't change the past, you can learn from it.

Choosing a Hospital or Birthing Center

Today, where you choose to have your baby—whether it's a hospital or birthing center—is influenced not only by location and personal preference. The decision increasingly is dictated by insurance policies, HMOs, and physician-hospital affiliations. Nevertheless, an extremely

competitive market makes hospitals and birthing centers keenly sensitive to consumer preferences, especially when it comes to childbearing.

Despite relatively short postpartum hospital stays, the hospital experience has a powerful impact on the long-term success of breastfeeding. Tour the facility where you plan to deliver and ask about their maternity policies. If pro-breastfeeding policies are not the standard, write out your specific requests and discuss them with your obstetrical and pediatric care providers. Enlist their support in agreeing to write specific breastfeeding-friendly orders for your baby's care.

Fortunately, most U.S. hospitals and birthing centers have modified their maternity practices to better support breastfeeding, so it should be relatively easy to find a facility where you can receive the necessary information, assistance, and encouragement to increase your chances for breastfeeding success. In 1991, the United Nations Children's Fund (UNICEF) and the World Health Organization (WHO) jointly launched the Baby-Friendly Hospital Initiative (BFHI) to promote, protect, and support breastfeeding by encouraging and recognizing hospitals and birthing centers that implement "The Ten Steps to Successful Breastfeeding," as outlined by UNICEF and WHO. (See pages 36–37.) To learn more about the Baby-Friendly Hospital Initiative in the United States, contact www.babyfriendlyusa.org.

Getting Started: The Hospital Experience

After months of preparation and anticipation, your baby has finally arrived. Exhausted and exhilarated, you are eager to get to know your new baby and hold him close. After carrying and nourishing him in your body for months, you are equipped to continue to provide all your baby's nutritional needs outside the womb. Breastfeeding allows you to nourish your baby with everything he needs to thrive, as well as provide him essential skin-to-skin contact. The atmosphere of closeness and security you create for your baby is a great start to nurturing a lifelong relationship with your new son or daughter. Congratulations!

Early Skin-to-Skin Contact

Until modern times, babies remained with their mothers continuously after delivery, but once hospital births became the norm, babies were separated from their mothers shortly after birth for observation, routine weighing, measuring, bathing, needle-sticks, and eye medication. Now, recent research has confirmed the importance of early skin-to-skin (STS) contact between newborns and their mothers. Instead of being whisked away after birth to be poked and prodded, the American Academy of Pediatrics (AAP) recommends that healthy infants be placed skin-to-skin with their mothers immediately after birth and remain in direct contact with their mothers until the first feeding occurs.

Most babies are vigorous and healthy at birth and require little immediate care beyond being dried off and having their mouths and nasal passages cleared. Ideally, your baby should be placed tummy-down on your bare chest immediately after birth. A health-care provider should dry him off, put a hat on him to prevent heat loss from his head, and cover him with a warm blanket while you hold him in a

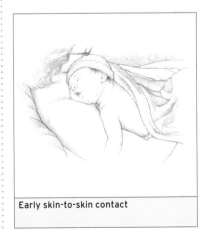

Early skin-to-skin contact

calm and soothing manner. An *Apgar score* (see box below) can be assigned and other postpartum assessments performed while your baby remains with you. Weighing and measuring, bathing, eye medication, and a vitamin K injection all can wait an hour or so until your baby has adjusted to life outside the uterus and has breastfed for the first time. This uninterrupted close contact provides warmth, a sense of security, ready access to breastfeeding, and the opportunity to get to know each other. When skin-to-skin contact is begun immediately after birth, many full-term infants are able to use their inborn reflexes to find their mother's nipple and latch correctly within the first hour. By two hours of age, infants typically become sleepy and may be difficult to rouse for the next three to four hours.

If you have had a cesarean birth, you can still experience skin-to-skin contact and breastfeed your baby in recovery or as soon as you are able to respond to your new baby. Meanwhile, Dad can get into the picture and begin fostering a strong bond with his baby by also holding him skin-to-skin. Everyone benefits from this closeness.

Your Baby's Apgar Score

Your baby's Apgar score, assigned at one and five minutes of life, is a brief evaluation of his adjustment to life outside your body. Named after Dr. Virginia Apgar, who developed the scoring system in the 1950s, the evaluation covers five categories—using the letters in Dr. Apgar's name—for assessing your baby's condition. Your baby is assigned a 0, 1, or 2 score for each of the five categories, so that an Apgar score can range from 0 to 10, with 10 being the highest.

A = **Appearance** (color blue, partially pink, or totally pink)

P = **Pulse,** or heart rate (absent, slow, or normal)

G = **Grimace response** (no response to stimulation, slight response, or vigorous response)

A = **Activity** and muscle tone (limp, moving slightly, or moving actively)

R = **Respiration,** or breathing (not breathing, weak breaths, or good breathing effort)

Most healthy babies receive an Apgar score at one minute of at least 7; the five-minute score is typically higher. The one-minute Apgar score quickly tells the attending health professionals whether a baby needs immediate medical intervention. Nearly all babies will have a five-minute Apgar score of 7 or higher, indicating that he is adapting well to life outside the womb. Good prenatal care, careful monitoring during your labor, and the availability of expert medical care at delivery all contribute to a high Apgar score for your baby.

SECURITY, BONDING, AND READINESS TO NURSE

The success of kangaroo care in fragile premature infants spurred studies of skin-to-skin contact in healthy newborns shortly after birth. Following this early contact, most babies show signs of readiness to feed. Not surprisingly, several recent studies have found that spending time in skin-to-skin contact immediately after birth promotes successful early breastfeeding and has a positive effect on long-term breastfeeding. There are other health benefits of skin-to-skin contact as well: Infants stay warmer and calmer, cry less, sleep more soundly, and have more stable blood sugar levels. Even better, the sight, feel, and smell of your baby produce powerful feelings of caretaking and love that help you develop a close bond with your baby. Families typically report that

Kangaroo Care

The benefits of mother-infant skin-to-skin contact were originally studied in premature infants. A novel method of premature infant care—known as kangaroo care—was first developed in 1979 in Bogotá, Colombia, where incubators for high-risk babies were in short supply. As a substitute for incubators, infants were placed skin-to-skin, upright, and tummy down between their mother's breasts, where they were allowed to breastfeed at will. The technique was initiated in the hospital and continued at home, with close monitoring of the infants' progress. The babies fared surprisingly well, spurring numerous worldwide studies of the technique.

More Advantages of Skin-to-Skin (STS) Contact

- Early STS contact exposes your baby to the normal bacteria on your skin, which helps protect him from harmful, disease-causing bacteria in the hospital.

- STS contact—your baby's first experience after birth—has been shown to shield newborns against the stress of birth and the sensory bombardment they experience during their transition to life outside the womb and eases their adaptation to the world.

- Round-the-clock rooming-in with your baby provides ample opportunities to hold him skin-to-skin. This vital contact helps promote infant feeding behaviors and contributes to successful breastfeeding.

- Because STS contact helps calm and settle your baby, you gain confidence in your ability to soothe him when he is upset.

skin-to-skin contact makes their birth experience even more special and memorable.

EVERYONE BENEFITS

Skin-to-skin contact continues to be beneficial long after you go home from the hospital. Cradling your baby between your breasts can both pacify him when he is fussy and provide a calming and relaxing experience for you. There are benefits for your partner, too. By snuggling and holding his baby close to his chest, a father can strengthen the bond with his baby and feel intimately connected from day one. Human touch communicates powerful feelings without the use of words. No wonder babies thrive best when their parents hold, touch, stroke, and massage them to convey their love and protection.

Hospital Policies That Promote Breastfeeding

It is no great mystery which hospital practices promote breastfeeding and which policies undermine its success. Fortunately, most U.S. hospitals have made great strides in implementing breastfeeding-friendly practices. (See Chapter 2, pages 36–37.) The higher the breastfeeding rates where you live, the more likely the hospital where you deliver will have maternity policies that foster breastfeeding success.

A recent large study in Colorado found that five specific breastfeeding-friendly hospital practices have a significant impact on breastfeeding success among mothers of all socioeconomic groups. More important, the combined effect of experiencing *all five practices* provides the greatest boost to successful breastfeeding over the long term. Ask your health-care providers and the hospital nursing staff to help assure that you experience these five supportive hospital practices:

1. **Your baby is breastfed in the first hour after birth.** Babies who latch on and breastfeed well shortly after birth are likely to continue breastfeeding effectively. Early, effective nursing is key to establishing an abundant milk supply. Colostrum—the first thick yellowish milk your breasts produce—is rich in immune benefits and growth factors that help your baby's gut mature and reduce his risk of infection. In addition, a successful early first breastfeeding experience promotes confidence in your ability to nurse your baby successfully.

2. **Your baby is fed only breastmilk in the hospital.** Many studies show that giving formula supplements to breastfed infants is linked with a shorter duration of breastfeeding. Supplements should be given only for valid medical reasons. When babies are supplemented with formula, they breastfeed less often, since

formula takes longer to digest than breastmilk. Infrequent breastfeeding may interfere with establishing an abundant milk supply.

3. **Your baby stays in the same room with you.** By keeping your baby in your room throughout your hospital stay, you are better able to recognize your baby's feeding cues, interpret his other needs, and rapidly learn to care for him. Breastfeeding on demand occurs readily when you and your baby room together—and studies show that babies are less stressed and do not cry as much when they are cared for in your room. Rooming-in is a great confidence builder. When you keep your baby with you and—with the help of knowledgeable, supportive staff—succeed in providing most of your baby's care yourself in the hospital, you leave knowing that you will be able to meet your baby's needs at home.

4. **Your baby does not use a pacifier in the hospital.** Several studies have found an increased risk of early weaning when a pacifier is introduced to breastfed infants in the first weeks of life. For some babies, early exposure to an artificial nipple can interfere with learning to breastfeed. Once your baby is latching on to your breast without difficulty, is drinking plenty of breastmilk and gaining weight steadily, and breastfeeding is well-established, you can introduce a pacifier. By waiting about a month, you will be much more experienced in distinguishing your baby's hunger cues from his comfort sucking needs and will be less likely to overuse the pacifier. To reduce the risk of sudden infant death syndrome (SIDS), the AAP recommends that babies use a pacifier when falling asleep. The pacifier can be introduced at one month in breastfed infants. (See Chapter 5, page 113.)

The Problem with Early Pacifier Use

Many new mothers offer a pacifier to quiet a fussy newborn without correctly interpreting whether their baby needs to be changed, held, soothed to sleep, or fed. Overusing a pacifier in the early weeks of life can limit how often your baby nurses, which may prevent him from drinking enough breastmilk and may keep you from bringing in a generous milk supply. The American Academy of Pediatrics recommends delaying the use of a pacifier until breastfeeding is well established (about a month). During this time, your baby's sucking efforts should provide him with the milk he needs and should stimulate your breasts to produce a generous supply. If your newborn frequently needs a pacifier, this could be a sign of difficulty getting enough breastmilk. Contact your baby's doctor and arrange to have your baby weighed.

5. You are given a telephone number to call to get help with breastfeeding after you go home from the hospital. In all likelihood, you will be discharged before your milk has come in and before your baby has had the chance to become proficient at breastfeeding. Even when breastfeeding has gone well in the hospital, problems commonly arise in the early days after going home. The top reasons for discontinuing breastfeeding in the first month are infant difficulty latching on or sucking, insufficient milk, inability to satisfy the baby, and sore nipples. If you know where to turn for help after going home, you can remedy common early problems and get breastfeeding back on track.

The Importance of Frequent, Unrestricted Breastfeeding

It was once commonplace for hospitals to restrict the duration of breastfeeding sessions until a mother's milk came in. Mothers were advised to nurse for only three to five minutes per breast, perhaps increasing the feeding time a few minutes per day, based on the mistaken belief that very short feedings would prevent sore nipples. Babies were made to wait four hours between feedings, and they often were removed from the breast before the letdown reflex had been triggered and before they had taken enough milk. Most hospitals now recognize that frequent, unrestricted breastfeeding is the best way for newborns to learn to nurse effectively and for mothers to establish an abundant milk supply.

Nurse your baby whenever he shows signs of being interested in feeding. (See page 57.) Offer your breast as often as necessary to satisfy him, typically every two to three hours since the beginning of his last feeding. The best advice is "watch your baby, not the clock." You may nurse as frequently as every hour or so, if your baby gives feeding cues. However, don't let more than about three and a half hours pass without attempting to rouse your baby to breastfeed, even if he does not seem interested. Frequent feedings are important to help your baby learn how to latch on, suck properly, and bring in a milk supply that satisfies his needs and promotes normal growth.

We now know that the key cause of sore nipples is improper infant latch-on, not lengthy breastfeeding sessions. A newborn who is latched well should be allowed to nurse at least fifteen to twenty minutes at each breast. During the first few days of breastfeeding, however, when your milk production is low, your baby may create excessive negative pressure while nursing and can cause nipple damage, even when he is latched on correctly. If your nipples become tender—and your lactation consultant agrees that your baby's latch looks good—try limiting feedings to about ten minutes per side until your milk starts coming in.

Your Baby's First Feeding

Babies were meant to breastfeed as soon as possible after delivery. Early breastfeeding is linked to more successful early nursing and a longer course of breastfeeding. With such high expectations of the first breastfeeding experience you may feel a little nervous, but there's no need to be intimidated. Try to view your baby's first feeding attempt as relaxing, intimate, get-to-know-you time. At first, your baby may simply lick your nipple and act content to be snuggled at your breast, and that's just fine. On the other hand, he may actually attach to your breast, suck briefly, then stop and look around. Or, he may latch on and suck rhythmically, as if he's done this many times before. Any of these responses is perfectly normal. The main thing is to relax and enjoy being with your new baby.

Colostrum, the very first milk your body produces, beginning in pregnancy and continuing though the first few days of breastfeeding, is the perfect first food for your baby. The small quantity your body manufactures is just the right amount to make it easier for your newborn to coordinate sucking, swallowing, and breathing after birth. Colostrum can vary in appearance from watery and clear to thick and yellow. It is easily digested, has a gentle, laxative effect, and contains important growth factors that prepare your baby's intestines to digest and absorb milk nutrients. Colostrum is also rich in antibodies, white blood cells, and other immune properties that help protect your baby against

The Free Formula Controversy

Infant-formula companies supply hospital nurseries with free formula and giveaways for new mothers. This practice reduces costs for the hospital and provides a marketing opportunity for manufacturers—they know that new mothers are likely to purchase formula brands that are familiar to them. Both breastfeeding mothers and those who feed formula routinely receive formula-company gift packs in the hospital, though the contents may differ according to the mother's feeding method.

Giving expectant or new mothers products with a formula logo can imply a hospital endorsement of formula feeding and promote the early use of supplemental formula, which may undermine your breastfeeding success. Many breastfeeding advocates insist that hospitals should stop accepting giveaways and should purchase their own formula, just as they buy other patient supplies. As a result, a growing number of hospitals have stopped giving formula freebies or provide their own gift packs without formula products.

swallowed bacteria and viruses. Not only is colostrum produced in much smaller quantities than mature milk, it contains higher levels of minerals and protein, and lower levels of calories, fat, and the milk sugar lactose.

A LEARNED ART

Breastfeeding doesn't come as naturally as you might think it does—for either you or your baby! Even though babies have innate reflexes for rooting and sucking, in many respects breastfeeding is a learned art. In some societies, the art of breastfeeding is passed along from mother to daughter or sister to sister, but in the United States many grandmothers lack personal breastfeeding experience or live far from their daughters. Consequently new moms typically learn how to nurse their babies from a hospital maternity nurse. So when you're in the hospital, don't be shy about asking for extra help, and above all, take your time! Don't let anyone rush you through the learning process.

GETTING READY TO NURSE

Since you will spend hours breastfeeding each day for many months, positioning yourself properly will help you to be much more comfortable. Correct positioning of your baby will improve his attachment to your breast and increase his intake of milk. It definitely is worth spending time getting it right. Correct latch-on technique is discussed in pages 52–56.

- Whichever breastfeeding position you use (see pages 49–51), your baby should be well supported throughout the feeding to help him relax and feel secure. Use a nursing pillow, bed pillows, or your arm to support his head, neck, shoulders, back, and bottom.

- During your hospital stay, you may breastfeed while reclining or sitting in your hospital bed or sitting in a chair in your room. If you sit up in bed, elevate your head as much as possible and tuck some pillows behind you to keep your back straight. If you use a chair, select one that has ample back and arm support and is an appropriate height for you. Although a rocker or glider may seem like an attractive option, the back and forth motion might make it more difficult for your baby to grasp your breast properly as he learns to latch on.

- A pillow placed on your lap will help raise your baby to the level of your breast. A lap pillow is essential if you've had a c-section because you'll want to keep your baby's weight from pressing against the incision. Placing a footstool beneath your feet will also decrease the distance between your lap and breast and be more comfortable for your back, neck, and shoulders. You may choose to purchase a special nursing pillow to make breastfeeding more comfortable. (See Resources.)

Nursing Positions

Breastfeeding using the cradle hold

Cradle Hold. The cradle hold is the most popular nursing position after the learning period. In this hold you support your baby with your forearm underneath his back and his head resting in the crook of your elbow or on your forearm. Your hand can cup his bottom or thigh, and you may be able to hold his uppermost arm against his body using your thumb.

Tip

With your upper arm held against your side, rotate your forearm so your baby's whole body turns toward you, until the two of you are chest-to-chest. Your baby's mouth should be lined up with your nipple to allow him to attach readily. His lower arm can be tucked around your waist or under your breast.

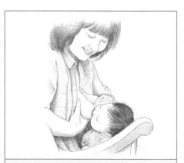

Breastfeeding using the cross-cradle hold

Cross-Cradle Hold. The cross-cradle hold is similar to the cradle hold, except that your arms switch roles. Your baby is supported by the forearm and hand opposite the breast being used, while your breast is supported by the hand on the same side. Rotate your baby's body on your arm so his chest and tummy are facing you. Your baby's upper back and the base of his head are supported in the palm of your hand. The arm supporting your baby can quickly guide him to your breast to help him latch on.

Tip

The cross-cradle hold is an excellent learning position, especially if your baby is small or has trouble latching on, as it provides you a good view of your baby's mouth on your breast.

Breastfeeding using the football hold

Football Hold. In this hold, also known as the clutch hold, you position your baby so that he can nurse on the same side as your supporting arm. If you've had a cesarean birth, this hold will keep your baby's weight comfortably off the incision. Hold your baby like a football along your forearm, against your side, with his feet pointing toward your back and his head near your breast. If you are seated in a chair, your baby's body can be flexed at the hips, with his bottom at the back of the chair and his legs pointed up. His shoulders, neck, and base of his head are supported by your hand and fingers, while his upper back rests against your forearm.

Tip

The football hold is another popular position for small babies as well as babies who have trouble latching on. It also works well for women with larger breasts or flat nipples. This position allows you to see your baby's mouth on your breast and to adjust the position of his head as needed. Move your baby's shoulders, neck, and head together, since direct pressure against his head can trigger a reflex that causes him to arch his head back away from the breast.

- When you breastfeed, you always want to bring your baby to your breast, not your breast to the baby. When your breast has to be pulled to reach your baby, it is dislodged easily from his mouth during feeding.

- During pregnancy, it's natural for your bra size to increase considerably, and when you begin producing abundant milk for your baby, your breasts get even larger.

Supporting your heavy breast from beneath will make it easier for your newborn to keep it positioned correctly in his mouth during nursing. With one arm supporting your baby, use the opposite hand to cup your breast, placing four fingers underneath and your thumb on top. The placement of your fingers on your breast is very important. Fingers should be well behind the areola, far back from

Breastfeeding in a reclining position

Reclining or Side-Lying Position. It is not necessary to get into a sitting position to nurse your baby. If you've had a cesarean birth you might prefer to nurse while lying down to avoid putting pressure on your incision. Or you just may not want to sit upright for long periods to nurse, preferring instead to nurse while lying in bed or resting. To nurse while lying down, roll onto one side and ask a helper to place several pillows against your back. You will probably want a pillow under your head, and perhaps another one between your knees for additional comfort. Try to keep your back and hips in a straight line. Place your lower arm around your baby and draw him close to you so that your bodies are touching. Your baby should be on his side and facing your breast, with his mouth lined up with your nipple. You can use your opposite hand to support your breast, if necessary.

Tip

The AAP recommends that you return your baby to his crib after nursing him in your bed. (See Chapter 5, page 113.) The risk of sudden infant death syndrome (SIDS) is increased when babies sleep in an adult bed. The safest place for your baby to sleep is in his own crib in your room. *Never leave your baby lying on your bed on top of a comforter or surrounded by pillows and other soft bedding—they can suffocate your baby.*

---

the nipple, so that they don't get in the way of the baby's mouth.

- Eventually babies learn to breastfeed without having the breast supported throughout the feeding. In the beginning, however, breast support will be a big help to your baby. If your breasts are very large, roll up a cloth diaper or receiving blanket and put it under your breast to elevate it.

DEALING WITH SELF-CONSCIOUSNESS

When you first start breastfeeding, it really helps to have both of your breasts exposed to help your baby latch on correctly. As the two of you gain experience, you'll discover how easy it is to nurse discreetly. While you're learning, your bra and other clothing can get in the way of your baby's efforts to latch on, so it's best to forgo modesty in favor of technique. During the learning stage, feel free to ask visitors to step out of the room. Pull the curtain around your bed or ask the nurse to put a DO NOT DISTURB sign on your door if you are concerned that a visitor might enter your room unannounced while you are learning to breastfeed. Eventually you'll become comfortable nursing almost anywhere without feeling self-conscious. In fact, most people won't even notice that you're feeding your baby! But when you're still figuring things out you probably don't want an audience. Relax, make yourself comfortable, focus on your baby, and don't be embarrassed about giving yourself the privacy you need.

Helping Your Baby Latch On and Nurse Effectively

Your baby is born with multiple natural reflexes that help him learn to breastfeed. For example, an infant automatically will turn his head toward a stimulus that brushes against his cheek, a reaction known as the rooting reflex. He will open his mouth wide and put his tongue down and forward when his lips are lightly touched. Your nipple touching the roof of your baby's mouth triggers rhythmical cycles of sucking and tongue compressions against

Nursing Tips for C-Section Moms

Although a cesarean birth poses unique challenges, successful breastfeeding is certainly possible for you if you have had a c-section. In fact, many moms who deliver by cesarean appreciate the extra teaching opportunities they receive by having a longer hospital stay. If you are having a scheduled c-section, ask in advance about breastfeeding-friendly practices at the hospital where you will deliver, including early skin-to-skin contact. Arrange to have a support person stay in your room at all times to help you with your infant. Share this responsibility among several people, such as your partner, your mother, and a sister or close friend.

If you have an epidural or spinal anesthetic, you can be awake for your baby's birth and can breastfeed shortly after birth. Even if you require a general anesthetic, you can start breastfeeding with assistance as soon as you feel ready. You may want to place a pillow over your lap or choose a nursing position that keeps the baby's weight off your incision, such as the side-lying position or the football hold. Resist suggestions to have your baby fed in the nursery. Ask for extra help (if you need it) at each feeding. Although the medications you take will pass into your milk, in general the antibiotics and pain relievers prescribed after a cesarean birth are safe for breastfeeding newborns when taken as directed. (See Chapter 8, page 218.)

your nipple and areola. With all these built-in reflexes, many babies latch on to the breast with minimal assistance and eagerly begin nursing. However, some babies require extra help as they learn to breastfeed. Once you are positioned comfortably with your breast cupped in your hand, and when your baby is well supported and his mouth is aligned with your breast, you are ready to help him latch on.

ASYMMETRIC LATCH

In the past, breastfeeding mothers were often advised to center their nipple in their baby's mouth. We now recognize that breastfeeding is more comfortable and a baby is better able to remove milk while nursing if he has a greater amount of breast tissue next to his tongue and lower jaw. This off-center positioning is known as the asymmetric latch and allows him to use his tongue and jaw effectively to remove milk as it is letting down. **The key to an asymmetric latch is to aim your baby's lower lip as far from the base of your nipple as possible. Bring his chin and lower jaw into contact with your breast first, while his mouth is still wide open and before his upper lip touches your breast. (See illustrations, page 55.)**
     The following tips will help you ensure that your baby achieves an effective, comfortable asymmetric latch:

- Using the cross-cradle hold, bring your baby's body close to you so that your breast is within

easy reach. You don't want your breast to pull away from him as he tries to latch and nurse.

- A newborn can latch on more easily if you gently compress your breast between your fingers and thumb to narrow the width of the areola as he tries to latch—just as you might compress a thick sandwich to flatten it before attempting to take a bite. Your fingers and thumb should be aligned with your baby's mouth by positioning them parallel to his jaw before compressing them together.

- Your baby's head should be tilted back slightly, as if he were sniffing a flower. This head tilt will help you bring his chin to the breast first. His legs and body should be pressed firmly against your body.

- Move your baby toward your breast and lightly stroke your nipple against the midpoint of his upper lip to stimulate your baby to open his mouth. Repeat the light touch against his lip and patiently wait for him to open his mouth very wide, as if he is yawning. Do not attempt to latch your baby when his mouth is only slightly open, since he may grasp only the tip of your nipple, which can cause nipple discomfort. Instead, take the time to keep lightly tickling his upper lip until he gapes really wide, with his tongue down.

- When your baby has opened wide, use your arm to quickly pull his whole body toward you so he grasps a large mouthful of your breast. Your baby needs to draw the entire nipple and enough surrounding breast tissue into his mouth to compress the milk ducts beneath the areola to obtain milk easily. (Many women make the mistake of trying to push their nipple into their baby's mouth, just as you might do with a baby bottle.) Instead, quickly bring your baby to your breast, with the base of your hand pressed against his shoulders and upper back.

- Bring your baby's chin and lower jaw (not his nose) into contact with your breast first. Once your baby has latched on, you should see more areola above his top lip than below his lower lip. The latch should feel comfortable. Continue to support your breast to help your baby stay attached correctly.

- Since the size of the areola can vary tremendously from woman to woman, your baby may need to take all of the areola into his mouth (if your areola is small), or he may leave a margin visible beyond his lips (if your areola is large). Grasping the entire nipple and a large mouthful of breast will assure that the nipple is far back in your baby's mouth so it won't be damaged by friction or pressure. Sucking is triggered when your nipple touches the midpoint of your baby's palate (roof of the mouth).

- When your baby is attached correctly, his mouth should be open wide, his lips flared out, and his chin pressed against

the underside of the breast. You should feel his jaws compressing your breast at a point well behind the nipple. His sucking should feel like slight tugging and should not be uncomfortable. The tip of your baby's tongue might be visible between his lower lip and your breast as it lies over his lower gum. If your baby's nose is touching your breast, try pulling his lower body closer to you, which will open a space between his nose and your breast.

- When you're first learning to nurse, you may want to keep your baby's hands out of the way so they don't wind up in his mouth or next to your nipple. You may be able to hold his arms against his body as you position him to nurse.

- When your baby comes off the breast, your nipple should look rounded—not flattened on one side, like a new tube of lipstick, or creased.

- For the first few days, you may feel slight nipple discomfort when your baby latches on and begins to nurse. This tenderness at the beginning of feedings typically subsides within a minute. Severe discomfort, continuous pain, or pain that does not improve within a day or two after your milk comes in usually means that your baby is not grasping your breast properly. (See Chapter 8, pages 196–197.) If he has not latched on correctly, do not continue the feeding. Instead, unlatch him from your breast, and re-attach him so that nursing is comfortable.

• Use breast compressions to help your baby keep drinking milk. With your hand supporting your breast, compress the breast firmly but gently, in a rhythmic pattern. You can either hold the compression or just compress, release, then compress and release again. This technique can keep a sleepy baby interested in nursing by increasing milk flow. Breast compressions can also enhance your letdown and improve milk drainage. (See Chapter 4, page 96.)

REMOVING YOUR BABY FROM THE BREAST

When a baby has nursed well and is satisfied, he usually will stop sucking and come off the breast on his own. Do not attempt to remove your nursing baby from your breast by pulling him off. Breaking suction in this way is likely to cause trauma to your nipple and make it sore. Instead, slide your finger between your baby's gums and press down on your breast to break the suction and comfortably remove your nipple.

Asymmetric Latch Technique

1. Lightly stroke the midpoint of your baby's upper lip with your nipple to stimulate him to open his mouth.

2. Repeat the light touch against your baby's lip until he opens his mouth very wide, as if yawning, with his tongue down.

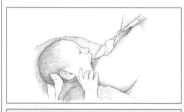

3. Bring your baby's chin and lower jaw (not his nose) into contact with your breast first, aiming his lower lip as far from the base of your nipple as possible.

4. When your baby is attached correctly, his jaws should be open wide, his lips flared out, and his chin pressed against the underside of your breast.

WHEN BREASTFEEDING BECOMES SECOND NATURE

All these details about correct breastfeeding technique make nursing sound complicated and hard to do. But remember, when you are learning the basics of almost any new skill, each step seems awkward and painstaking. Before long, though, you will be nursing without giving any thought to the fundamentals. A toddler learning to walk has to concentrate on every step. In a matter of weeks, the child becomes more surefooted, and before long, walking is automatic. Breastfeeding is like that. You and your baby have so much to learn in the first days that you may wonder if nursing will ever feel natural. Rest assured, by the time your baby is a month old, breastfeeding will be so routine that you may find yourself multi-tasking by reading, eating, talking on the phone, comforting an older child, or checking your e-mail while nursing your baby.

Correct Latch-on and Nursing

You can assume your baby is properly latched on to your breast and nursing effectively if you notice the following:

- Your baby's eyes are open.

- His mouth is open wide and his lips are flared out.

- He grasps the entire nipple plus a large amount of the areola into his mouth.

- His jaw moves in wide, slow motions as he sucks deeply and rhythmically. When he opens his mouth to the widest point while nursing, you see a pause as his mouth fills with milk. Although you can't see inside his mouth, this pause when his jaw drops is a helpful sign that he is getting milk.

- He swallows regularly, heard as a soft "cuh, cuh, cuh" sound when he exhales.

- Your nipple feels comfortable after the first few sucks.

- Your baby's cheeks do not sink inward, and you do not hear any clicking or smacking sounds as he nurses. Smacking and cheek tugging suggest that your baby is breaking suction instead of securely keeping the breast in his mouth.

- Your baby becomes full and drowsy as your breasts soften.

Reading Your Baby's Feeding Cues

Many new parents expect their baby to cry when he is hungry, but crying is a late sign of readiness to feed. If you wait until your baby is crying loudly before you prepare to nurse him, both of you may become frustrated if his hunger is not satisfied fast enough. Worse yet, your baby may become so exhausted from crying, that by the time you offer your breast, he nurses poorly. Instead of waiting for your baby to cry, look for one or more of these earlier clues (see illustrations on page 66) that tell you he is ready to nurse:

- rapid eye movements
- starting to rouse from sleep
- increased alertness
- flexing of arms and legs
- squirming or grimacing
- making small sounds
- bringing a hand to his mouth
- turning the head
- moving his mouth or tongue

NURSING FREQUENCY

When your baby is just learning to nurse, don't worry about how far apart you should space his feedings. That implies that feedings should occur at

Incorrect Latch-on and Nursing

In all likelihood your baby is *not* properly latched on to your breast or nursing correctly if you notice any of the following:

- He grasps just your nipple and none of the surrounding breast tissue.
- Your baby's chin is not pressed against the underside of your breast.
- His lips are curled in.
- He keeps falling off the breast.
- He closes his eyes as soon as he latches on and falls asleep.
- He does not suck deeply and regularly. (Simply keeping his mouth on your breast, without moving his jaw, or a rapid, light, sucking action—flutter sucking—are not effective.)
- You seldom hear swallowing sounds.
- Your baby's cheeks are tugging inward or you hear clicking noises.
- You feel significant pain while nursing.
- Your baby still acts hungry after "feeding."

predictable intervals. But an early breastfeeding session is less a meal than it is a learning experience that needs to be repeated over and over. In fact, your baby is learning how to signal his interest in feeding, how to correctly grasp your breast, how to remove milk efficiently, how to suck and swallow and breathe without choking, and how to soothe and pacify himself at your breast. That's a lot for a tiny person to master. Instead of waiting for an arbitrary number of hours between feedings, give your baby as much breastfeeding practice as possible by offering him your breast as often as he shows interest. Breastfed newborns typically nurse at least eight, and as many as ten to twelve, times a day during the first month. If your baby does not wake up or give feeding cues after about three and a half hours from the beginning of his last feeding, try to wake him up. Frequent skin-to-skin contact will encourage your baby to want to nurse. Staying close to him while he sleeps nearby is the best way to learn to recognize and respond to his feeding cues.

BURPING YOUR BABY

All babies swallow some air during feeding. Although many will burp easily without any special positioning, most parents make a ritual of helping their baby burp after feeding from each breast. Some babies need to be burped more often. Trapped air in his stomach can make your baby uncomfortable, either during or after feeding. Releasing the air can allow him to continue feeding more comfortably. A bubble of air in his stomach also can make your baby feel full too soon and cause him to stop feeding before he has taken enough milk. Burping your baby after the first breast not only makes room in his stomach for more milk, the positioning and handling involved in burping can help rouse a sleepy infant into taking the second side. If your baby is actively nursing, do not interrupt the feeding to burp him. Rather, take advantage of natural pauses for burping and use the time to socialize with your baby as you gently pat and stroke him.

Several popular techniques are effective for burping your baby. You can sit him in an upright position on your lap, with your hand cupped under his chin to support his chest and head. Lean him forward slightly while you rub and pat his back.

Another popular burping method is to support your baby in an upright position over your shoulder (protected with a burp cloth to catch any spit-ups) and pat his back. Or you can place your baby across your lap, with his head slightly higher than the rest of his body, and gently rub and pat his back.

STAYING HYDRATED

Make sure you have something to drink each time you nurse your baby. Milk production requires extra fluids, and you may become thirsty when your milk ejection reflex is triggered. (See Chapter 4, page 81.) Keep a pitcher nearby while you are in the hospital and at home—and pour yourself a tall glass of water or a nutritious beverage, such as low-fat or fat-free milk or 100 percent fruit or vegetable juice, each time you sit down to nurse your baby. Placing a straw in the glass will make it easy for you to take sips when the glass is offered, since you will need to use both your hands when you first start breastfeeding. The ritual of drinking a beverage as you prepare to nurse also helps trigger milk letdown.

NIGHTTIME FEEDINGS

It is tempting to skip nighttime breastfeeding sessions in the hospital in hopes of getting extra sleep. In fact, you'll get more sleep in the long run if you leave the hospital knowing how to feed and care for your baby. And both of you will rest more soundly at night, sensing that the other is nearby. Also, if nurses give your baby a bottle feeding during the night, he may have trouble latching on when you try to resume breastfeeding in the morning. Round-the-clock nursing helps stimulate a generous milk supply to meet your baby's needs. These days, hospital stays are so short that you can't afford to miss even one breastfeeding opportunity before going home.

Getting the Most from Your Hospital Experience

There is so much to learn about baby care, it's hard to take it all in during your brief hospital stay. Still exhausted from labor and birth, you may be tempted—and even encouraged—to delegate much of your baby's care to the nurses. Remember that, while they can provide expert care for your baby at the moment, they won't be going home with you! Your top priority in the hospital is to transfer as much of the nurses' expertise as possible to yourself and your partner. Don't be afraid to ask even the most basic questions. Plenty of mothers have asked them before you, and the nurses are well prepared to fill you in. Other sources of information in the hospital may include:

- **Educational programming**
  New parents can get instruction on closed-circuit television, from in-house productions aired at specific times to continuous commercial programming, and educational DVD recordings. While such programming cannot replace one-on-one guidance from an experienced nurse, viewing them can make your interactions with the nurses more worthwhile.

- **Group classes**
  Group instruction is offered on a variety of baby-care topics,

from changing diapers to breastfeeding. Take advantage of hospital-sponsored breastfeeding support groups after discharge.

- **One-on-one instruction** Hospital maternity services have one or more lactation consultants on staff to help women who are having breastfeeding difficulties, and sometimes are able to meet and assist every nursing mother in the mother/baby unit. More hospitals now offer follow-up lactation services after you go home.

Visitors

The popular trend toward family-centered maternity care is highly commendable. It can be a wonderful thing to bring a child into your family surrounded by all your loved ones, but you should avoid turning your hospital room into a block party. Having your extended family and friends share in celebrating your new baby can be fun for a time. On the other hand, too many visitors can leave you feeling like an entertainment coordinator and wishing you had more private time to get to know your baby and to sleep between feedings.

Even without well-meaning visitors and phone calls, frequent interruptions by hospital personnel moving in and out of your room can interfere with learning to recognize your baby's feeding cues and his learning to latch on correctly. You and your baby will be visited by nurses for routine care, and other staff will enter your room to screen your baby's hearing, take his picture, deliver flowers, empty wastebaskets, replenish water and supplies, deliver and pick up menus and food trays, take him to the nursery for procedures, and advise you about obtaining his birth certificate and social security card.

A recent study found that new mothers in the hospital experienced an average of fifty-four interruptions (either by people entering the hospital room or receiving phone calls) during a twelve-hour period of observation on the first day after giving birth! Try to limit visitors to those you really want to see, and then keep visits short. Remember, the purpose of your hospital stay is to learn to care for and feed your baby and to recover from childbirth. There will be plenty of time later to introduce your baby to your friends and family. Inquire whether your hospital has a designated nap time each afternoon, or a DO NOT DISTURB sign that you can hang on your door when you need to rest. Have your phone calls held for a few hours and turn off your cell phone. Your nurse or partner will probably be happy to help monitor visitors and make sure they don't stay too long.

Baby's Second Night

Many lactation consultants have noticed that a baby's second night can be particularly difficult for families. A new mom who has sailed through the first twenty-four hours of breastfeeding may feel blindsided when her baby cries excessively on the second night. This common—and distressing—infant behavior can derail breastfeeding, since many new moms assume that they don't have enough milk to satisfy the baby's hunger. The leading explanation for this "second night" behavior is that a newborn becomes overwhelmed by all the new sights, sounds, smells, and sensations outside the womb. He longs for the snug, cozy environment inside of your uterus, and the familiar sound of your heartbeat. He feels most secure and comforted when nestled at your breast or held against your chest. Each time he falls asleep at your breast and you try to settle him into his bassinet, he vigorously protests against being separated from you. His cry of distress is instinctual behavior. From his point of view, as a tiny newborn human, being separated from caretaking adults is a life-threatening situation!

Hunger may contribute to your baby's second-night behavior as well. Your milk production may lag slightly behind his increasing appetite, especially if he is a larger baby. Within another twelve to twenty-four hours, however, your milk production will surge, and your baby will easily be satisfied.

Whether the second night of breastfeeding happens in the hospital or at home, the following strategies can help you cope:

- When your baby falls asleep at the breast, hold him upright between your breasts for another twenty minutes until he transitions from light sleep (REM) into deep sleep. If you move him before he has settled into deep sleep, he will awaken easily and cry out for you.

- Hold him skin-to-skin as often as possible to help him feel calm and secure.

- If he cries inconsolably, try the five S's for settling a crying baby. (See Chapter 5, pages 117–119.) Do your best to comfort your newborn and never leave him to cry alone.

- If your baby still acts hungry after nursing frequently, using proper breastfeeding technique, consider offering a small amount (approximately a half ounce) of supplemental milk. (See pages 66–71.)

Urination and Bowel Movements

The first bowel movement your baby passes is known as *meconium*, and it will look tarry black. Meconium is present in your baby's intestines before he is born. Because colostrum is a natural laxative, frequent nursing will help expel the meconium. During your hospital stay, your baby's stools may change to a greenish black. As your baby drinks more milk, his bowel movements turn yellow-green. By the fourth day, they should start to look yellow-gold, with little seedy curds, and the number of movements should

Common Early Breastfeeding Problems

Don't be discouraged if breastfeeding isn't picture-perfect during the first few days of learning. With patience and practice, both you and your baby will become more proficient in your roles. If you continue to have difficulty after your milk has come in, however, you should seek expert help right away. The sooner you address a breastfeeding problem, the easier it is to remedy. Since poor feeding can be a sign of a medical problem in an infant, it is essential to evaluate babies who are not feeding well for possible illness.

The following problems are common during the get-acquainted phase of breastfeeding. Since the same problems also commonly occur during the first week at home, many of these challenges are discussed in depth in Chapter 4. Typical early breastfeeding concerns include:

•Your baby will not awaken to nurse.

•He has trouble latching on.

•Your baby stops sucking.

•He prefers one breast over the other.

•Your baby acts unsatisfied after nursing.

•Your nipples hurt.*

•Your breasts are hard and swollen.

* See Chapter 8 for information about treating sore nipples.

---

increase to four or more each day. (See Chapter 4, pages 87–88.)

Your baby may urinate only a few times a day the first two days after birth because the amount of colostrum he drinks is low. When your milk comes in (about the third day after birth), he will start to drink more, and the number of wet diapers should increase to about six or eight each day. Keeping a record of your baby's feeding times, wet diapers, and bowel movements can be very helpful in monitoring his progress with breastfeeding. (See Chapter 4, page 88.)

If Your Baby Won't Latch On

While many babies attach to the breast virtually unaided, others cry, act distressed, and do not seem to know what to do when Mom's breast is offered. An infant's refusal to latch on can feel like outright rejection and leave you feeling helpless. The problem is especially frustrating if you expected breastfeeding to be as easy as it is natural. After unsuccessfully trying to get your baby to latch on, you may hear yourself lament, *"My baby doesn't want my breast."*

Nothing could be further from the truth! All babies naturally want to breastfeed—some just take a little longer than others. If your baby is having trouble latching on, try the following techniques:

- Don't worry about nursing for the moment if your efforts are upsetting you and your baby. Take a deep breath, try to relax, and soothe your baby with your voice.

- Review the basics of breastfeeding technique: positioning yourself and baby, supporting your breast, tickling your baby's upper lip and bringing him to your breast chin-first to achieve an asymmetric latch. (See pages 53–55.) If you're still at the hospital, ask the lactation consultant to evaluate your technique and offer suggestions.

- Keep feeding attempts to a reasonable length. Try settling your baby by letting him suck on your little finger. Make sure your hands are clean, of course, and insert your little finger, with the fleshy part (palm side) up against the roof of his mouth. Then offer your breast again. Remind yourself that latch-on difficulties are common and that many women have felt exactly as you do right now.

- Help your baby enjoy being close to your breast. Hold him securely between your breasts skin-to-skin as much as possible and speak reassuringly. This "breast-friendly" time will help offset any frustration that either of you might experience from unsuccessful breastfeeding attempts. Offer your breast again as soon as your baby shows an interest in nursing.

- Use a breast pump or hand expression (see Chapter 6, pages 137–138) to collect some of your milk. Even half a teaspoon of colostrum can settle a fussy baby and encourage him to try to nurse. You can also drip some of your expressed milk on your nipple to entice him to latch on.

- If you have flat or inverted nipples, try wearing breast shells between feedings. (See Chapter 2, pages 31–32.) Stimulate and shape your nipples to make them protrude more. Compress your breast to narrow the width of your areola in line with your baby's mouth. You also can use a breast pump before each feeding to pull your nipples out and start some milk flowing.

- A baby who had been nursing well may have difficulty latching on to engorged breasts. (See page 100.) Use hand expression or a breast pump to soften your areola and help your milk begin flowing before you try to latch your baby.

- Try to avoid the use of artificial nipples (pacifier or bottle nipples) in the hospital, and delay introducing a pacifier until breastfeeding is going well. (See page 45.) If your baby requires supplemental milk while in the hospital, consider offering it by cup or spoon rather than by bottle. (See pages 69–70.)

- If your baby isn't latching on well within twelve to twenty-four hours, begin pumping your breasts approximately every three hours, preferably with a hospital-grade double electric pump to bring in and maintain your supply. (See Chapter 6, pages 145–146.) Offer your expressed milk by bottle or other method to keep your baby well nourished and continue to try to latch him at every opportunity. As long as he remains well fed and your milk supply is maintained with pumping, your baby can still learn to breastfeed. Don't give up! Regular pumping will also help flat or inverted nipples protrude more.

- If your baby still hasn't learned to latch on by the time you are to be discharged, talk with your pediatrician about your plan to continue pumping and feeding your expressed milk to your baby. Arrange for close follow-up to monitor your baby's weight, and ask for a referral to a lactation consultant who can offer additional strategies for helping your baby learn to nurse.

Using a Nipple Shield

Temporarily using an ultra-thin, soft silicone nipple shield over your breast can help your baby overcome a latch-on problem and learn to breastfeed.

If your baby continues to be unable to grasp your breast correctly, your lactation consultant may recommend that you place an ultra-thin, soft silicone nipple shield over your nipple to help your baby latch on more easily. When your baby begins sucking, your own nipple is drawn into the shield, and milk flows through holes at the tip.

It's important that you use a nipple shield with the guidance of a lactation consultant who is familiar with its use. She can help you select the appropriate size, position the shield correctly over your nipple, ensure that your infant is able to drink milk using the shield, monitor his weight gain closely, and give you tips for how to wean from the shield as quickly as possible. Some babies need to use a nipple shield for only a few feedings, while others may require it for several weeks or more. After nursing with the shield for several minutes, try to remove it and latch your baby directly to your breast.

When using a nipple shield, you should pump after breastfeeding three or more times each day to express remaining milk, since nursing with the shield may not fully drain your breasts. If you maintain an abundant milk supply, it will be easier for your baby to learn to latch on directly to your breast and nurse effectively.

If Your Baby Is Too Sleepy

As a result of a long labor, birth trauma, immaturity, medications you received during childbirth, or other reasons, some newborns sleep longer than desired in the early days of life. You might be anxious to begin breastfeeding only to discover that it takes two cooperative partners to make the process work. While some newborns awaken every few hours and let you know they are hungry, others do not give regular feeding cues (see page 57) and must be coaxed to nurse. At a time when you may be exhausted and overwhelmed, an apparently contented, non-demanding infant can seem like a blessing. Well-meaning family and friends may reinforce this misperception by telling you how fortunate you are that your newborn sleeps through the night. Before long, however, ineffective and infrequent nursing can result in an underweight infant and an inadequate milk supply. If you are having trouble waking your baby, try the following techniques:

- If your newborn is not displaying feeding cues (see illustrations on the next page) at least every three and a half hours, try to wake him and offer your breast. He will be easier to rouse from light sleep (look for rapid eye movements, arm and leg movements, facial twitches, or mouthing motions).

- Try dimming the lights. Babies are more likely to open their eyes in subdued room lighting and often close their eyes in bright light.

- Un-swaddle your baby and unfasten or remove some clothing. To wake him and interest him in feeding, you may need to undress your baby down to his diaper and make him less cozy.

- Stimulate your baby by changing his diaper, wiping his bottom with a wet wipe, gently rubbing his arms and legs, stroking his head, or massaging the soles of his feet. Pat his back or walk your fingers along his spine.

- Gently run your finger along his upper lip. Start in the midline and move toward the outer edge, one side at a time.

- Place your baby skin-to-skin upright between your breasts. Skin-to-skin contact promotes feeding behaviors, and babies naturally open their eyes when placed upright.

- Hold your baby on your arm, with his head in the palm of your hand and his back supported on your forearm. Use your other hand to support his bottom. Moving both arms together, gently lift your baby upright against your chest; then slowly lower him to your lap. Gently move him several times from your lap to your chest and see if his eyes open.

- Talk to or sing to your baby. Use a high-pitched voice and exaggerate your intonation as you accentuate each syllable.

- After washing your hands and being careful of sharp fingernails, place the nail side of your pinky finger against the baby's tongue and stimulate the roof of his mouth with the fleshy part of your finger. After your baby starts sucking, remove your finger and offer your breast.

- Some drowsy babies who appear to be uninterested in feeding actually have borderline low blood sugar. (See box, next page.) Giving a sleepy baby a little nourishment can perk him up and bring him to

an alert state so he can nurse effectively.

If Your Baby Needs Supplemental Milk

Ideally your baby will be solely breastfed during your hospital stay, without receiving any additional fluids. However, sometimes a valid medical reason—such as premature birth, significant jaundice, or low blood sugar—makes it necessary to give extra milk to a breastfed newborn until your milk production increases or your baby is able

Feeding Cues

 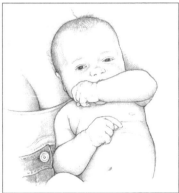

Your baby will signal that he is ready to nurse by rousing from sleep, moving his tongue or mouth, or trying to suck on his fingers, hand, or wrist.

Low Blood Sugar (Hypoglycemia)

Sometimes health professionals prescribe supplemental formula for a breastfed newborn to correct low blood sugar. Glucose, a simple sugar, is your baby's most important source of energy. Glucose is carried in the blood to every cell in the body, including brain cells, and provides essential fuel for body functions. During fetal life, a baby gets glucose from its mother through the umbilical cord. During the last three months of gestation, babies store some of this glucose to maintain blood glucose levels during the first few days of life, until they are feeding well. Lactose in breastmilk converts to glucose during digestion, and regular feedings maintain steady blood glucose levels.

A baby's blood sugar level usually is lowest one to two hours after birth as he adjusts to life outside the womb. Ordinarily blood glucose levels spontaneously rise at two to three hours after birth, as sugar is released from normal glucose stores. Some babies are at risk for persistent low blood glucose in the first hours and days of life, including (1) premature babies and babies who are considered small for their birth dates (who may have fewer sugar stores), (2) babies who have had a complicated delivery or respiratory distress after birth (who may rapidly use up their sugar stores), (3) large-for-date infants and babies born to mothers with gestational diabetes (who may be affected by their mother's hormonal imbalance), and (4) babies with rare medical conditions causing low blood sugar.

During the first two days of life, hospitals follow guidelines for periodically checking blood sugar levels in at-risk infants. While a brief drop in blood sugar below normal levels is harmless, prolonged periods of hypoglycemia can cause long-term developmental problems. Damage to the brain is more likely to occur when hypoglycemia causes symptoms, including tremors, a high-pitched cry, seizures, lethargy, limpness, rapid breathing, poor feeding, or blue color. Your baby's doctor may prescribe extra milk temporarily (your own expressed milk, donor breastmilk, or infant formula) to raise your baby's blood glucose level and protect him from possible harm. Rarely, IV (intravenous) glucose must be given to correct hypoglycemia.

Even if your baby requires supplemental milk, you can still continue breastfeeding. To prevent low blood sugar and help stabilize your baby's glucose level, begin breastfeeding as soon as possible after you give birth and offer your breast often for both comfort and food. Hold your baby skin-to-skin as much as possible and avoid letting him cry excessively, which can use up glucose stores. If he is not nursing well, the hospital staff can help you offer some of your expressed milk by spoon or cup.

to nurse effectively. The most important thing is to tend to your baby's welfare first and then focus on improving the effectiveness of breastfeeding and discontinuing the supplemental milk.

OPTIONS FOR SUPPLEMENTAL MILK

When supplemental milk is needed, the ideal choice is your own expressed breastmilk. You may be able to obtain sufficient colostrum or milk using hand expression or a hospital-grade electric breast pump, available on the maternity ward. If a larger volume of milk is needed than you can express, infant formula may be required (unless you have access to screened, processed donor breastmilk from a distributing Mothers' Milk Bank). (See Chapter 8, pages 231–233, and Resources.) Often, only a minimal amount of supplement is necessary until your own milk increases in volume. Many formula choices are available, including cow's milk–based, soy-based, and hypoallergenic formulas, which may be appropriate if you have a family history of allergic disease (asthma, eczema, food allergies, or hay fever).

METHODS OF FEEDING SUPPLEMENTAL MILK

The most common method of feeding supplemental milk to a newborn is with a bottle and a nipple. If you prefer to avoid bottle feeding your baby, however, ask for an alternative method described below. Many lactation consultants prefer alternative feeding methods over bottle feeding, especially for a baby who has not yet learned to breastfeed effectively. However, cup feeding is the only alternative feeding method that has been studied, and research shows no significant benefit of cup feeding over bottle-feeding in maintaining breastfeeding beyond hospital discharge. Before using an alternative method of supplementing, be sure you're carefully instructed in its proper use by a health professional with experience using the method. (See Chapter 8, pages 233–236.)

Bottle and Nipple. Bottle feeding—the traditional method of supplementing breastfed infants—is familiar, fast, and convenient, and most newborns have no difficulty drinking from a bottle. However, it is widely believed that early bottle feeding of breastfed infants causes "nipple confusion," or a preference for bottle feeding over breastfeeding. Yet many breastfed newborns receive one or more small supplemental feedings by bottle during the first week of life and go on to breastfeed exclusively. Other infants, including some whose mothers work outside the home, accept a bottle readily and resume breastfeeding without apparent difficulty.

On the other hand, exposing breastfed newborns to artificial nipples may make it more difficult for them to learn to breastfeed. Newborns who are just learning to nurse are more susceptible than older babies to being "seduced" by bottles, because the amount of colostrum a baby gets during early breastfeeding is relatively low compared to the free flow of milk from a bottle. If a baby who does not yet breastfeed well is offered a bottle, he may find the longer and more rigid artificial nipple that supplies him with more and faster-flowing milk to be easier and more rewarding than being breastfed. This preference is more likely to occur with babies having difficulty latching on or getting insufficient milk when they breastfeed.

Nipple confusion is less likely to occur if: (1) your baby has already nursed well numerous times, (2) your nipples protrude well, and (3) your milk flows easily. Fortunately even if supplemental bottle feedings have contributed to nipple confusion, all is not lost. By applying the basics of good breastfeeding technique, using a pump to keep your milk supply abundant (see Chapter 6, pages 145–146), and getting help from a breastfeeding specialist, your baby eventually can learn to nurse effectively and be breastfed exclusively.

Cup. Cup feeding is common around the world. Done properly, it can be safe and effective for newborns. There are several options—from using a one-ounce plastic medicine cup to special cup-feeding devices, such as Medela's SoftFeeder, designed for supplementing breastfed newborns. (See Resources.)

Spoon. Your baby can also eat from a plastic spoon used in a similar manner to a cup. You can hand-express a small amount of colostrum directly onto the spoon, and offer this to your baby, placing

Supplementing a Breastfed Newborn by Bottle

• Keep your baby semi-upright during the feeding.

• Use a slower flowing nipple.

• Stroke your baby's upper lip with the nipple and wait until he opens his mouth wide, similar to breastfeeding.

• Let your baby take the nipple into his mouth, instead of pushing it in.

• Hold the bottle as horizontally as possible—rather than vertically— to reduce the rate of milk flow.

• Remove the nipple from your baby's mouth from time to time or tilt the bottle so that milk doesn't flow into the nipple. This will give your baby a chance to pause, rest, and catch his breath.

• Don't overfeed. In the first two days your newborn requires relatively small feedings. He should be ready to try nursing again within one and a half to three hours. (Also see Chapter 6, pages 156-158.)

How Much Breastmilk Your Baby Takes

You might be surprised to know how little milk your baby requires during the first two days of life, and how rapidly your milk increases in quantity. Healthy full-term infants are born with extra water and sugar stores that help supply their needs until your own milk production surges around the third day postpartum. Although some women produce much more colostrum than others, the average feeding in the first twenty-four hours is less than half an ounce of milk—often just a teaspoon or so! Ordinarily this small amount is all that your baby needs. Between twenty-four and forty-eight hours after your baby's birth, your milk production increases and your baby takes up to half an ounce or more at a feeding. By the third day, as your milk comes in, your baby probably will drink at least an ounce at each feeding. And by four to five days of age, his intake will increase to about two ounces per feeding. By the end of the first week, if your baby has been nursing well, you can expect to produce about twenty ounces of milk each day. Within another week or so, he may drink twenty-four to twenty-eight ounces each day.

Feeding from a Cup

To feed your newborn from a cup, fill the cup with half an ounce of milk. Begin when your baby is calm and alert. Hold him upright, place an absorbent bib under his chin to catch spilled milk, and rest the brim of the cup gently on his lower lip. Tip the cup slightly so that the milk just touches his lips. It is important *not to pour* the milk into his mouth. Instead, allow him to lap or sip and swallow the milk at his own pace. Do not try to cup-feed your baby if he is not alert or is crying or drowsy.

Babies need to suck, both for comfort and for proper development of their palate, jaw, and the muscles of their face, lips, and tongue. Consequently cup feeding is not recommended for the long term. Rather it is intended as a temporary method of giving necessary milk supplements in the hospital while your baby is learning to breastfeed.

the tip of the spoon on his lower lip. Sometimes even a tiny amount of milk will rouse a sleepy newborn so he is able to latch on and begin nursing.

Dropper or Syringe. Some lactation consultants use a plastic eyedropper to feed small amounts of milk in the same way oral medications are given to babies. Others have experience feeding newborns with a regular syringe (without the needle, of course) or a periodontal syringe that has a curved plastic tip. Hold your baby upright and begin by giving only drops at a time, making sure he swallows before giving more. This method, like using a spoon, is suitable only for giving small amounts of milk in the first day or two after birth.

Supplemental Nursing System (SNS). If your baby is able to latch on and breastfeed yet still requires supplemental milk, it is possible to feed the supplement at the same time you breastfeed by using a special feeding device, known as the Supplemental Nursing System (SNS). This method causes no nursing disruption and actually enhances your baby's breastfeeding technique by giving him an immediate reward for his efforts. Convenient starter SNS kits are available for short-term use, or your lactation consultant can fashion a similar feeding device using a hospital feeding tube and a feeding bottle. You will need assistance from a lactation consultant at your hospital who has experience using the device. The SNS works best when a baby already knows how to nurse. Babies having latch-on problems may not be able to correctly grasp both your breast and the SNS tubing. (For more information on the SNS, see Chapter 8, page 234.)

Finger. Finger feeding is an alternative method used when your baby has not yet learned to latch on to your breast. The method uses the SNS or a similar system, with the tubing taped to your finger (usually the index finger). As your baby sucks your finger, milk flows through the narrow tubing into his mouth. Some lactation consultants also use the method with a plastic eyedropper or feeding syringe placed against the finger. When your baby starts sucking, the consultant rewards his efforts with a small amount of milk. Advocates of finger feeding argue that it provides "suck training" for an infant, but no research has been conducted to support this claim. Many lactation consultants use finger feeding for only a minute or two to get a reluctant nurser sucking before attempting latch-on.

Late-Preterm Infants

Infants born at thirty-four, thirty-five, or thirty-six weeks' gestation are known as "late preterm." The proportion of all U.S. births that are late preterm has increased over the past fifteen years. Late-preterm births now approach 10 percent of all births and represent more than 70 percent of all preterm births.

Although the reason that late-preterm births are on the rise is not fully understood, contributing factors include: (1) an increase in elective inductions of labor, (2) the need to deliver some infants early due to medical complications, (3) more pregnancies occurring among older women, and (4) the increased use of fertility treatments, which has led to a rise in pregnancies of twins and higher multiples.

Late-preterm infants have been called "imposter babies" because they often look like full-term infants. Hospital personnel and parents tend to treat these apparently healthy infants as if they were developmentally mature. In reality they have more medical problems and longer hospital stays than full-term infants. Late-preterm infants are at increased risk for poor feeding, low blood sugar, severe jaundice, breathing difficulties, infections, difficulty maintaining body temperature, and excessive weight loss after birth. These babies often have trouble latching on and breastfeeding effectively because they have lower muscle tone, are sleepy, and tire easily. Mothers of preterm infants are more likely to have a medical condition, such as gestational diabetes, high blood pressure, or cesarean birth, that may make breastfeeding more challenging.

In addition to immediate skin-to-skin contact and early, frequent breastfeeding, you may need to begin prevention pumping (see opposite page) to ensure that you bring in and preserve a generous milk supply until your baby matures enough to breastfeed effectively. (See Chapter 6, pages 145–146.) To assist your baby in latching on, you may need to temporarily use an ultra-thin, soft silicone nipple shield. (See page 64.) Close follow-up after discharge is essential because late-preterm babies have a higher rate of hospital readmission, commonly due to poor feeding, infections, and severe jaundice. (See Chapter 4, pages 97–99.)

Extra Breastfeeding Help for You

You may need extra help getting breastfeeding off to a good start for various reasons that require close follow-up and support after you've been discharged from the hospital, such as:

• A previous breastfed baby did not gain weight well.

• You have flat or inverted nipples.

• There is a variation in the appearance of your breasts (such as a marked difference in size between your breasts or if you have tubular-shaped breasts).

• Previous breast surgery has damaged your milk ducts or the nerves involved in milk production.

• You have had a breast abscess.

• Your nipples are extremely sore.

• Your breast size increased minimally during pregnancy.

• Your milk has not come in abundantly within three days of birth.

• You are experiencing severe postpartum breast engorgement.

• You have a medical problem, such as a postpartum hemorrhage, high blood pressure, or an infection.

Prevention Pumping or Insurance Pumping

In the past, it was thought that all babies took as much milk as they needed, but it is now understood that some at-risk infants need more time to learn to nurse effectively. Meanwhile, "prevention pumping" is a way to protect your milk supply from rapidly dwindling if your baby is not able to drain your breasts well. By using a "mechanical baby" to regularly remove any remaining milk at the end of each feeding, you can establish and maintain an abundant supply. Furthermore, having a generous milk supply allows a baby who does not nurse well to obtain milk more readily. And if supplemental feedings are needed, your own expressed milk makes the ideal supplement. Chapter 6 covers "prevention pumping" for at-risk newborns, as well as a variety of other situations in which using a breast pump can help you overcome breastfeeding problems.

Extra Breastfeeding Help for Baby

If you have an at-risk baby you may need to begin "prevention pumping" (see above) to bring in and maintain an abundant milk supply until your baby is able to breastfeed effectively. He may need extra help learning to breastfeed if any of the following is true:

- Your baby weighs less than six pounds or is premature (born at fewer than thirty-seven weeks' gestation) or is a late-preterm infant (born between thirty-four and thirty-six weeks).

- He has difficulty latching on to one or both breasts.

- Your baby has difficulty sucking.

- He has an abnormality of the tongue, jaw, or palate.

- You have twins or greater multiples.

- Your baby has a medical problem, such as jaundice, heart or breathing difficulties, an infection, or other illness.

- He has a developmental problem, such as Down syndrome.

Your pediatrician needs to monitor your at-risk baby's weight closely until breastfeeding is going well. Ask to be referred to a lactation consultant, who can help with your breastfeeding technique, show you how to use a breast pump, and communicate with your baby's doctor about feeding expressed milk, donor milk, and/or supplemental formula.

Monitoring Your Baby's Weight at Home

New technology now makes it possible to follow your baby's weight at home. You can rent an accurate, portable, user-friendly electronic scale to weigh your baby periodically between medical visits until you are confident that your breastfed baby is thriving.

These scales also allow you to measure your baby's milk intake by weighing him before and after nursing. This pre-feed and post-feed weighing procedure is known as *infant feeding test weights.* Your baby's weight change after feeding represents the amount of milk he just drank. (See Chapter 4, page 90, and Chapter 8, pages 227–228.) This method is highly accurate if a reliable scale is used and you are taught how to perform the procedure correctly. Weighing your baby at home can be very helpful in monitoring infants at risk for inadequate breastfeeding. If you have a breastfeeding problem and decide to use infant feeding test weights at home, your lactation consultant and your baby's doctor can help you modify your feeding plan as needed. Of course, a scale cannot substitute for your baby's health-care provider. Rather, the information should make you and your health-care professionals a stronger team. To locate a rental-grade electronic infant scale, see Resources.

The Importance of Early Follow-up

Many new mothers are discharged from the hospital before they feel confident about breastfeeding or other baby care. The American Academy of Pediatrics (AAP) recommends that all infants be seen by an experienced health-care provider within forty-eight hours of discharge. Early follow-up within two days is essential to ensure that: (1) your milk has come in and is flowing well, (2) your baby is nursing effectively, and (3) he has not lost too much weight or developed newborn jaundice. (See Chapter 4, pages 97–99.) While a telephone call from your lactation consultant is a nice addition to a follow-up visit, it is not an adequate substitute for being evaluated in person.

If your baby is not nursing well by the time the two of you are discharged, arrange for an appointment the following day with the hospital lactation consultant, your baby's doctor, or at a private breastfeeding clinic. Whenever you seek breastfeeding help from someone other than your baby's doctor, be sure to keep him or her informed of all visits and feeding recommendations from other professionals. Your baby's doctor should coordinate all aspects of your infant's health care. The WIC program and La Leche League are additional sources of valuable breastfeeding information and support.

The First
Weeks of
Breastfeeding

4

The first few days and weeks at home with your new baby are a precious time. Breastfeeding will be the most time-consuming, most intimate, and possibly, the most satisfying aspect of new motherhood. In fact, getting breastfeeding off to a good start is one of the most important things you can do to smooth your adjustment to new parenthood. At the beginning, learning to care for and getting to know your baby can feel overwhelming. This is a perfectly natural reaction, given the newness of the experience and the fact that you will undoubtedly be tired and excited at the same time. You may also expect everything to fall into place perfectly right away. Don't be disappointed if there are some fits and starts—this is completely normal. Try to relax, ask for plenty of support from your partner and family, and grab a few hours of sleep whenever you can. You may be surprised by how energized you feel after even a short break. If you encounter breastfeeding difficulties, rest assured that expert help and support are available from many sources.

Getting Comfortable

At first you will probably nurse your baby in a few comfortable places around the house, such as your bed, sofa, or cozy chair or rocker. For first-time moms, privacy may be a priority, while those of you with small children may prefer a convenient central location, where you can keep an eye on things. Plan to have several pillows or cushions and a footstool on hand. Eventually you will find that you can nurse with ease almost anywhere.

Keep a supply of clean diapers, infant wipes, and extra infant clothing nearby, so you can feed and change your baby without having to leave your favorite nursing spot. In addition to having your phone and a trash can handy, stock your nursing nook with some enjoyable reading materials for leisurely breastfeeding. Believe it or not, you will soon be able to nurse without feeling like you need a third hand. If you have other children, fill a basket or box with a few favorite toys and storybooks to occupy them in your presence while you nurse. Finally, be sure to keep a pitcher or sports bottle handy so that you can sip water conveniently while you breastfeed.

Asking for Help

Breastfeeding is easier and more successful when you have a strong support system. Ideally your partner will be your chief source of help and encouragement. Your mother, mother-in-law, sister, or friend might also be able to help out for a period of time. Your support person can do household chores such as laundry, prepare meals, encourage you to nap, occupy an older child, bring you a beverage, burp and change the baby, handle callers and visitors, and bolster your spirits. You may also want to hire a postpartum doula (see Chapter 2, page 22) to ease your transition to new motherhood.

Wait a while before inviting relatives, no matter how well intentioned they may be, if you are not completely comfortable with them, if they tend to criticize your parenting choices, or if you feel they are not genuinely helpful. Instead, choose a compatible helper whom you can count on to encourage and assist you. Even if no one can help in your home, you can get telephone support by calling your own or your baby's doctor, a hospital lactation consultant, local WIC clinic, peer counselor, La Leche League, or experienced friend.

A Family Honeymoon

While you are getting to know your new baby, keep visitors to a minimum except for those whose help you can trust. The fact is, a steady stream of visitors not only exposes your newborn to germs, it inevitably interrupts or postpones breastfeeding, and this can be very frustrating for both you and your baby. For now, discourage drop-in visits and use your caller ID or answering machine to screen calls. Ask your partner or helper to protect your need for privacy and nursing time with your little one with comments like, "She's with the baby now," or "She's finally napping, and I don't want to disturb her." Experiencing an intimate family honeymoon—a secluded cocooning period—is the best way to get to know your baby and establish your breastfeeding routines. Once she is nursing well and you are more rested, you will have plenty of time and energy to receive visitors and truly enjoy their company.

Sleep, Glorious Sleep . . .

In the first weeks after the birth of your baby, you can expect to be seriously sleep deprived. There's no gentle way to break this news, I'm afraid. Nighttime feedings, continuous baby care, and sheer physical depletion after giving birth inevitably take their toll. No matter how often you are warned about how little sleep you will get in the first few weeks and months of motherhood, the reality of constant fatigue can make you feel discouraged and depressed, but even a little rest can change your whole perspective. Many new moms make the mistake of coming home from the hospital and diving into ambitious projects such as finishing the nursery or completing work assignments. The best advice to counteract drop-dead exhaustion is to simply rest and sleep when you are not feeding your baby or giving her other essential care. Since your nighttime sleep will be interrupted, make a habit of napping when your baby naps. Wearing your bathrobe during the day may serve as a physical reminder to slow down and rest. Be assured that once breastfeeding is going smoothly and a daily routine emerges, you will find time to get other things done.

When Your Milk Comes In

On the second to third day after giving birth, your breasts will become quite full and firm. The small amount of yellowish colostrum your breasts have been making changes to creamy-white transitional milk and greatly increases in quantity. This surge in milk production, accompanied by breast swelling and firmness, is commonly referred to as your "milk coming in," or postpartum breast engorgement.

The sudden increase in milk production is triggered by the abrupt fall in your blood levels of estrogen and progesterone after delivery, together with the high level of prolactin in your blood at the end of pregnancy. Although early and frequent nursing is thought to help increase milk production sooner, postpartum breast engorgement also occurs in new moms who feed formula to their babies. Medications to suppress milk production are no longer routinely prescribed for women who don't choose to breastfeed. What this means is that if you change your mind, you can easily switch from formula feeding to breastfeeding in the first few days after delivery.

How Breastmilk Is Made and Released

Whether or not you intend to breastfeed, your milk production

Transitional and Mature Milk

The milk you produce—beginning around three or four days after your baby is born to about ten to fourteen days—is no longer colostrum but not yet mature milk. Since the composition of your breastmilk changes daily during this time, it is commonly known as *transitional milk*. The amount you produce steadily increases, and your baby begins to gain weight rapidly. At the same time, the proportion of protein, fat, and lactose gradually changes to that of mature milk.

The breastmilk your body produces after about ten to fourteen days, known as *mature milk*, is whiter and is produced in much greater quantities than colostrum. The composition of mature milk remains fairly stable as you continue breastfeeding, although the fat content steadily rises throughout a feeding.

surges a few days after delivery. However, production quickly stops if you feed your baby infant formula rather than breastmilk. Breast engorgement usually subsides within three to four days in mothers who feed formula, although some may leak milk for a few weeks. If you breastfeed, you will continue to produce milk as long as you nurse your baby regularly or use a breast pump. Although many hormones are involved in making and releasing milk, attention is usually focused on the roles of *prolactin* and *oxytocin*. Both hormones are made by the pituitary gland, located at the base of your brain. Infant suckling is the driving force that controls the release of these hormones. The act of nursing stimulates nerve endings in your nipple and areola, causing a message to be carried to your brain, which, in turn, triggers the release of prolactin and oxytocin.

PROLACTIN

Prolactin is the key hormone that causes your milk glands to manufacture milk. Prolactin is especially important for triggering abundant milk production after delivery. Your prolactin level is high during pregnancy and right after you've given birth. If you begin breastfeeding, your prolactin level remains elevated—with even higher spikes after each nursing—and milk production continues. However, if you feed your newborn formula, your prolactin level rapidly declines, and your body stops producing breastmilk.

OXYTOCIN

Oxytocin, the same hormone that causes your uterus to contract during labor, also plays a key role in lactation. When your baby starts to suckle at your breast, oxytocin is released from your pituitary gland into your bloodstream and causes the muscle cells surrounding your milk glands to contract. The squeezing action of these tiny muscle cells forces milk and fat particles out of your milk glands and into the ducts that carry milk to your nipple openings. The effect of oxytocin on milk release is known by two common terms, the *letdown reflex* or the *milk ejection reflex*. The letdown reflex is triggered in both breasts simultaneously and typically occurs within a minute or two of breastfeeding or using a breast pump.

When your letdown reflex propels milk out of the glands into your milk ducts, it is easily available to your nursing infant if she has correctly grasped your nipple and surrounding areola. With the nipple positioned well back in her mouth, your baby's tongue and jaws compress the areola and the underlying milk ducts, and milk is removed by a wave-like movement of her tongue, from the tip to the back. With this milking action and a brisk letdown reflex, your baby is able to drink milk easily.

When you begin breastfeeding after delivery, oxytocin not only causes milk to be ejected from your breasts, but also triggers uterine contractions that help shrink your

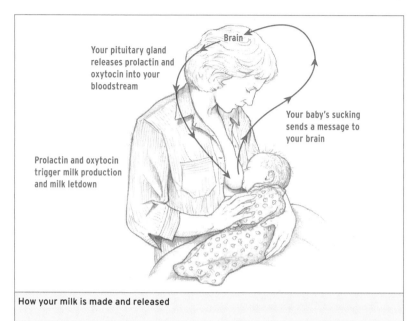

Your pituitary gland releases prolactin and oxytocin into your bloodstream

Brain

Your baby's sucking sends a message to your brain

Prolactin and oxytocin trigger milk production and milk letdown

How your milk is made and released

uterus back to its normal size. These contractions can cause some cramping in your lower abdomen during the first week or so of breastfeeding. This temporary discomfort, known as afterpains, is a telltale sign of oxytocin release.

Signs of Letdown

After about two weeks of breastfeeding your baby, the letdown reflex is well-conditioned and your milk supply should be quite abundant. The sudden stretching of your milk ducts as they rapidly fill with milk can create a sensation in the breasts that many women describe as a slight "pins-and-needles" feeling, or as "tingling" or "tightening." Some women experience milk letdown as mildly uncomfortable, while others don't notice any sensation. Most perceive letdown as soothing and pleasant. In addition, you may feel thirsty, relaxed, or even sleepy when your milk lets down. One of the most dramatic signs of letdown is seeing your milk drip rapidly or spray from your breasts in multiple jets. Your baby may start gulping milk or even pull away to catch her breath when the reflex is triggered shortly after she starts nursing. You can wear disposable or washable breast pads inside your nursing bra to absorb any milk that leaks between feedings. It's typical to experience milk letdown more than once during a feeding, but most women aren't aware of this. Research shows that babies drink about one ounce of milk with each letdown. Letdown sensations and milk leakage are usually less dramatic after six to eight weeks postpartum.

The Lowdown on Letdown

Although milk letdown is triggered by breastfeeding (or pumping), it also can be conditioned to occur simply by hearing your baby cry, smelling the top of her head, or looking at her. Because stress and anxiety can interfere with breastfeeding, it helps to relax and develop familiar routines that help promote letdown. Sitting in a favorite chair, pouring a glass of water to drink, or gently massaging your breasts can trigger milk flow before you actually begin to nurse. Some mothers find their milk lets down at work if they look at a picture of their baby while pumping. On the other hand, pain, negative emotions (such as embarrassment or fear), interruptions, and time pressures can impair the letdown reflex and limit the amount of milk you pump or your baby takes during a feeding.

Staying Well-Drained: It's Essential

While prolactin and oxytocin play an important role in making and releasing milk, hormones alone do not fully explain why nursing moms continue to produce milk. For example, we know that if you nurse from one breast only, the other, unsuckled breast soon stops producing milk. The unused breast dries up, even though nursing on the other side releases prolactin and oxytocin into your bloodstream and both breasts continue to be exposed to these lactation hormones. We now know that the amount of milk produced in each breast over the long term mainly depends on how much milk is drained through active nursing or pumping. Milk that accumulates in the breast contains a protein inhibitor that scientists call *feedback inhibitor of lactation* (FIL). When milk is not removed regularly, the amount of FIL builds up and sends a signal to the milk-producing glands to decrease the rate of production. In addition, over-full breasts create excessive pressure that can damage milk glands and decrease your supply.

For these reasons, your body produces more milk when your baby nurses frequently and effectively drains your breasts. Of course the flipside of this equation is that you will produce less milk if your baby nurses infrequently or ineffectively. Common examples of breastfeeding problems that can lead to poor milk drainage and a low milk supply include infant difficulties latching on correctly or lack of vigorous sucking, severely sore nipples that interfere with feedings or inhibit milk letdown, and being separated from your baby and unable to nurse regularly. To prevent an unwanted decrease in your milk supply in cases like these, it's important to drain milk from your breasts frequently with an effective breast pump until the breastfeeding problem can be remedied. Hospital-grade rental models or highly effective daily-use pumps can empty both breasts well in ten to fifteen minutes. If a breast pump is not available, you can express milk by hand. (See Chapter 6 for more information on breast pumps and hand expressing.) It's especially important that your breasts get drained regularly and effectively once your milk starts to come in.

Foremilk and Hindmilk

On average, fat makes up about four percent of your breastmilk and provides more than half of its calories, but the fat content of your breastmilk doesn't stay the same—it varies according to how full your breasts are. The milk your baby first drinks from a full breast is known as *foremilk*. This milk is somewhat watery and has a lower-than-average fat content. As the feeding progresses, and the more your breast is drained, the fat content of your milk steadily rises. The high-fat milk your baby drinks later in a feeding is known as *hindmilk*. The fat content of hindmilk can rise to 12 percent or more, but the amount of this high-fat, creamy milk is very small—like having dessert. At the second breast, your baby begins again with a lower-fat milk, but as the fat content climbs during the feeding, she becomes full, sleepy, and thoroughly satisfied.

Some lactation consultants place great emphasis on draining the first breast very well to ensure your baby gets enough calorie-rich hindmilk. However, trying to manipulate your baby's fat intake is almost always unnecessary, and may be counter-productive. After all, the fat content of your milk goes up as the amount of available milk goes down. Nursing your baby longer on a well-drained breast may give her only a tiny amount of additional high-fat milk, when she could easily drink much more milk if she were offered the second, fuller breast. Your healthy baby is quite capable of consistently regulating her daily fat

> **Tip**
>
> Instead of focusing on whether your baby is getting enough hindmilk, give her the opportunity to drink from both breasts if she wants. Allow her to nurse at the first breast until her sucking and swallowing slow down, which usually signals that milk flow has tapered and the breast is well drained. Then burp her and offer the other side, where plenty of milk is easily available.

> **Tip**
>
> In almost all cases where a breastfed baby is not growing well, the problem is caused by drinking *too little milk*, rather than failing to get enough hindmilk.

intake through different patterns of breastfeeding. She may take frequent smaller feedings or fewer larger feedings; she may prefer to nurse from both breasts at each meal or take only one side.

The First Weeks of Breastfeeding: What to Expect and When to Get Help

Breastfed babies have a wide range of feeding patterns. Each baby is a unique individual, with her own nursing habits. Even in the same family, mothers notice that different siblings have different nursing styles. Some babies breastfeed at closer intervals than others or take longer to complete a feeding. Some like to nurse in a leisurely fashion, while others get right down to business. Mothers often find a nickname for their baby's particular nursing style, ranging from the "nibbler" to the "barracuda."

While no two mother-baby pairs are alike, the following typical breastfeeding routines will help prepare you for what to expect during your first weeks at home. Beginning when your milk comes in, these guidelines will help you recognize the range of what are considered normal breastfeeding patterns, and give you guidance about when to seek help. It is

natural to have questions, doubts, or concerns after going home. Fortunately there is plenty of expert help and encouragement for overcoming any early glitches. Breastfeeding problems are always easier to remedy if you get help early.

LATCHING ON AND SUCKLING

By the time you go home from the hospital, your baby should be able to latch on to both breasts without much difficulty and suck actively for at least ten minutes per breast at each feeding. It is not uncommon for a baby to have an easier time latching on to one breast or to prefer one side, but do keep encouraging your baby to take both breasts. (See pages 95–96.)

Once your baby is latched on correctly, allow her to suck for as long as she wants. She may pause periodically and need some gentle prodding, but, in general, she should suck actively throughout most of the feeding. She probably will start sucking less vigorously, fall asleep, or come off the first breast after ten to fifteen minutes. This is a good time to burp her, change her diaper, and help rouse her to take the second side.

A baby usually takes more milk by nursing at both breasts than by taking one side only, so try to encourage her to nurse from both breasts at each feeding whenever possible during the early weeks. Allow her to stay at the second breast as long as she wants, although she may not nurse as long on this side. An infant nurses more vigorously at the first breast and usually takes more milk from that side. Alternate the side on which you start feedings, so that both of your breasts receive about the same stimulation and drainage. A lopsided milk supply can develop in a matter of days if you consistently start feedings on the same breast or if your baby favors one breast over another.

Get Help: If your baby is unable to latch on to one or both breasts, or latches briefly but does not suck effectively, try the strategies in Chapter 3, pages 52–56. If these techniques don't help, seek assistance right away. An infant latch-on problem is not only frustrating for both you and your baby, it can prevent your baby from getting enough milk and can cause your supply to go down. A lactation consultant can help you overcome the latch-on problem, thereby ensuring that your baby is well-fed and your milk supply plentiful.

SWALLOWING WHILE FEEDING

Your baby first starts nursing with short, fast bursts of sucking. As milk flow begins, the sucks get longer and slower. Swallowing is triggered when your baby's mouth fills with milk. Before your milk comes in abundantly, your baby may not swallow often during nursing, since the amount of colostrum is low. Once your milk has come in (usually on the second to fourth day), you should start to hear your baby swallow—a soft

"cuh, cuh, cuh" sound when she exhales—after every one or two sucks.

When your letdown is triggered, your baby may swallow after every suck in order to handle the rapid flow of milk. Audible swallowing after every one or two sucks should continue for most of the feeding. As milk flow slows down, your baby takes less milk per suck, and the frequency of swallowing will decrease. When your baby goes to the second breast, rapid swallowing should begin again.

Get Help: If you do not hear frequent swallowing when your baby nurses—and suspect that she is not drinking much milk—contact your baby's doctor. Infrequent swallowing may be due to a low milk supply or ineffective suckling that prevents your baby from getting enough milk.

> **Tip**
>
> Another way to tell that your baby is drinking milk is to watch for the distinct pause in the movement of her chin as her jaw drops to the lowest point during sucking. This is the point at which her open mouth fills with milk.

NURSING FREQUENCY

On average, your baby will show signs of wanting to nurse every two to three hours. Feedings are timed from the beginning of one nursing to the beginning of the next. Expect your newborn to nurse frequently—at least eight times every twenty-four hours, for about ten to fifteen minutes per breast at each feeding. In fact, ten or twelve feedings a day are not uncommon during the early weeks. Your baby may pause periodically but in general she should suck actively throughout most of the feeding. Burp her when she switches breasts. (See Chapter 3, page 58.)

After your baby finishes a feeding, she will probably be ready to nurse again within the next two hours. Don't be surprised if she sometimes wants to nurse only an hour or so after finishing her last feeding. Babies often cluster several feedings close together, especially in the late afternoons or evenings, and then sleep for a longer stretch at other times, such as the middle of the night (or so you can hope!).

Some new breastfeeding moms are not prepared for quite so many feedings. They may even assume they don't have enough milk. Instead of focusing on the clock, though, follow your baby's cues about how often she needs to nurse. Remember that feeding frequently in the early days and weeks after giving birth is the way you "place your order" for the amount of milk your body eventually will produce for your baby. Early frequent feeding ensures that your milk supply adjusts to match your baby's requirements. This is a classic example of supply meeting demand!

Although most babies will let you know when they are hungry, your baby may not make her needs known as often as she should. If she does not give feeding cues at least every three and a half hours during the daytime, you *should* gently rouse her from sleep, especially if she is starting to stir or having rapid eye movements. (See Chapter 3, pages 57, 66.) Pick her up, change her diaper, and remove some of her clothing to awaken her, and offer your breast.

Get Help: If your baby often sleeps through feeding times, seldom demands to be fed, or frequently needs to be awakened to nurse, contact her physician and have her weighed and checked. You should also let your baby's doctor know if she nurses more than twelve times each day or frequently acts hungry after breastfeeding. A lactation consultant can evaluate your breastfeeding technique, help you start using a breast pump to effectively drain your breasts, and make suggestions for improving your baby's intake of breastmilk.

Tip

To ensure that your baby breastfeeds often enough each day, don't let more than a single four- to five-hour interval go by without nursing her until she is at least a month old. Of course, you will want this longer interval to occur at night, if at all possible!

The Long and Short of It

Both very short and extremely long nursing sessions can signal a feeding problem. If your newborn suckles too briefly (only a few minutes per feeding), she probably isn't getting enough milk. On the other hand, if she nurses for more than about forty-five minutes total, or often seems hungry again shortly after feeding, it could mean that she is not being satisfied. When babies don't get enough milk there are generally two reasons: They're not nursing effectively or your milk supply is low. Often it is a combination of both. Contact your baby's doctor if you suspect your baby is not getting enough milk.

ACTING CONTENT

Generally, a well-fed baby is a contented baby. Breastfed newborns usually fall asleep at the second breast and act satisfied between feedings. Sometimes new parents don't recognize their baby's hunger cues because they mistakenly assume that an infant who has just finished nursing has automatically taken enough milk. However, an infant can nurse from both sides, and still not drink much milk. There are several explanations for this: your baby may have latched on incorrectly or maybe your milk letdown reflex wasn't triggered, or your milk production is low.

Get Help: If your baby acts hungry after most feedings (for example, if she is crying, sucking on her hands, rooting, or needs a pacifier to be consoled), she may not be getting enough milk—even if she is feeding frequently. Contact your baby's doctor who can check things out and refer you to a lactation consultant for additional help with breastfeeding.

Tip

The first thing to do when your baby appears hungry after nursing is return her to the fullest breast for another chance at feeding.

Tip

Not all fussiness in a breastfed baby is due to hunger. Babies need human contact as much as they need food. Your baby may be crying because she doesn't want to be separated from you and wants you to hold her close. Even if your baby is well fed she may want to be carried and held to make her feel safe and secure.

DIAPER CLUES– BOWEL MOVEMENTS

During the early weeks of breastfeeding, the contents of your baby's diaper will be of surprising interest to you and provide a valuable tool to assess how she is breastfeeding. In the first few weeks, it can be very helpful to keep a daily record of your baby's feedings, wet diapers, and bowel movements.

Your baby's frequency of stools is a sensitive indicator that she is getting enough to eat. Expect your newborn's bowel movements to start to turn yellow by the fourth or fifth day after birth. Yellow "milk stools" typically appear within twenty-four hours after your milk comes in abundantly and your baby starts drinking generous amounts of milk. The stools are loose, about the consistency of yogurt, with little seedy curds. They often look like a mixture of cottage cheese and mustard or butterscotch pudding. A normal-sized milk stool is at least a tablespoon in amount, and often represents a sizeable clean-up job. (A dot or streak of stool on your baby's diaper should not be counted as a bowel movement.)

Your baby should pass four or more sizeable bowel movements each day for at least the first four to six weeks after her birth. Many breastfed newborns will pass a yellow milk stool with every nursing during the early weeks of life. This frequent stooling pattern is not diarrhea. It is entirely normal and indicates that your baby probably is getting plenty of milk.

After the first month or two, the number of daily bowel movements gradually declines. Some older exclusively breastfed infants continue to pass at least one stool each day, while others may go for several days—even a week or more—without having a bowel movement. In the first month of life, however, frequent bowel movements is a reassuring sign that your baby is getting enough milk.

Get Help: If your baby is still passing dark meconium or greenish brown "transition" stools by five days of age and has not yet had a yellow bowel movement, or if she has fewer than four stools each day or her bowel movements are very small (just a stain on the diaper), she may not be drinking enough milk. Contact your baby's doctor and have your little one checked and weighed to see whether she is getting all the milk she needs.

DIAPER CLUES– URINATION

Expect your baby to urinate six or more times a day. In the first two days, your baby may wet only a few times in twenty-four hours. As your milk production surges, though, the number of wet diapers should steadily increase. By the fourth or fifth day your baby should urinate after most, if not all, feedings, and produce at least six to eight wet diapers every twenty-four hours. The urine should be colorless (dilute), not yellow (concentrated).

Get Help: If your breastfed baby has a pinkish or orange-colored "brick dust" appearance in her diaper (a sign of concentrated urine) after the third day of life, contact her physician and have your baby checked. Show the diaper to her doctor, who will weigh your baby to tell if she is getting enough to eat. You also should notify your baby's doctor if your baby has fewer than six wet diapers each day after the fourth day or if her urine is dark yellow (not clear) or scant in quantity. These could be other indicators that your baby is not taking in enough breastmilk. You can work with a lactation consultant to increase your milk supply and improve your baby's nursing technique.

Tip

Because disposable diapers are so absorbent, it can be difficult to tell whether your baby has urinated. To get an idea how a wet diaper feels, pour one to two ounces of water onto a dry diaper. Or, you can place a tissue inside the diaper to tell if your baby has urinated.

WEIGHT LOSS

Your baby's weight is the most reliable way to tell if she is getting enough to eat. All babies lose some weight in the first days after birth. Peak weight loss typically occurs on the third day, just before your milk comes in. On average, breastfed babies lose a little more than formula-fed infants. This is because the amount of colostrum, or early milk, you produce is relatively low in the first two days. It is considered within the range of normal for a breastfed baby to lose up to 10 percent of her original birth weight in the first three days of life. This amounts to about eleven ounces for a seven-pound baby. However, most babies lose less than 10 percent of their birth weight (more like seven or eight ounces for a seven-pound baby) before they start gaining. Larger babies can lose a greater number of ounces than smaller babies yet still fall within the range of normal. Your baby is likely to lose more than the expected amount of weight after birth if your milk comes in later than usual (more than seventy-two hours after delivery).

Get Help: If your baby loses more than 8 to 10 percent of her original birth weight—either while she is in the hospital or by her early follow-up pediatric visit—or, if she continues to lose weight beyond four days of age, it is very likely that she is not getting enough milk from breastfeeding. If your baby is not taking enough milk, your breasts soon will stop making enough milk. The result will be an underweight infant and a low milk supply. Your baby's doctor should check your newborn and decide whether supplemental feedings of expressed breastmilk and/or formula are required. Meanwhile, you can keep your milk supply plentiful by using an electric breast pump to regularly drain your breasts after your baby has nursed. (See Chapter 6, pages 145–146.) Ask to be referred to a lactation consultant, who can help you with your breastfeeding technique and get your infant back to full breastfeeding as soon as possible.

WEIGHT GAIN

During the early weeks of life, breastfed infants usually gain weight at a surprisingly rapid rate. Most begin gaining weight by four to five days of age and will regain their lost weight and surpass their birth weight within ten to fourteen days. Although every baby's growth pattern is unique, most babies will gain about one ounce each day between birth and three months. This amounts to about ten to sixteen ounces (close to a pound) every two weeks. Many breastfed babies gain even more. After the first several months of life, the rate of weight gain gradually tapers off.

Get Help: If your baby is still below her birth weight by two weeks of age or has not started to gain at least five to seven ounces a week after your milk has come in, she may not be getting enough milk or breastfeeding effectively.

Your doctor can check her and decide whether supplemental milk is required and refer you to a lactation consultant. She can help you keep up your milk supply with pumping until your baby learns to breastfeed effectively. The sooner the problem is addressed, the easier it is to remedy.

BREAST ENGORGEMENT

Making milk that provides everything your baby needs to grow and develop is nothing less than a miraculous "super power." No wonder your breasts, which have already changed considerably during your pregnancy, undergo an even more incredible morphing act the first week after giving birth. Here are some of the ways you can expect your breasts to change and how these changes offer clues about how well breastfeeding is coming along.

Weighing Your Baby at Home

You can rent lightweight, user-friendly, affordable, and accurate electronic baby scales for weighing your baby at home, if you are concerned about whether or not she is getting enough milk. (See Resources.) Some health professionals discourage the use of scales at home, assuming they are inaccurate or that using a scale will be intimidating for parents. However, modern digital infant scales are highly accurate, and many new moms report that they can breastfeed with greater confidence knowing their baby is gaining weight. Home monitoring of your baby's weight is especially helpful for at-risk infants, such as babies born before term, twins, infants with jaundice, or any infant with a feeding problem. Accurate electronic scales also can be used to measure how much milk your baby drinks when breastfeeding by weighing her before and after nursing. As long as you don't change her clothes or her diaper, the difference between the pre-feeding and post-feeding weight represents the amount of milk your baby drank. (See Chapter 8, pages 227-228.)

Your milk comes in usually within two to four days after your baby's birth. It may come in a little earlier if you've given birth previously or delivered vaginally, compared to first-time moms or women who have had cesarean births. With engorgement, your breasts become larger, firmer, heavier, warmer, and may feel tender. While these changes are more dramatic in some women than in others, you can expect to know when your milk comes in. Rarely, breast engorgement and abundant milk production are delayed as long as five to seven days, sometimes due to medical complications or emotional stress. Although your baby may temporarily need supplemental milk, it's still possible to produce a full milk supply if your milk comes in late.

Get Help: Excessive engorgement can be a problem for some women, especially first-time moms. Occasionally a woman's breasts become extremely swollen, tense, and uncomfortable, temporarily making it difficult for her baby to latch on correctly and get milk. If your breasts are not well drained, severe engorgement can cause your milk supply to decrease within a few days. Contact your own and/or your baby's doctor if your breasts are severely engorged and you are having trouble latching your baby or getting your milk to flow. Ask to be referred to a lactation consultant who can help you use an electric pump to express your milk, soften your breasts and areola, and latch your baby. Meanwhile, hand expressing some milk and applying cool compresses can help decrease swelling and improve milk flow, making it easier for your baby to nurse. (See pages 99–101, later in this chapter.)

In a tiny percentage of women—sometimes those who are very ill postpartum—breast engorgement does not occur after delivery and milk production does not climb sufficiently to nourish their babies. If your baby seems hungry after most feedings or you do not think your milk has come in by four days postpartum, you should contact your baby's doctor and have your infant weighed to make sure she has not lost too much weight. Using an electric pump in addition to nursing your baby may help stimulate more milk production.

BREAST DRAINAGE

Your breasts should feel full before each feeding and become softer after your baby has nursed. The second breast suckled may be fuller at the next feeding because babies typically take more from the first side. After your longest night interval between feedings, your breasts should feel particularly full and they may leak milk at night or become so full that you awaken before your baby does. This is normal.

Get Help: If your breasts are engorged and do not soften when your baby suckles, this suggests that she is not draining much milk. This is especially likely if your baby is having trouble latching on, keeps coming off your breast, or does little sucking. At the other extreme, if your breasts do not feel fuller before feedings and your baby acts hungry after nursing, your milk may not have come in yet, or you may have a supply problem. Using a breast pump can be helpful in both situations by getting milk to flow and stimulating more production. Contact your baby's doctor, who can evaluate your infant and refer you to a lactation consultant for additional solutions.

NIPPLE TENDERNESS

Any early nipple tenderness should be much improved by the end of the first week. Your nipples might feel mildly tender for the first several days of nursing—usually at the beginning of feedings and subsiding as the feeding progresses. Nipple tenderness generally does not interfere with feedings and should dramatically improve once your milk has come in.

Get Help: If you are experiencing severe nipple pain that makes you dread nursing your baby, pain that lasts throughout a feeding or persists beyond a week, it may be that your baby is not breastfeeding correctly and is causing nipple injury. Severe nipple discomfort is not a normal part of breastfeeding! A lactation consultant can help you get your infant latched on comfortably for effective breastfeeding and give you tips for healing damaged skin. Since damaged nipples can be infected with bacteria or yeast, contact your doctor to see if you need a prescription to speed healing. (See this chapter and Chapter 8, pages 199–203).

MILK LETDOWN

You will notice the sensation of milk letdown within two to three weeks of birthing. Letdown usually occurs shortly after you begin nursing, and it can be triggered by the sight, sound, or smell of your baby. Once your milk supply is well established, letdown (the milk ejection reflex) causes noticeable but very brief breast sensations in many women—such as a slight tingling or pins-and-needles feeling, tightening or heaviness, or slight burning. Most women feel pleasantly relaxed when their milk is letting down. The rapid flow of milk during letdown may cause your baby to start gulping milk, and her rate of swallowing will increase. You may see your milk drip or spray from the other breast. These are reassuring signs that your baby is getting plenty of milk.

> **Tip**
>
> Have a cloth diaper handy to collect dripping milk while you're nursing. Disposable or reusable breast pads inside your nursing bra absorb milk that leaks between feedings and protect your clothing. Excessive milk leaking and sensations of milk letdown tend to diminish after about eight weeks. (See Chapter 8, page 209–210.)

Early Breastfeeding Screening Form

Even though you can't actually see how much milk your baby takes while nursing, the preceding guidelines can help you know whether your newborn is breastfeeding effectively and getting plenty of milk. If your baby can latch on well to both breasts, nurses often with frequent audible swallowing, seems contented after feedings, wets six or more diapers, and has at least four yellow bowel movements each day, she is most likely thriving, and your breastfeeding is off to a great start. Similarly, if your milk has come in and is flowing well, if your letdown reflex is well conditioned, and your nipples are not very sore, then breastfeeding is working well for you, too. However, if you have any doubts about how breastfeeding is going during the first few weeks, the following questions can help you know whether you would benefit from getting extra help as early as possible.

1. Do you feel breastfeeding is going well for you so far? **Yes No**
2. Has your milk come in yet (i.e., did your breasts get firm and full between the second to fifth postpartum days)? **Yes No**
3. Is your baby able to latch on to both breasts without difficulty? **Yes No**
4. Is your baby able to sustain rhythmic suckling for at least ten minutes total per feeding? **Yes No**
5. Does your baby usually demand to feed? (Answer No if you have a sleepy baby who needs to be awakened for most feedings.) **Yes No**
6. Does your baby usually nurse at both breasts at each feeding? **Yes No**
7. Does your baby nurse approximately every two to three hours, with no more than one long interval of up to five hours at night (at least eight feedings each twenty-four-hour period)? **Yes No**
8. Do your breasts feel full before feedings? **Yes No**
9. Do your breasts feel softer after feedings? **Yes No**
10. Are your nipples extremely sore (i.e., causing you to dread feedings)? **No Yes**
11. Is your baby having yellow bowel movements that resemble a mixture of cottage cheese and mustard? **Yes No**
12. Is your baby having at least four good-sized (at least a tablespoon) bowel movements each day? **Yes No**
13. Is your baby wetting her diaper at least six times each day? **Yes No**
14. Does your baby appear hungry after most feedings (i.e., sucking hands, rooting, crying, often needing a pacifier, etc.)? **No Yes**
15. Do you hear rhythmic suckling and frequent swallowing while your baby nurses? **Yes No**

If you circled any answers in the Right-hand column, seek advice from your baby's doctor or a lactation consultant. Be reassured that most early breastfeeding problems can be successfully resolved with timely help.

Get Help: Although women vary in the way they experience milk letdown, it is unusual not to notice any signs of the reflex by three weeks postpartum. In general, the more abundant your milk supply, the more dramatic the signs of letdown. If you are concerned about whether you have an adequate milk supply, schedule a weight check with your baby's doctor to make sure your baby is gaining as expected.

Common Early Concerns About Breastfeeding

Your baby was born to breastfeed, and your body is well equipped to make abundant milk. Most mothers and newborns quickly become a successful breastfeeding team: You offer your breast often and your baby does her part by latching on and draining your milk well. Yet you may be surprised to learn that many mothers and their babies need extra help fine-tuning the "natural" art of effective breastfeeding. Some breastfeeding difficulties, such as a sleepy baby or infant latch-on problems, may begin in the hospital and persist after you go home. Other challenges, such as breast engorgement, sore nipples, and infant jaundice may not surface until after you have been discharged. The following common early breastfeeding concerns typically arise during the first week after your baby's birth. Fortunately workable solutions exist for all of these early problems, and you can have every expectation of meeting—or even exceeding!—your breastfeeding goals.

Q & A

Q: How can I keep my baby sucking after latching on?

Some babies will attach to the breast, but suck only a few times before coming off and crying. Usually these babies are frustrated at not receiving an immediate reward of milk. Perhaps they have had one or more bottle feedings and expect a rapid flow of milk as soon as a nipple enters the mouth. Or, perhaps a baby is not able to draw the breast far enough into her mouth to touch the midpoint of her palate and trigger sucking. Here are some scenarios and solutions for successful breastfeeding:

- If previous feeding attempts have been negative experiences, perhaps due to aggressive efforts to get her to latch, she may react to sensory overload by shutting down and going to sleep when brought to the breast. Other signals include hiccups, yawning, and the "stop sign" (raising her hand with the palm facing outward). To encourage your baby to nurse well, hold her skin-to-skin as much as possible, and offer your breast as soon as your baby shows feeding cues. (See Chapter 3, pages 57 and 66.) If you wait until your newborn is crying, she may tire easily and fall asleep before taking much milk.

- Babies get drowsy when they are overly warm and swaddled. Being at your breast can be so cozy that your baby forgets why she is there and falls asleep. You may need to undress her down to her diaper before offering your breast to help her stay awake.

- Try "switch nursing" to help your baby keep sucking and take more milk. When your baby's sucking and swallowing slow down, remove her from the first breast. Try to bring her to a more wakeful state, and offer the second side, where the milk flow is usually faster. Keep switching sides each time your baby stops sucking at one breast.

- Use hand expression or a breast pump to start some milk flowing before you latch your baby. Trickle a little of the expressed milk onto your nipple to rouse your infant and interest her in feeding.

- Notify your baby's doctor if your baby does not nurse very well for more than a feeding or two. Unless she sucks actively and swallows often, she will not get much milk, even if you invest a lot of time in trying to feed her, so do take your baby for an evaluation. You will need to use a pump and feed your expressed milk to your infant until she is more vigorous and able to nurse effectively.

Q: How can I get my baby to take my other breast?

Often, a baby latches on more readily to one breast than the other. Perhaps one nipple is easier to grasp, or milk flows more freely on that side. Your baby's preference for using one breast results in greater milk production on that side, which in turn makes her prefer the better-producing breast even more. It is important to keep working with your baby to take the less-preferred side as quickly as possible, to assure that both breasts receive adequate stimulation and drainage. To encourage your baby to take the less-preferred side:

- Try starting feedings on the "difficult" side and see if your baby cooperates more when she is hungry. If she starts to fuss, calm her with your voice, then switch her to the preferred breast.

- After she has successfully nursed on the favored side (a cross-cradle hold works best—see Chapter 3, page 49), slide your baby over to the second breast without changing her position, and try offering the

---

Tip

If the above techniques do not work, an ultra-thin, soft silicone nipple shield might help. Babies often begin sucking when the tip of the nipple shield strokes the midpoint of their palate. (See Chapter 3, page 64.)

---

less preferred breast again. As one mother has explained, "My baby just thinks I have two left breasts."

- If your baby isn't taking both breasts well by the time your milk comes in, use a fully automatic electric breast pump to regularly remove milk from the breast that is not being suckled. Better yet, pump both breasts simultaneously, since it takes no longer than pumping one side and will help keep your overall milk supply generous.

Breast Compressions

Breast compressions can be used to keep your infant drinking milk after her sucking has slowed down or becomes less effective. The technique also can help you remove more milk when using a breast pump. To perform breast compressions, support your breast during feedings with your fingers below and your thumb above. Your fingers should be placed far back from the areola, with your hand close to your chest wall. When your baby stops her slow, deep sucking and begins "nibbling," you can deliver a spray of milk by compressing your breast, which may entice her to start drinking again.

Close your hand around your breast—not to the point of discomfort, just a firm, steady squeeze. If your baby starts drinking milk again, just hold the compression as long as she is getting milk. Often you will trigger another letdown this way. Then release the compression when your baby stops sucking. When she starts trying to get milk again, use another breast compression to squirt a spray of milk into her mouth and keep her drinking. Some mothers prefer to compress and release the breast intermittently to keep the baby sucking. When your baby no longer drinks, even when you use compressions, or if she gets sleepy and comes off the breast, you can switch her to the other side.

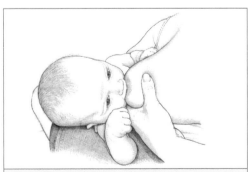

Use breast compressions to deliver a spray of milk into your baby's mouth and entice her to start drinking again.

Q: Why isn't my baby satisfied after nursing?

You may become frustrated during the first few days of breastfeeding if your baby nurses for prolonged periods but doesn't seem to be satisfied. This is sometimes true of larger babies weighing more than eight or nine pounds, who act persistently hungry until milk production surges around the third day. If your milk is not in yet and your baby remains unsatisfied after nursing, try some of these ideas:

- Cuddling your baby skin-to-skin against your chest will usually settle and calm her. Reviewing the basics of correct latch-on technique will help ensure that your baby nurses effectively. (See Chapter 3, pages 52–57.)

- Use breast compressions during feedings to help your baby take more milk.

- Although pacifiers are not generally recommended for newborns, a large hungry newborn might benefit from using one for a day or so until your milk comes in.

- Occasionally a small supplemental feeding may be required to satisfy an inconsolably hungry baby until your milk comes in abundantly.

- Be sure to nurse as often as possible and to try to discontinue any supplements as soon as your milk production increases (usually by two or three days after birth).

- If your baby is not being satisfied by the fourth day of life, notify her doctor and ask for additional help with breastfeeding. A lactation consultant can evaluate how well your baby nurses and make suggestions to improve your milk production and your baby's milk intake.

Q: What is newborn jaundice?

Jaundice is a medical term that describes a yellowish skin discoloration. While jaundice is an uncommon symptom in older children and adults, more than half of newborn infants develop a visible but harmless yellow tinge in the first few days of life (called *physiologic jaundice*). The color comes from a yellow pigment in the blood known as *bilirubin*, which is produced when hemoglobin in red blood cells breaks down. Bilirubin usually is processed quickly by the liver and expelled in the stool. Jaundice results when either an excess of bilirubin is produced (often as a result of bruising from birth trauma or the rapid breakdown of red blood cells) or the elimination of bilirubin is impaired (often due to poor feeding and infrequent bowel movements). Physiologic jaundice usually appears on the second or third day of life and clears by the seventh day. No treatment is necessary beyond frequent feedings.

Although slight newborn jaundice is considered benign, very high levels of bilirubin can be toxic to a baby's brain, causing seizures, permanent brain damage, hearing loss, cerebral palsy, and even death. As a precaution, it is now recommended that all babies have their bilirubin level measured before discharge, and the American Academy of Pediatrics recommends all newborns be screened for jaundice by their doctor within forty-eight hours of hospital discharge.

Jaundice first becomes visible on a baby's face and in the whites of her eyes. As the bilirubin level rises, the yellow color progresses downward to her chest, abdomen, and eventually her legs. Infants with severe jaundice are typically lethargic and feed poorly.

To check for jaundice at home, examine your baby in natural daylight or in a room that has fluorescent lights. Press your fingertip gently against the tip of your baby's nose or forehead. The skin should look white (for babies of all races). If the skin looks yellowish when you press with your finger, jaundice is present to some degree and should be reported to your baby's health-care provider.

If your baby looks jaundiced, her doctor can perform an exam and order a blood test (taken from the heel) to accurately measure the bilirubin level. Although many health professionals believe they can estimate the severity of jaundice by looking at an infant's color, the educated guess is notoriously inaccurate!

If necessary, infant jaundice can be treated with phototherapy, which involves placing an undressed baby under special lights and/or fiberoptic blanket to break down bilirubin in a baby's skin. Frequent breastfeedings ensure hydration and help eliminate bilirubin in stools.

Q: What can I do about uncomfortable breast engorgement?

Babies Likely to Develop Severe Jaundice

Some babies are more likely to develop higher levels of bilirubin than others. The following infants are monitored more closely for jaundice, so that treatment, if needed, can be started early:

- Breastfed babies with feeding difficulties

- Premature babies, born before thirty-seven weeks' gestation

- Babies with a sibling who had jaundice

- Babies who develop jaundice in the first twenty-four hours of life

- Babies with large bruises at birth

- Babies of East Asian or Mediterranean heritage

- Babies with certain blood-group mismatches between mother and infant that cause the baby's red blood cells to break down rapidly (most often an O mom and a baby with blood type A or B).

Postpartum breast engorgement is highly variable. Some women scarcely can tell that their milk has come in, while others have extraordinary breast swelling, firmness, and discomfort. In addition to being more dramatic in first-time mothers, the amount of engorgement is influenced by the number of milk glands, the rate at which pregnancy hormones decline after delivery, the frequency of milk removal, and other individual differences. Fortunately, postpartum breast engorgement is a temporary condition, usually lasting only a few days until your body adjusts to the process of making and releasing milk. By the end of the first week postpartum, milk flow is usually well established and breast engorgement has subsided considerably.

The rapid surge in milk production is a critical transition in the first week of breastfeeding. If milk flow is easily established and your breasts are regularly drained, then full milk production continues and you are well on the way to establishing a comfortable,

Breastfeeding and Jaundice

It is important to know that both the intensity and the duration of jaundice may be increased in breastfed infants compared to formula-fed infants. The two causes of increased jaundice in breastfed infants are known as *breastfeeding jaundice* and *breastmilk jaundice*.

- With breastfeeding jaundice, ineffective breastfeeding and low milk intake (usually due to infrequent feedings or problems with latch or sucking) cause the baby to have infrequent stools. This leads to increased absorption of bilirubin from the baby's intestines and a rise in bilirubin level, usually between three and five days of age. The baby's poor feeding aggravates jaundice, and jaundice contributes to poor feeding by making the baby more sleepy. In addition to treating jaundice with phototherapy—if necessary—it's also important to begin pumping to drain the breasts well. The expressed milk can be fed to the baby by bottle until she is able to nurse effectively. As the baby drinks more milk, she will pass more bowel movements, which will help her bilirubin level fall. Sometimes supplemental milk is required temporarily.

- With breastmilk jaundice, the bilirubin level is increased in otherwise healthy, well-fed infants as a result of an unknown factor in the breastmilk of some mothers. Jaundice typically appears late in the first week and can persist for many weeks. Fortunately the baby's bilirubin level seldom gets high enough to require treatment. Rarely, your baby's doctor may recommend interrupting breastfeeding for twenty-four to thirty-six hours, which will cause the bilirubin level to fall. You will need to pump your breasts during this time to maintain your supply. You can save the milk you express to feed your baby later. (See Chapter 6, pages 151-157.)

mutually satisfying nursing routine for you and your baby. However, if your engorged breasts remain full and tense and your milk is not drained by frequent feedings or pumping, the accumulated milk and increased pressure in your breasts will decrease your milk production. Postpartum breast engorgement is usually short-lived; but for a few women, it can pose the following additional challenges that can threaten to derail the best-laid breastfeeding plans:

- Breast swelling and firmness can make the nipple and surrounding areola less elastic and more difficult to grasp, making the tissues more prone to injury. As a result, your baby may latch on incorrectly, taking only the tip of the nipple, limiting the amount of milk she takes and causing nipple discomfort and damage (cracking, bruising, or abrasions). Babies who learn to attach correctly in the first day or two, when the nipple and areola are soft and pliable, are better prepared to nurse effectively if excessive engorgement occurs.

- Severe breast engorgement can make it difficult for your baby to obtain sufficient milk with nursing. Not only is correct latch-on more difficult when your breasts are swollen and firm, but excessive pressure can impair milk flow when your baby attempts to nurse. The result can be a frustrated, hungry baby and a dwindling milk supply.

Treatment Strategies

- Severe engorgement may be prevented—and definitely is reduced by—early, frequent, and effective nursing. Encourage your baby to nurse at least every two to three hours around the clock. Offer your breast sooner if she gives you any feeding cues such as squirming, moving her mouth or tongue, or bringing her hand to her mouth. Use breast compressions while your baby nurses to help her take more milk. (See page 96.)

- Express some milk before nursing, preferably using a hospital-grade electric breast pump or by hand expression. Softening the nipple-areola area will make it easier for your baby to grasp correctly, and getting some milk to flow will help entice your baby to latch on. Gently massage your breasts before and while expressing to improve milk flow with pumping. (See Chapter 6, page 137.) Review the basics of correct positioning and latch-on. (See Chapter 3, pages 48–57.)

- Apply cool compresses to your breasts between feedings to relieve discomfort and reduce swelling, as cold therapy reduces inflammation and pain. Try applying traditional ice packs, cool compresses, commercial cold packs, or even bags of frozen vegetables wrapped in cloth, to engorged breasts for fifteen to twenty minutes at a time. Cold therapy reduces blood congestion, inflammation, and tissue swelling, and helps milk move through the ducts to the nipple openings.

- Apply moist heat to your breasts just prior to feeding to help trigger the milk ejection reflex (letdown) and start milk flowing. Standing under a warm shower, wrapping your breasts in warm, wet washcloths or towels for a few minutes, or applying commercial hot packs may help relieve discomfort and start milk dripping. Be careful not to apply excessive heat, especially in the sensitive nipple area. Limit the use of heat to about five minutes, as prolonged heat may actually increase swelling. Try both hot and cold applications to find which one best relieves discomfort, decreases breast congestion, and improves milk flow. You can alternate these two therapies in the most effective way for you.

- If your breasts remain uncomfortably full after breastfeeding, express some remaining milk to reduce breast firmness. Some women are reluctant to pump or express milk during engorgement for fear that they might stimulate more milk production and worsen the condition. But engorgement is more a problem of poor milk flow than excessive milk production. Ten to fifteen minutes of pumping usually is sufficient at one session, and longer pumping times can cause nipple damage. For maximum effectiveness and comfort, use a hospital-grade electric pump with a double collection system. If your pump has two-phase suction technology, keep it on phase 1 until your milk lets down, or longer if desired. (See Chapter 6, pages 139–140.) Otherwise, use your controls to select a low-suction, rapid-cycling phase to trigger milk letdown. With severe engorgement, some women prefer to pump one breast at a time, instead of both breasts at once. You can use your free hand to gently massage your breast while pumping. Steady pressure applied to firm areas often starts milk flowing. When milk flow stops, switch to the opposite breast. Massage and pump on the second side as long as you are getting results. Then switch again when milk flow stops. Stop pumping after fifteen to twenty minutes of total effort. Wait an hour or two before trying again. Removing milk reduces the pressure in the breasts and improves the ease of milk flow, making it easier for your baby to nurse and get enough milk.

- To help trigger your milk ejection reflex (letdown), relax and visualize your milk flowing. Play calming music or practice relaxation techniques such as Lamaze breathing. Ask your partner to give you a neck massage or back rub. Extend your arms above your head and slowly bring them down to your sides. Repeating this "flying angel" exercise several times may help your milk letdown.

The Cabbage Cure

Some lactation consultants suggest wrapping engorged breasts in cabbage leaves to relieve discomfort and improve milk flow. For centuries cabbage has been used in many countries as a folk remedy for various ailments. Although many women attest to the benefits of cabbage wrap therapy, there is no conclusive proof that it is truly effective for breast engorgement. Here's the home remedy:

Thoroughly rinse and dry fresh green cabbage leaves, either refrigerated or at room temperature. Strip out the large vein before applying the leaves over the engorged breasts. The leaves can be worn either inside the bra or as compresses covered by a cool towel. The leaves can be cut, if necessary, to allow the nipples to stay dry. The cabbage leaf compresses are left in place for about twenty minutes, or until they have wilted, at which time they can be replaced by fresh leaves. Many women report significant relief within hours. The applications should be discontinued as soon as possible, as over-treatment is said to reduce milk supply. Only one or two applications are usually required to establish good milk flow. Do not use cabbage wraps if you are allergic or develop a skin rash.

Engorgement Beyond the Postpartum Period

After breastfeeding is well established, uncomfortable breast fullness and firmness can result whenever your breasts are not drained regularly. Allowing your breasts to become hard and overly full due to infrequent feeding or pumping can cause your milk supply to decrease, even after breastfeeding has been going along well. (See Chapter 7, page 177.) It also can place you at risk for plugged ducts or a breast infection.

Q: Should my nipples hurt this much?

Sore nipples are one of the most frequent complaints among breastfeeding women, and one of the chief reasons new moms discontinue nursing. Fortunately nipple pain is both avoidable and treatable! Temporary mild nipple tenderness, beginning on the second day, is common and considered normal. Usually the first minute after your baby latches on is the most uncomfortable. Once you begin to produce abundant milk, your baby will apply less suction while nursing, and initial nipple discomfort subsides. By the end of the first week, you should have little, if any, discomfort when breastfeeding.

Severe nipple pain, pain that lasts throughout a feeding or doesn't improve once your milk comes in, suggests that your baby is either attached incorrectly or not sucking properly. Severe pain means that something is wrong, so do not ignore this important clue! The most common problem is that your baby is not opening her mouth wide enough and is latching on to the tip of your nipple instead of taking a large mouthful of breast. In addition to correcting your baby's latch, here are a few other tips to keep nipple tenderness at bay:

- Pat your nipples dry after feedings and apply ultra-pure, medical-grade lanolin (Lansinoh or PureLan). Or, you can wear new, soft hydrogel pads over your nipples to provide soothing relief.

- Nurse for shorter periods at more frequent intervals.

- Start feeds on the less sore side, then move your baby to the more painful side once your letdown has been triggered.

For in-depth information about the causes and treatment of sore nipples, see Chapter 8, pages 195–204.

Q: Can I feed my baby on a schedule instead of on demand?

The vast majority of breastfeeding experts strongly recommend feeding your new baby around the clock whenever she gives hunger signals. Most parents, however, wish they could help their babies establish regular patterns of feeding and sleeping. After all, it is very appealing to imagine that your baby could be fed on a predictable schedule and sleep

through the night at an early age. However, infant development experts agree that parents should make every effort to meet their infant's individual needs promptly—no matter what time it is. Meeting your baby's needs as consistently as possible helps her feel loved, safe, and secure. It forms the basis for a strong love bond with your baby and helps her build trust in the world. Remember, too, that waking up to feed your baby in the wee hours (or every other hour!) will not last forever. With the support of your partner or other helpers and as many naps as you can possibly steal over the course of the day, you'll soon find that your baby develops her own routines. This, in return, will give your days and nights more predictability—even without "scheduling" your baby.

Q: When is poor feeding a sign that my baby is sick?

One of the most important clues to your baby's well-being is the frequency and quality of her feedings. As a breastfeeding mom, you'll quickly become attuned to your baby's usual feeding patterns and notice any changes in how often, how long, or how vigorously she nurses. Although young babies don't have many ways to communicate illness, poor feeding is one of the strongest indicators of a medical problem. Sleeping through feeding times, showing less interest in feedings, suckling for a shorter period of time, or nursing with less vigor than usual—all could indicate some type of medical problem. Always promptly report any change in your baby's feeding pattern to her doctor.

Q: How can I express some of my milk?

During the course of breastfeeding, most nursing moms will choose—or need—to express some of their milk, often beginning during the early weeks after delivery. Various milk expression options and guidelines for storing and handling expressed breastmilk are covered in detail in Chapter 6.

Q: Where can I find help for breastfeeding problems?

If breastfeeding does not seem to be going well, get the help you need right away, before the problem becomes compounded by low milk or slow weight gain in your baby. While you may have to pay directly for some specialized services, the expert care you receive is well worth the investment. You can request help from one or more of the following sources:

- **Your own or your baby's doctor**
  He or she may have experience managing breastfeeding difficulties. If not, ask for a referral to a lactation clinic or consultant. Your baby's doctor should weigh your infant and make sure that no underlying medical problem is contributing to her breastfeeding difficulties. If you seek advice from other health workers or from

breastfeeding support groups, your baby's physician should remain the primary coordinator of her overall care. Consult your own doctor for breast or nipple pain, or signs of a breast infection. Some physicians are board-certified lactation consultants (see below) and practice Breastfeeding Medicine.

- **The hospital where you delivered**
  Most hospitals that offer maternity services have lactation consultants (see below) or knowledgeable nurses on staff who can talk with you about your breastfeeding problem. Many hospital-based lactation consultants offer out-patient visits for women who encounter breastfeeding difficulties after discharge. The hospital may also sell breastfeeding supplies or have a breast pump rental station.

- **Individual lactation consultants**
  A lactation consultant (LC) is a health-care provider who focuses on breastfeeding education and helping nursing mothers overcome breastfeeding problems. A lactation consultant can provide personal assistance with breastfeeding technique, teach you how to use a breast pump and other breastfeeding supplies, evaluate your milk supply and recommend ways to increase your production, make recommendations about using supplemental milk when necessary, and offer essential

support and information. An International Board Certified Lactation Consultant (IBCLC) has completed academic prerequisites and required practice hours assisting breastfeeding mothers, in addition to passing a comprehensive examination. The IBCLC designation is the most widely accepted standard for lactation consultants, although some highly skilled breastfeeding specialists have not pursued this credential.

Your obstetrician, family physician, or pediatrician may work with lactation consultants to whom you can be referred. You also can locate an LC in your community by contacting the International Lactation Consultant Association (see Resources) or the lactation consultant at the hospital where you delivered. Close communication among your health-care team is essential to ensure the best care for you and your baby.

- **Lactation centers**
  Some communities may have a specialized breastfeeding center, staffed by lactation consultants who provide in-depth breastfeeding consultations for nursing mothers and their babies. These centers may be free-standing clinics or affiliated with a hospital, and some are directed by a physician who practices Breastfeeding Medicine.

- **The WIC Program (Supplemental Nutrition Program for Women, Infants, and Children)**
  Local WIC clinics provide helpful counseling for their breastfeeding clients, and many offer peer counselors. In addition, WIC sites provide electric and manual breast pumps for women who need them. Some WIC clinics have lactation consultants or lactation educators. WIC also can refer clients with complex breastfeeding problems to other community resources. (See Chapter 2, pages 22–23, and Resources.)

- **La Leche League International (LLLI)**
  LLLI is an excellent source of information and mother-to-mother support for breastfeeding women. (See Chapter 2, pages 21–22, and the Resources.) If this reputable group is present in your community, it will be listed in the white pages of your phone book. LLLI holds regular meetings, and accredited leaders provide telephone counseling. LLLI also offers recorded information on selected breastfeeding topics and provides telephone assistance to health professionals and mothers through its Center for Breastfeeding Information (see Resources).

Adjusting to Parenthood

Among life's many transforming events, nothing compares to becoming a mother for the first time. You may alternate between feeling excited and hesitant, exuberant and drained, triumphant and anxious—if not downright scared. In assuming total responsibility for a new little person, you will probe the depths of your love, creativity, and resilience. You'll find that no matter how many prenatal classes you and your partner may have attended or the number of baby books you've read, there is simply no way to prepare yourself for the colossal changes of first-time motherhood! Inevitably, the joys will be intermixed with questions and doubts, but as the days and weeks pass you'll discover new strengths and resources (and even regain your sense of humor). With support from your partner, family, and friends during the first few weeks of being a new mom, you will make significant and satisfying connections with your baby that will last a lifetime.

The first and most fundamental task of caring for your new baby is the ability to feed him successfully. This is crucial, since the most important activity of a newborn is eating. When feedings go well, your confidence soars. Conversely, when feeding difficulties arise, you may doubt your ability to care for your baby. But take heart: you can have a successful and enjoyable breastfeeding experience. This chapter addresses some key concerns among new mothers and is aimed at reducing your stress and magnifying your rewards as you make the amazing transition to parenthood.

Sleeping Through the Night

Everyone knows that sleep deprivation is a normal part of new motherhood, but few parents are prepared for the physical and emotional toll that chronic fatigue exacts. Your young baby's ongoing need for nighttime feeding and care means that your sleep will be disrupted for a number of months.

Bleary-eyed new parents inevitably ask, "When will my baby sleep through the night?" While you can't make your baby sleep through the night, you can provide a safe sleep environment and take steps early on to establish a structured routine that will help promote healthy sleep habits and a well-rested baby. Good infant sleep habits don't just benefit parents. When your baby is well-rested, he is content, energized, and better able to concentrate. By contrast, overly tired babies are irritable and less alert.

THE SLEEP LOTTERY

Some parents are blessed with babies who easily nod off and sleep soundly. Others have babies who have difficulties making the transition from wakefulness to sleep and who need help returning to sleep after routine wake-ups. Fortunately babies gradually consolidate their nighttime sleep as they get older.

Newborn. Although your newborn sleeps sixteen to eighteen hours a day, his sleep is divided into six or seven short periods of two to four hours each, evenly distributed between day and night. It'll take several months for your baby to consolidate his sleep into a long night interval and regular daytime naps and to develop self-soothing skills that will allow him to fall asleep easily and return to sleep.

One to Three Months. Initially your newborn's longest sleep period may be only three to four hours long. By six weeks—or when your baby weighs about ten pounds—he will probably become more "settled" and start sleeping longer at night—perhaps up to five hours at a stretch. Gradually your baby will start falling asleep earlier in the evening and sleep longer, so that by the time he is three months old, he may sleep for eight or more hours at night. Although infants continue to awaken several times each night, they gradually acquire more self-comforting behaviors that allow them to return to sleep quickly.

Three Months and Older. By the time your baby is three or four months old, daytime sleep becomes more regular and is organized into two to three longer naps instead of brief, irregular sleep periods. By the time he is four to eight months old, he'll be sleeping nine to twelve hours at night and consolidating his daytime sleep into two naps, usually totaling between two and a half and four hours each day. While some babies (especially breastfed infants) still require one or more nighttime feedings after six months of age, continued middle-of-the-night feedings after nine months are unnecessary and are based on habit.

PROMOTING HEALTHY SLEEP HABITS

Just as your baby needs to be fed when he is hungry, and changed when his diaper is wet or soiled, he needs to be put down to sleep when he is tired. You can expect your newborn to become drowsy after a one-to-two-hour period of wakefulness. While you can't predict exactly when he will become sleepy, you can approximate a time, just as you anticipate when he might be hungry again. For a number of months, it will be unlikely for him to remain alert for more than two hours at a time. As your baby gets older, he will gradually remain awake for longer periods.

Observe your baby closely to learn his individual sleep signals, so that you can recognize that precise moment when he becomes drowsy but not yet too fatigued to settle easily. Common drowsy signals include decreased movement, drooping of the eyelids, less intense eye contact, weaker or slower sucking, or yawning. Other signs you may observe when he is a little older include decreased activity, becoming more quiet and calm, being less responsive to you or less interested in his toys, staring into the distance, and rubbing his eyes. If you begin a soothing sleep routine at just the right time, there will be little or no crying. However, if you miss your baby's drowsy signals and allow him to become overtired, he may become irritable, may start crying, and will be more difficult to get to sleep.

For a newborn, your soothing, wind-down routine can include dimming the lights, cuddling, breastfeeding, playing calming music, singing softly, patting, rocking, swinging, offering a pacifier, or swaddling. Many newborns sleep better when swaddled securely in a receiving blanket to re-create a womblike environment. As your baby gets older and consolidates his nighttime sleep, you can add other soothing bedtime rituals, such as an evening bath, reading books, dressing him in a sleep sack, and using reassuring words ("It's time for night-night; it's sleepy time now; sleep tight; there, there, you're okay" etc.) as you place him in his crib.

- Gradually try to increase your baby's sleep at night. During nighttime feedings, keep the lighting subdued and don't stimulate your baby. Make night feedings "no-nonsense" events. To increase nighttime sleep, try not to let your newborn sleep longer than three and a half hours during the daytime before trying to rouse him.

- Learn to distinguish your baby's normal "sleeping sounds" (occasional grunts, whimpers, brief cries) from his legitimate awake and hungry signals. Over-responding to normal sleeping noises may actually teach your baby to awaken more often. When he does wake up and need to be fed, tending to him promptly—before he escalates his crying—will make it easier to settle him back to sleep afterward.

- A young baby should not be left to cry alone in his crib. Always respond to your baby's cries and hold him as long as necessary to soothe him and help him make the transition to sound sleep.

- When he's around four months old, your baby can begin to learn to go to sleep on his own. This will be easier if you have made his crib feel welcoming, safe, and comfortable. Place your baby in his crib several times each day with a favorite toy or stimulating mobile and sit nearby while he briefly entertains himself. At bedtime play a familiar soft lullaby and keep using other sleep cues from your established bedtime routine. Now that pacifiers at bedtime are recommended to prevent SIDS (see facing page), many babies associate a pacifier with sleep. If your baby cries for more than a few minutes, check on him, pat him gently, talk to him reassuringly, replay his music, or re-insert his pacifier. Little by little, you can fade out the interval between your return visits and decrease the amount of time and physical contact with your baby during repeat checks.

SAFE INFANT SLEEP

Sudden infant death syndrome (SIDS) is both a medical mystery and one of the greatest fears among new parents. SIDS refers to the sudden death of an infant (younger than one year of age) that cannot be explained through investigation, autopsy, and review of the baby's medical history. SIDS rates have dropped dramatically over the last decade—from 1.2 per 1,000 live births in 1992 to 0.54 per 1,000 in 2005—as we've learned more about this silent killer. Yet SIDS still remains the leading cause of death for infants between one month and one year of age.

The main hypothesis to explain SIDS is that certain infants—for unknown reasons—have an impaired ability to rouse from sleep when they encounter a potentially life-threatening situation. Ordinarily if an infant's breathing becomes hampered—such as re-breathing his own expired air or by having his head covered—the lack of oxygen will trigger a response that causes him to change his breathing or start crying. However, some infants sleep too deeply and lack this protective arousal response when their breathing becomes impaired.

Helping Your Baby Fall Asleep on His Own

Everyone awakens several times each night as part of the normal cyclical process of sleep. Ordinarily we are able to go right back to sleep because we immediately recognize our surroundings and know how to fall asleep on our own. Babies who are consistently rocked, held, or nursed until they are sound asleep will come to depend on these "props" to carry them to dreamland and won't be able to return to sleep readily when they awaken. Instead, they must summon their parents to come and re-create their familiar bedtime environment—breastfeeding, rocking, and being held. To help your baby learn to fall asleep on his own, put him in his crib when he is drowsy but not yet asleep, whenever possible. If his last waking memory is the crib, he will awaken under the same conditions that he has learned to fall asleep in, and he will be able to soothe himself and return to sleep without needing your help. If your baby falls asleep at the breast, you do not need to wake him before placing him in his crib to sleep. Just don't always wait until he is fully asleep before putting him down.

American Academy of Pediatrics Recommendations to Reduce the Risk of SIDS

- Place your baby on his back for every sleep—not on his stomach or side, since side sleeping also increases the risk of SIDS compared to sleeping on the back.

- Use a firm crib mattress covered by a sheet. Infants should not be placed to sleep on waterbeds, soft mattresses, sofas, or other soft surfaces.

- Keep soft materials and loose bedding—including comforters, blankets, quilts, pillows, stuffed toys, sheepskins, and other soft objects—out of your baby's crib.

- Do not smoke during pregnancy and avoid exposing your baby to second-hand smoke. Smoking during pregnancy is a major risk factor for SIDS, and being around second-hand smoke after birth also poses a risk.

- Have your baby sleep in your room but not in your bed. Room sharing without bed sharing has been found to have a protective effect against SIDS. You may bring your infant into your bed for breastfeeding and return him to his own crib in your room afterward.

- Offer your baby a pacifier when you put him down to sleep for every sleep session in the first year of his life. Several recent studies have shown a strong protective effect of pacifiers on the incidence of SIDS—particularly when the pacifier is used when placing an infant down for sleep. Because you are breastfeeding, you can delay introducing a pacifier until your baby is one month old. You don't need to reinsert the pacifier after he falls asleep, and if he refuses a pacifier, you don't have to force him to take it. Do not dip the pacifier in honey (which can cause infant botulism) or other sweeteners. Clean your baby's pacifiers often and replace them regularly.

- Avoid overheating or over-bundling your baby. He should be lightly clothed for sleep, and the bedroom temperature kept comfortable for a lightly clothed adult.

- Provide your baby with daily "tummy time" opportunities, when he is awake and under your watchful eye, to avoid flattening of the head from sleeping on his back. Minimize the time he spends in his car-seat carrier and give him liberal upright "cuddle time" each day. Regularly alternate your baby's head position between facing right and facing left when placing him to sleep. You also can alternate which end you place him in his crib, so he will have to turn in a different direction to face the door when you enter. This will prevent his head from flattening.

(continued)

•Do not use commercial products marketed to reduce the risk of SIDS, as none has been adequately tested for safety or effectiveness. Safety standards have not yet been established for infant beds that attach to the mother's bed. Home monitors are not recommended as a SIDS prevention strategy.

Using a Fan to Reduce the Risk of SIDS

A new study has found that running a fan while your baby sleeps significantly reduces the risk of SIDS. It is possible that a fan—by increasing room ventilation—reduces a baby's risk of re-breathing his exhaled carbon dioxide that accumulates around his nose and mouth. The protective effect of running a fan is even more pronounced when a baby is in an adverse sleep environment (such as a warmer room, prone sleep position, or with no pacifier use).

Known Risk Factors for SIDS

Although the precise cause of SIDS remains unknown, the following factors have consistently been found to place infants at increased risk:

•Sleeping in the prone position (on the tummy)

•Sleeping on a soft surface

•Smoking by the mother during pregnancy

•Overheating

•Late or no prenatal care

•Young age of the mother

•Preterm birth

•Low birth weight

•Male gender

The incidence of SIDS is low during the first month of life, peaks between two and three months, and decreases thereafter. Rates are several times higher among black infants and those of Native American or Alaskan Native ethnicity.

Guidelines for Co-Sleeping

While bed sharing with a baby—as practiced in the United States and other Western countries—increases the risk of SIDS, some parents choose to co-sleep with their infants as part of their parenting philosophy or to make nighttime breastfeeding easier. The following guidelines can help reduce the risks to your baby that are associated with co-sleeping:

•Sleep on a firm mattress, never on a waterbed, sofa, couch, armchair, daybed, or other soft surface.

•Do not smoke or allow others to smoke in your home. Do not share a bed with your baby if you smoked during your pregnancy, as your baby already has an increased risk of SIDS.

•Do not have a headboard or furniture next to your bed, or a wall touching your bed. Babies can become trapped between an adult bed and furniture or walls.

•Always place your baby on his back for sleep.

•Keep all bedcovers and pillows away from your baby.

•Do not co-sleep if you or your partner is extremely tired, has taken a sleeping pill or pain medication, or has consumed drugs or alcohol.

•Do not co-sleep if you or your partner is obese.

•Do not allow siblings or pets in bed with an infant.

•Do not co-sleep with a very young infant, since the risk of bed sharing is greatest for infants younger than twelve weeks.

•Temporarily place your baby in a separate crib during your intimate moments with your partner.

Coping with Crying

A baby comes into the world totally dependent on his parents and other caretakers to meet his physical and emotional needs. Crying is the earliest vocalization in your baby's communication repertoire and one of the main ways he lets you know when he's hungry, wet, sleepy, lonely, bored, uncomfortable, or unwell. Since the very survival of babies depends on adults responding to their needs, don't be surprised if your baby's crying evokes powerful feelings that compel you to feed, comfort, and care for him from the very first signal of distress. You are doing exactly what nature intended to keep your baby healthy and well nourished.

Dunstan Baby Language

The inability to console a crying baby is one of the most frustrating aspects of new parenthood, but Pricilla Dunstan, an Australian mother with a rare photographic memory for sound, began studying the cries of infants to help new moms and dads respond appropriately to their baby's crying. She was able to identify specific cry sounds in young infants that conveyed distinct needs, which Dunstan believes represent a universal baby language. Each unique cry is created when sound is added to a baby's natural reflexes. For example, the baby word Dunstan identifies as *neh* translates as "I'm hungry." The phonetic sound is created when your baby raises his tongue to the roof of his mouth to start the sucking reflex. Other easily identifiable baby sounds form a fascinating vocabulary, according to Dunstan, that makes it easier to interpret what your baby is trying to communicate.

You can learn more about how to use Dunstan Baby Language to guide your own natural mothering instincts by visiting www.dunstanbaby.com.

INTERPRETING YOUR BABY'S CRIES

Although all crying may sound alike to you at first, babies actually have their own consistent and unique patterns of crying that convey hunger, pain, fatigue, and other forms of distress. Fortunately new parents are highly motivated to interpret their baby's vocalizations and respond with the appropriate behavior to meet his needs. At first, this is accomplished mainly by trial and error, as you attempt to console your distressed infant with feeding, burping, changing, holding, rocking, and soothing words. Over time, your baby will gain greater skill and clarity in transmitting cues that are easier for you to read, making the reason for his tears more understandable. In turn, you too will gain more confidence and competence in understanding your baby's cries and knowing how to satisfy his needs. Some new parents find it helpful to keep a daily diary of their baby's sleeping, feeding, and crying patterns during the early weeks of life. Keeping a record of this kind can help establish some structure and a routine for your baby's care and help you learn to decode what your baby's cries really mean. (Possible causes of excessive infant crying are reviewed in Chapter 8, pages 221–225.)

CRYING ISN'T "GOOD" FOR A BABY'S LUNGS

Contrary to what some parents are told, responding quickly to a baby's crying won't "spoil" him. All babies need extensive physical contact with their parents. In fact, research has shown that the more you carry your baby, the less he will cry over the long term. Babies who are picked up as soon as they begin to fuss will cry less often and for shorter periods than babies whose parents do not respond quickly. By promptly attending to your baby's crying, you are teaching him to trust you. When he has a need and it is satisfied, he learns that the world is a safe place and he is loved. Your baby's trusting relationship with you becomes the foundation for communication and relationships with others. Eventually your baby will learn to associate feeling better with the mere sight of you, the sounds you make as you draw near to him, your unique smell, and your familiar touch. By the time your baby is three and a half months old he may stop crying simply by hearing you approach, since he can now anticipate that you will make him feel better.

Despite your best attempts, however, you're not always able to respond immediately to your baby's distress signals. Your response might be delayed because you are driving on the freeway, taking a shower, or tending to another child. And of course there will be times when even your best efforts fail to relieve your baby's distress. Rest assured, however, that as long as you are generally consistent in responding to his needs promptly and with affection, he will be convinced that the world is a safe and friendly place and will form a strong, loving bond with you.

DR. HARVEY KARP'S FIVE S'S FOR CALMING A CRYING BABY

Pediatrician Harvey Karp, who has studied the reasons and remedies for infant crying, suggests that the root cause of infant colic is "the missing fourth trimester." Dr. Karp explains that human infants are born after only nine months of fetal development because the human brain is too big to permit a longer gestation. In the early months of life, Karp maintains that a baby benefits when his parents re-create the sensory environment of the uterus, thus simulating a "fourth" trimester of gestation.

The Calming Reflex. While in the womb, your baby is snugly enclosed, frequently jiggled by your body motions, and exposed to the constant whooshing sound of blood flowing through the placental arteries. Dr. Karp hypothesizes that these calming uterine rhythms trigger a profound soothing response that he calls the "calming reflex." Karp believes that this calming reflex serves to relax your baby during the last months of pregnancy, when he keeps his head down and moves less, in preparation for vaginal delivery. While some babies handle the birth transition without difficulty, others become overwhelmed by the diverse stimuli of life outside the womb and the loss of calming uterine rhythms. These babies cry excessively to convey their distress and bring adults to their aid.

Dr. Karp has found that the calming reflex can be activated by five strategic maneuvers that mimic uterine sensations. Because each of these techniques starts with the letter *S*, Karp calls them the Five S's in his book *The Happiest Baby on the Block* and companion video. (See Resources.) The Five S's described here can help you calm your fussy baby, enhance your confidence in meeting his needs, and promote positive breastfeeding routines.

1. Swaddling

Swaddling a fussy baby in a large, thin square blanket helps re-create the snug environment of the womb during the last months of pregnancy and helps him feel secure. Restraining your baby's arms with snug wrapping helps keep them from flailing and startling him. This step is recommended first because wrapped babies respond better to the other calming techniques. Studies show that swaddled babies have fewer startles, rouse less, and sleep longer. Of course, with his arms restrained, your baby will not be able to signal hunger by bringing his hands to his mouth, so you will need to stay tuned to other hunger cues, such as alertness, rooting, or mouthing movements.

Tip

Only swaddle for fussy times, not continuously, and never use bulky blankets or allow the blanket to cover your baby's face. Stop swaddling for sleep when your baby can roll to the prone position (on his tummy). Avoid over-heating your baby when swaddling.

2. Side or Stomach Position

Although the risk of sudden infant death syndrome (SIDS) is lowest when babies sleep on their backs, infants actually calm down faster when placed on the stomach or side. If your baby is lying on his back, his crying or movement easily triggers the startle reflex, causing him to throw his arms out. After swaddling, hold him up against your chest or shoulder. You also can use side positioning with the cradle or cross-cradle hold while breastfeeding. Stomach positioning can be achieved by holding your infant against your shoulder for burping or by placing him across your lap, tummy down, while patting his back. Or you can carry your baby facedown on your forearm, patting his back with the other hand while walking or rocking side to side. He can then be placed to sleep on his back.

3. Shushing

Many babies quickly calm down when they hear a loud, repetitive "shhh" sound that mimics the familiar whooshing noise of blood flowing through the placental arteries in their mother's womb. Your own voice—or anything mechanical that makes continuous white noise, such as an electric fan—can help soothe and calm your crying baby. Steady rhythmic sound from a vacuum cleaner, soothing words, or repetitive singing can have a similar effect.

4. Swinging

Gentle rhythmic motions such as rocking or swinging can be very effective in calming your upset baby because they remind him of the comforting lulling motions he'd grown accustomed to while he was inside your uterus. Countless parents will attest to the wonders of a car ride when it comes to soothing an upset baby. Simply secure him in his car seat and go for a drive. The sound of the engine and the motion of the car will usually lull your baby to sleep in no time at all.

> **Tip**
>
> Another calming strategy that involves rhythmic movement—and easily gets Dad involved—is pushing your baby around the block in his stroller until he nods off.

5. Sucking

Offering your breast, even if you don't think your baby is hungry, is another good way to help your baby settle down if he is crying. Nursing—whether for comfort or nutrition—calms your upset baby. No wonder, since he undoubtedly comforted himself by sucking his fingers while he was in the womb.

Your crying baby may respond immediately to swaddling, or he may require three to five of Dr. Karp's S's before calming down.

The beauty of this approach is that not only does it curb your baby's crying, it also empowers you and restores your confidence—all of which can mean the difference between successful breastfeeding and a sense of despair.

> **Tip**
>
> Don't hesitate to nurse your fussy baby again, even if you just finished feeding him. His crying may be a signal that he is still hungry. Excessive crying in a breastfed baby may be due to unrecognized hunger, so it's always best to get a weight check to be sure your baby is gaining well before assuming that his frequent fussy behavior is due to "colic."

OTHER WAYS TO COPE WITH CRYING

Above all, remember that your baby's crying is a distress signal, and crying babies need to be held and comforted whenever possible. Ignoring your young baby's cries or responding to them in an inconsistent manner will cause him to feel insecure, unloved, and hopeless. Holding your baby doesn't reinforce crying any more than feeding him reinforces hunger.

> **Tip**
>
> An ideal way to hold your baby for long periods without restricting your own activity (and that keeps your hands free) is to use a front carrier or baby sling. If you invest in one of these devices, you can securely hold your little one close to your body while going about your assorted daily activities. (See Resources.)

- Contact your baby's doctor, who can examine your infant and reassure you that he is healthy and that the crying is not your fault. If your baby is diagnosed with infant colic, you can expect excessive crying to diminish by three months. (For more information about colic, see Chapter 8, pages 224-225.).

- Ask your baby's doctor about prescribing probiotics (dietary supplements containing potentially beneficial bacteria or yeast). A recent study found that daily crying time decreased significantly within one week in colicky breastfed infants who were given the probiotic Lactobacillus reuteri compared to infants treated with gas drops.

- If hearing your baby's crying becomes stressful and you feel especially tense and anxious, take a break. Ask your mother, partner, or a close friend to watch your baby for a while. Just getting outside and walking around your neighborhood or running a short errand while someone else cares for your baby can renew your perspective.

- Conserve your strength and renew your energy by napping whenever you can.

- Minimize housework and, if possible, ask other caregivers to look after your baby for short periods each day.

- Call your baby's doctor if your baby cries for more than two hours, if he seems to be in pain, if other symptoms of illness are present, or if you feel you might lose control.

> **Tip**
>
> If you ever feel you could lose control with your baby, place him in his crib, close the door, and leave the room until you have calmed down. Return periodically to comfort your baby, and call someone to relieve you. Never shake your baby. Violent shaking can cause severe brain injury and even death!

Crisis-Nursery Care

Ask your baby's doctor if your community has a federally funded crisis nursery that offers safe, supportive, and non-judgmental temporary care to relieve a potential or existing family emergency. Most crisis nursery programs also provide support services or referrals for stressed-out parents who fear they could lose control.

At Risk for PPD

Although the exact cause of postpartum depression (PPD) is unknown, various factors associated with new motherhood—including hormonal fluctuations; sudden lifestyle and role changes; and physical stressors, such as fatigue and discomfort—may contribute to the disorder. Women who have experienced PPD are at higher risk of suffering future bouts of depression, both postpartum and unrelated to childbirth. Other identified factors for PPD include:

- A previous history of depression

- Depression or anxiety during pregnancy

- A recent stressful life event (such as the death of a loved one, loss of a job, or divorce)

- A family history of any psychiatric condition

- Lack of prenatal social support from family and friends

Feeling Blue

Despite having every reason to be thrilled about your new baby, you may be distressed about feeling more emotional, moody, tearful, anxious, or irritable than usual. You may notice a loss of appetite, trouble concentrating, or difficulty sleeping. These symptoms—known as the "baby blues"—usually occur three to seven days after you've had your baby, and are attributed to the rapid fall in pregnancy hormones after delivery. Don't worry—you're not losing your mind. The "baby blues" are considered a normal part of early motherhood, affecting up to 80 percent of new mothers. The situation no doubt is made worse by fatigue, physical discomfort, too many visitors, and worries about your brand-new baby. Fortunately symptoms typically resolve by ten days after your baby's birth, and no treatment is required.

POSTPARTUM DEPRESSION (PPD)

While most new mothers experience temporary baby blues, 10 to 15 percent develop full-blown postpartum depression

(PPD) requiring treatment with medication and psychotherapy. (Among teen mothers, rates can run as high as 25 percent.) PPD can begin from two weeks to twelve months after delivery, with most cases occurring in the first six weeks after delivery. Symptoms include depression; lack of pleasure; sleep disturbance; irritability; crying; poor appetite; anxiety; loss of energy; feelings of being overwhelmed, worthless, or guilty; indecision or diminished concentration; and thoughts of death or suicide. Many women do not realize they are suffering from PPD, however, since changes in weight, sleep, energy, and emotions may be dismissed as routine consequences of childbirth. Contact your obstetrician or midwife or other trusted health-care provider if you think your own postpartum feelings may be more than just the "baby blues." Your doctor can recognize PPD and refer you for essential help and support.

Effects of PPD. Untreated postpartum depression can adversely affect your baby's long-term personal, social, behavioral, and cognitive development. This is because depressed mothers interact differently with their infants, and babies are very sensitive to the emotions of their caregivers. Depressed mothers have lower activity levels, talk to their infants less, and use a flat tone. They may be withdrawn, show little emotion, and play with their babies less. Infants of mothers who were depressed for longer than six months show growth and developmental delays at one year of age.

Treatment of PPD. Do not try to manage postpartum depression on your own—get help as soon as possible. You are not alone and are not to blame for how you feel. And there is help: Individual counseling, group therapy, professional and social support, exercise and diet, and antidepressant medications are all helpful in the treatment of PPD. (See Resources.)

Tip

Although antidepressants appear in breastmilk, you don't have to compromise your well-being in order to safeguard your milk. Some antidepressants are considered safe for breastfeeding mothers. (See Chapter 10, pages 281-282.)

PREVENTING BABY BLUES AND PPD

There are a number of things you can do to promote your physical and emotional well-being after delivery and help thwart the baby blues and avoid PPD. Here are a few suggestions:

• Communicate your needs and wants. Make requests of others, rather than hoping they will notice your distress and step in to help. Readily accept any offered assistance, whether it comes in the form of meals, errands, or household help. Build a support system of trusted friends and relatives that you can count on and talk to.

- Make an effort to get out of the house every day, if only for a few minutes. Just walking around the block with your baby in a carrier or stroller and appreciating nature can change your whole outlook. Arrange to drop your baby off at Grandma's or with a trusted friend for an hour while you shop alone, get a massage, or indulge in a manicure.

- Join a new moms' support group or participate in a mother's day out program at your place of worship. Connecting with other new moms will reassure you that what you are experiencing is common and normal. Share your own parenting successes and try some helpful tips that others offer.

- Set realistic expectations for yourself in your new role as a mother. Consider your parenting responsibilities to be your full-time job as you become more comfortable and confident as a mom. Give yourself permission to be less than perfect and recognize that no other parent does everything right.

- Combat sleep deprivation by retiring earlier in the evening and taking daily naps, especially in the afternoon and while your baby sleeps.

- Eat a healthy diet, limit your caffeine intake, and avoid alcohol and tobacco.

- Make sure you have an adequate intake of the long-chain omega-3 fatty acids EPA and DHA, which are found in oily fish (such as salmon, herring, and sardines), some plant and nut oils, and fish oil supplements. Both EPA and DHA show promise in the treatment of depression. Ask your doctor about taking a fish oil supplement containing both EPA and DHA and to recommend a brand that is safe for pregnant and breastfeeding women.

- Exercise (either strength training or aerobic) a minimum of two to three times a week for twenty minutes at a moderate level. Exercise has been found to reduce depression and stress and to provide a healthy lifelong coping skill. If you can't get to a gym, just going for a regular walk each day with your baby in a stroller will reduce stress and give you a sense of well-being.

- Adopt regular relaxation techniques to reduce stress, such as joining a postnatal yoga class, practicing meditation or deep breathing, praying, listening to music, or soaking in the tub.

- Take heart in knowing that the hormones released during breastfeeding have a calming and relaxing effect on mothers. Breastfeeding also helps strengthen the mother-infant bond. When your baby needs to be fed, consider breastfeeding to be a therapeutic break from your other duties and a thoroughly enjoyable part of your day.

Postpartum Psychosis

This rare but extremely serious postpartum mental disorder occurs in only two in one thousand childbearing women. Women with bipolar disorder are most likely to be affected. Symptoms appear within the first two weeks of delivery, and include rapid mood swings, disorientation, disorganized behavior, hallucinations (hearing voices and seeing things that are not there) and delusional thoughts (thoughts not grounded in reality), usually concerning the infant. Because affected women are at great risk for harming themselves or their infants, postpartum psychosis is considered a psychiatric emergency. It requires immediate hospitalization and expert treatment.

- Talk to your obstetrician or other health-care professional if you (or your partner) have been feeling down, depressed, or hopeless or have had little interest or pleasure in doing things during the past month. You owe it to yourself and your baby to receive treatment for PPD!

Feeling Tired

New parenthood and sleep deprivation go hand in hand, since essential night feedings will inevitably disrupt your sleep. Although you may be wisely admonished as a new mom to "sleep when the baby sleeps" during the day, you may succumb to the temptation to do laundry, mail baby announcements, prepare and clean up meals, or perform other chores whenever your baby dozes off. Resist these temptations as often as you can! It's all too easy to underestimate the magnitude of your exhaustion and the vital importance of rest.

Even if things are going relatively smoothly, round-the-clock care of your new baby day after day, week after week, takes a physical toll. When breastfeeding is not going well, your exhaustion is even greater. Chronic sleep deprivation can change your perspective, cloud your judgment, make you vulnerable to illness, predispose you to depression, and squelch some of the joys of new parenthood. Here are a number of strategies that can help keep you rested and on an even keel.

- Divide the nighttime duties, whenever possible. Ask your partner to bring the baby to you for nursing, then let your partner doze off while you breastfeed. Afterward, let your partner burp the baby, change his diaper, and settle him while you return to sleep. If your partner can't get up on weeknights because of work responsibilities, ask him to help out on weekend nights.

- In the early weeks, try to compensate for nighttime awakenings by taking daytime naps when your baby sleeps. Go to bed earlier. Try nursing in a reclining position to make nighttime feedings easier. Opt for an extra hour of sleep instead of watching TV or a newly released DVD. Record your favorite shows for later viewing.

- Postpone all duties that can wait until later, including sending thank-you notes, birth announcements, and buying non-essential additions to the nursery. Once you and your baby have settled into a routine, and you are less sleep deprived, you can efficiently complete those lingering "to do" items.

- Remember, babies are nurtured from your own emotional overflow. Taking time to attend to your own needs is fundamental to self-care. Structure your time to allow for a daily shower or bath at the minimum—it will be thoroughly rejuvenating, no matter how exhausted you are. Enlist the help you need to spend some precious time each day refreshing yourself.

Feeling Like Your Old Self Again

At first, your new role as somebody's mother feels all-encompassing. After receiving so much care and attention during your pregnancy, your baby now has become the center of attention, and his compelling daily needs leave little time for your old life or your own needs and wants. Your identity as a lover, partner, professional, and friend seem like a distant reality. You wonder how you can ever reclaim those diverse roles or if you ever will find time to work out, socialize with friends, or read a book for pleasure. The truth is that once you become comfortable and confident with breastfeeding and the basics of baby care, the rest of your life can begin to synchronize with your new routines as a mom.

Breastfeeding and caring for a newborn can be all-consuming at first. As a new nursing mom there'll be days when you have no hope of showering anytime soon, and you'll still be wearing your bathrobe in the middle of the afternoon. On those days, you may doubt that you will ever find time to put on makeup, fix your hair, take a bubble bath, or do your nails again. In the early weeks of nursing, feedings take longer, are closely spaced, and cannot be delegated to anyone else. Before long, however, feedings become more efficient and less frequent, your baby sleeps longer at night, and a comfortable routine emerges. Here are some suggestions for smoothing the transition to motherhood:

- Go easy on yourself and give yourself sufficient time to adjust to this major life change. Eventually you will find ways to resume many, if not all, of your previous roles, while juggling the joys and demands of having a breastfeeding baby in tow.

- Amid all that needs to be done for your baby, savor some daily moments of solitude and personal pampering by sipping

a cup of tea, enjoying a favorite snack, reading a magazine article, reviewing your e-mail, listening to music, or taking a bath.

- Carve out some precious couple-time, when you and your partner can focus on each other while the baby sleeps or is cared for by someone else. Schedule a weekly "date," if possible, and commit to making time for regular emotional or physical intimacy.

- Find ways to multi-task as you become more comfortable in your child-care responsibilities. Take a bath with your baby, or place him in a swing or bouncy seat in your room while you get ready in the morning. Carry him in a sling or front carrier and go about routine activities with your baby.

- Don't try to be "supermom" or make the mistake of returning too quickly to professional responsibilities, social commitments, or fitness routines. Your body needs time to recover, both physically and emotionally, from the passage into motherhood. Give yourself sufficient time to adjust to this major life change.

- Try to maintain your perspective. Life has many stages and passages. Despite the challenges of new parenthood, this is a unique, precious, and transient time in your life. Babyhood passes all too quickly, while career and educational opportunities, hobbies, and friendships can be resumed at a later time.

Avoiding Comparisons

Get any group of new mothers together and the comparisons start flying thick and fast. While you're swapping pregnancy stories; baby weights; and how often and how long he breastfeeds, sleeps, and cries, you may be tempted to feel like a less-than-competent mother if your baby doesn't quite "measure up" to the ideal (whatever that is). Just let go of those expectations and recognize that much of your baby's behavior is due to his unique personality. If he has trouble latching on or drifting off to sleep (while your friend's textbook baby sails effortlessly through it all), that is not an indictment of your parenting. Relax—and cherish your baby exactly for who he is.

New-mom comparisons also reveal very different choices, priorities, and values that are reflected in parenting styles. Perhaps your sister-in-law returned to her law practice at six weeks after she gave birth, while you left your job in the corporate world to stay home with your baby. Your girlfriend "wears" her six-month-old in a baby sling and has never left him with a substitute care provider, while you pump your breasts daily to allow Dad to give an evening bottle, and your mother watches your baby once a week while you go on a date with your husband.

Your friends and neighbors aren't the only ones with parenting opinions and experiences to share. Your mother and mother-in-law have their own childrearing stories that may translate into family legacies and expectations. Without intending to, they may represent an intimidating presence as you struggle to find your own path as a new mother. Remember that while others may have more experience or expertise, you are still the expert on your own baby. You can listen to the stories of others and take what you find useful. Thank them graciously and acknowledge what worked for them; then do what feels right for you and your baby. After all, parenting is not a competition, and there is no single "right" way to breastfeed and raise a child. So avoid the temptation to compare your baby with other babies or rate yourself against other mothers. Instead, recognize that this is your baby, your reality, and your life. Here are some strategies for avoiding comparisons:

- Consider spending some time alone—if only a day or so—integrating your new baby into your family before visitors arrive. This "cocooning" period is not unlike an intimate, secluded honeymoon that follows the hubbub of a marriage ceremony. A brief period of relative privacy will allow you and your partner to get to know your baby.

- The better you know your baby and the closer the bond you forge with him, the more you can trust your own intuition as you care for him. Make eye contact with him as often as possible, and explore his little body. Observe and record his feeding and sleeping patterns and his alert periods. Learn to distinguish his different cries—hunger, fatigue, over-stimulation, and pain.

- Talk to your baby as you would to an older child. Explain everything you do as you care for him, "Let's change this messy diaper. You'll feel better after you're clean and dry." "I know you're upset. You're probably getting tired now." Let your tone of voice reflect your baby's mood. Talking to your baby this way conveys your respect and empathy and helps him eventually learn what to expect next.

Dads and Breastfeeding

Many men mistakenly believe that breastfeeding involves only mothers and babies, and they see themselves as passive, outside observers who have little to contribute to the breastfeeding process. A common complaint among fathers of breastfed babies is that they feel excluded from the intimacy of the nursing couple. Although only mothers can breastfeed, there is no need for a father to feel left out of this special experience.

Here are some ways dads can get involved to support you and your growing family:

- When your husband or partner ranks breastfeeding as a high priority, you feel affirmed in your role as a nursing mother. By encouraging you to keep your baby nearby for unrestricted nursing, he conveys a positive family attitude toward breastfeeding that promotes success.

- Breastfeeding can be emotionally demanding, physically exhausting, and uncomfortable at times. Your partner can bolster your confidence by complimenting you, praising your efforts, and offering words of encouragement. His support role can be particularly helpful when you are feeling tired and discouraged. Even if he doesn't know exactly what to say, it doesn't matter: He can still be a sounding board and a source of emotional support for you. Just lending a sympathetic ear or helping you figure out how to treat a specific breastfeeding problem can be an enormous help and make you feel as if you aren't struggling all by yourself.

- In a very practical way, your partner can enhance your breastfeeding experience by spending extra time with older children, helping with household chores, screening phone calls, and running errands while you invest in nursing your baby. He can encourage you to nap when the baby naps, get the baby when he awakens, and bring him to you so that you don't have to get up. And while you're nursing, he can also bring you a cool glass of water and massage your shoulders. If all of these loving

ministrations haven't exhausted your partner, he can even burp the baby after the first breast and help rouse him for the second side. When the feeding is complete, he can change your baby and put him down to sleep. While these activities may not be as rewarding as feeding a baby, each contributes to your breastfeeding success and builds your partner's confidence as a loving parent and mate.

- Although the bond between a breastfeeding baby and his mother is one of the strongest in nature, this does not diminish the importance of a baby's early relationship with his father. Instead of feeling left out of the nursing relationship, a father can begin to cultivate his own unique bond with his baby by connecting with him through touch, one of the most powerfully developed senses at birth. He can hold, carry, rock, caress, massage, and stroke his baby and let him fall asleep against his bare chest (skin-to-skin contact is great for both baby and Dad). Bath time can be a special, fun activity for dads and their babies, too (and it can provide you with a little time to rest and restore your energy).

Sex After Baby

Having a baby transforms a couple into a family and surely represents one of the most significant transitions in adult life. Despite the temporary upheaval, increased stress, and new responsibilities,

Forging a Baby-Daddy Bond

Help your baby's father create a unique bond with his child. Because babies respond best to a higher-pitched voice, encourage Dad to use baby talk with him. Since your baby already recognizes the sound of his father's voice from hearing it while in the uterus, your baby will love it. Encourage your baby's father to sing, read aloud, or make silly noises. Fathers naturally engage in more physical play with their babies, compared to a mom's gentler face-to-face interactions. Within a few months, your baby will perceive that Dad is the source of more energetic, exciting, and stimulating play that is different, but no less important, than your own more verbal, tender exchanges.

A father can cultivate a unique and intimate bond with his baby.

Catch Him Doing Something Right

If you are more adept at comforting, bathing, diapering, and entertaining your baby, don't be tempted to be the only caregiver. Instead, show your partner how to perform certain infant-care tasks, and leave him alone with the baby, starting with brief periods. There is a big difference between merely "helping out," with you looking over his shoulder, and being "on his own" with the baby. Don't be too quick to try to "rescue" your partner when the baby cries. Help him gain confidence in his ability to soothe his baby by himself. Worry less about whether your partner is "doing things right," and let him know how much you appreciate him for "doing the right things."

most couples ultimately discover that parenthood brings a whole new dimension to their relationship that enhances their intimacy and strengthens their bond. At first, however, personal time for you and your partner is superseded by the pressing needs of the infant newcomer who becomes the focus of the family.

The spontaneity you enjoyed as a couple before your baby came along is soon replaced by the comfortable familiarity of his daily schedule and predictable routines. Former exciting leisure activities give way to new compelling interests in baby matters—the quality of a breastfeeding, the magnitude of a burp, or the color of a bowel movement. As a new mother, physically depleted at the end of the day, it is understandable that you might prefer a quiet evening at home over a night out with your partner. And weeks of nighttime feedings can make a little shut-eye seem more appealing than a romantic interlude with your mate. Before long, the enormous demands of parenthood can create tension between you and your partner.

THE BREAST-INTIMACY CONNECTION

Myths and misconceptions about a woman's lactating breasts can impact lovemaking. Men mistakenly may assume that, when a woman's breasts are used to nourish a baby, they become off-limits sexually. A nursing mother's nipples may be less sensitive to sexual arousal, or cracked, painful nipples may interfere with lovemaking. The intense physical intimacy of the nursing relationship leaves some breastfeeding women with little interest in their partner's sexual advances. With a baby at your breast for much of the day, you might view additional physical contact as just one more demand on your body. On the other hand, you might find that breastfeeding makes you feel more comfortable with and confident about your body, making you more sexually responsive than ever.

No generalities can be made about the impact of breastfeeding versus formula feeding on a couple's sexuality because individual differences vary so widely. After giving birth, women typically are advised to abstain from intercourse until they no longer have bright red vaginal bleeding. Most couples resume sexual relations between four and six weeks after the birth of their baby and eventually manage to reclaim the same level of sexual intimacy they enjoyed before pregnancy. Consider the following tips for understanding and rekindling physical intimacy after pregnancy:

- Because fatigue, depression, and preoccupation can diminish libido, it is not surprising that mothers who are particularly exhausted or overwhelmed often have little energy for sexual activity. Mothers with medical complications of pregnancy or delivery or those who have had cesarean births justifiably may take longer to recover from childbirth. Be patient with yourself. Begin by spending alone time with your partner, simply cuddling together, without the expectation of intercourse.

- Sometimes fear of discomfort during lovemaking causes women to avoid sexual intercourse, and fear of hurting their partner makes men reluctant to initiate sex. Excessive vaginal dryness (making intercourse more difficult) is a common complaint among breastfeeding women because estrogen levels are low during lactation. Your doctor can recommend a vaginal lubricant if this is a problem for you.

- While your breasts are producing milk, it is only natural for your partner to fantasize about tasting it. Some partners attempt to nurse from their mates during lovemaking and admit that doing so enriches the couple's intimacy. This is common and normal. However, some women feel overly protective about their breasts or their milk when they are nursing a baby. A woman may fear that her partner's mouth will contaminate her nipples (a herpes infection can be passed this way if your partner has a cold sore) or that his attempts at nursing will be uncomfortable for her. The best way to deal with any of these

uncertainties and concerns is to communicate openly about them with your partner—and enjoy the precious time you have together.

- For women, breastfeeding is an integral part of the full cycle of reproduction. The hormone oxytocin, which triggers letdown (the milk ejection reflex), is the same natural hormone that causes uterine contractions during labor, shrinks the uterus back to its normal size after delivery, and produces uterine contractions during sexual intercourse. Since breastfeeding and sexuality are seldom discussed in our culture, most couples discover quite by accident the startling connection between orgasm and milk ejection. As a woman climaxes during lovemaking, oxytocin is released and milk spontaneously sprays from her nipples as an amazing reminder of the inextricable link between the sexual and nurturing roles of the breasts.

- Despite your inevitable exhaustion and preoccupation with your new parental responsibilities, try to make time for being intimate with your partner on a regular basis. At a time when your relationship as a couple is undergoing so much change, maintaining an active sex life will help preserve and strengthen the love between you. While spontaneous romance is a nice ideal, many couples find it useful to actually schedule time for sex just as you schedule other priorities in your life. Make a bedroom date with your partner. Choose a time when your baby predictably sleeps soundly. Then plan ahead to be as rested and renewed as possible so you will be able to focus on giving and receiving pleasure from your partner.

Expressing, Storing, and Feeding Your Breastmilk

n the not-so-distant past, few women in North America breastfed their babies beyond the first few weeks or months after birth. Some stopped breastfeeding because they felt "tied down" by the need to be available for every infant feeding. Many women who faced common breastfeeding challenges—such as giving birth to a premature infant or returning to work—were not able to maintain an adequate milk supply when they were separated from their baby. The breast pumps of the past were limited in their ease of use, effectiveness, and comfort. When efficient hospital-grade pumps did become available, the rental costs were prohibitive for many women. Today, however, a wide array of highly effective, comfortable breast pumps is readily accessible, making it far easier and more convenient for nursing moms to express their breastmilk (and keep up an ample supply) for as long as they continue to breastfeed. Being able to express your milk greatly expands your breastfeeding options, and for many women, allows them to prolong the duration of breastfeeding. In this chapter you'll learn about various options for expressing your milk, storing it safely, and feeding it to your baby.

Reasons for Expressing Milk

By choice or necessity, just about every breastfeeding mom these days will express her milk at some point, either occasionally or regularly. In fact, breast pumps are now routinely recommended in treating countless breastfeeding problems. Here are some of the reasons why you may need or choose to express your milk:

- In the early weeks of nursing you may need to pump your milk if your breasts become uncomfortably engorged or if your newborn is not able to drink much milk when she nurses. If you have flat or inverted nipples, pumping briefly before feedings can draw your nipples out and make it easier for your newborn to learn to latch on.

- If your baby is born prematurely or has a birth defect such as a cleft palate that prevents her from nursing effectively, you may need to pump your milk for many weeks or months.

- If you are employed or attend school and must be separated from your baby each day, you will need to express your milk to maintain your supply and provide breastmilk for your baby's feedings.

- If you have an at-risk newborn who does not breastfeed effectively—such as a late-preterm infant born between thirty-four and thirty-six weeks' gestation or an infant with jaundice—you'll need to express any extra milk left in your breasts after most feedings to ensure that you continue to produce a generous supply of milk. Once your baby begins gaining weight and is able to drain your breasts well, you can cut back on pumping after feedings.

- If your milk supply is low, you can try to increase your production by pumping after each nursing to provide additional breast stimulation and draining.

- If you have extremely sore nipples or a breast infection, you may need to interrupt breastfeeding temporarily and express your milk, preferably with a hospital-grade electric pump, until your nipples have healed or your breast pain has subsided enough to tolerate nursing.

- If you are hospitalized because of an illness, surgical procedure, or injury—and your baby can't be brought to you for nursing—you will need to express your milk temporarily.

- If you produce far more milk than your baby requires, you may want to express some excess milk to prevent uncomfortable breast fullness, relieve a plugged duct, or donate to a Mothers' Milk Bank. (See Resources.)

- Expressing and storing extra milk can give you peace of mind, knowing that you have reserves available for your baby in the case of unforeseen events, such as an illness that temporarily decreases your milk supply or the need to take a medication that is not safe for nursing infants.

- Once breastfeeding is well established, you may choose to pump so that your partner can enjoy feeding your baby. For example, he can give a middle-of-the-night feeding while you pump both breasts for ten minutes and return to sleep. Dad then feeds your expressed milk by bottle, and handles burping, changing, and helping your baby settle back to sleep. Expressing your milk also gives you the flexibility of being able to leave your baby in the care of your partner or a relative for several hours, knowing that he or she can offer a bottle of expressed milk if your baby becomes hungry before you return.

- Many women, for a variety of personal reasons, prefer not to breastfeed directly, and opt instead to use a breast pump exclusively and feed their expressed milk to their infant by bottle.

Methods of Expressing Breastmilk

All breast pumps—whether hand varieties or high-end electric models—have three basic parts: a breastshield that fits over your nipple and areola, a method to create suction, and a milk collection container. Before modern electric breast pumps became available, breastfeeding women were advised, "There is no pump as effective as your baby." Today, however, some of the newer hospital-grade and daily-use electric pumps mimic the sucking action of a nursing infant and can actually remove more milk than your baby might take at a feeding!

HAND EXPRESSION

When you don't have access to a pump or can't use it effectively to express your milk, you can always use your hand. Not only is hand expression convenient and free, a few women prefer it over a mechanical pump. Plus, hand expressing before and after pumping may increase the amount of milk you are able to remove, compared to pumping alone.

> **Tip**
>
> Always be sure to wash your hands before handling your breasts or collecting expressed milk.

For best results expressing milk, first gently massage your breasts to help you relax and trigger your letdown reflex. Support your breast with one hand while you lightly stroke your breast from your chest toward the nipple, rotating around your breast. You also can massage more firmly, pressing with your fingers in a circular motion at one spot. Then gradually move around your breast and progress toward the nipple.

> **Tip**
>
> Massaging your breasts before and while using a pump can help increase the amount of milk you are able to express.

To express your milk by hand, place your thumb above your nipple and your first two fingers below, positioning them about one to one-and-a-half inches behind the base of your nipple. Next, press your thumb and fingers back toward your chest wall. Then gently compress your thumb and fingers together (rolling them forward as if you were simultaneously making thumbprints and fingerprints). The rolling motion will express milk from the milk ducts beneath your areola. Relax your hand before repeating the motions again. Lean forward slightly and collect the dripping or spraying milk in a clean cup or other wide-mouthed container. Try to keep the milk from dribbling over your fingers as you collect it. Repeat the press,

Every breastfeeding mother should learn the technique of hand expression.

Tip

Don't be frustrated if you're not getting much milk at first; just try to stay relaxed, and don't worry about volume right away. As you become accustomed to the method, the milk will follow. Hand expression truly is "handy," especially on those occasions when you don't have access to electricity and a pump is not an option.

compress, and roll motions until milk stops flowing easily. Alternate back and forth between your breasts each time the flow of milk slows down. When expressing colostrum, you might obtain only a few drops with each compression, but once your milk has come in and is flowing well, you may get sprays from several duct openings. Rotate your thumb and finger

positions around your nipple to empty milk from all the milk ducts. Hand expression requires a little practice, so take your time and be patient with yourself.

BREAST PUMPS

Countless breast pumps are available to meet your individual needs and lifestyle. Today's pumps offer diverse features, including a range of cycle and suction settings, power sources, sizes, and prices. Breast pumps are available at baby superstores, hospital breastfeeding boutiques, breastfeeding centers, WIC clinics, online from the pump manufacturers, and through lactation consultants. (See Resources.)

Occasional-Use, Single or Double Pumps. Occasional-use pumps are for moms who need to pump only a few times a week, or once or twice daily. Many models of breast pumps are available for purchase, including simple manual pumps, battery-operated models, and small, electric single or double pump options. Each has its own unique features and price range, and every woman's experience is different—all of which makes it difficult to generalize about which is the most effective, comfortable, or convenient choice in each category. The best advice is to explore several pump options, preferably with a lactation consultant who can help guide your decision. Before purchasing one of the smaller breast pumps, however, you might find that a hospital-grade rental electric pump or a daily-use double electric breast pump would better suit your needs.

Tip

Don't purchase a rubber bulb ("bicycle horn") pump, since these can't be cleaned adequately.

A relatively inexpensive, small manual breast pump

Daily-Use Double Pumps. If you are planning to return to work or school, highly effective, fully automatic, daily-use electric breast pumps with double collection kits are an increasingly popular pumping option for women who express their milk regularly. Your breast pump might be your biggest breastfeeding investment, so it is worth your time to choose an efficient, comfortable model that is easy to use. Owning a daily-use pump can prove to be very cost effective if you continue pumping for many months or use it again when your next baby comes along. These relatively lightweight pumps have dual-control mechanisms to allow you to regulate both the speed at which the pump cycles and the strength of the suction, to assure maximum comfort and efficiency. Some models are equipped with

a two-phase pumping action—a rapid, low-suction "letdown" phase and a slower, full suction, milk-expression phase. Daily-use pumps come in attractive carrying cases, including backpacks and shoulder bags that hold a cooler bag with milk storage bottles. They can be used with multiple power sources—AC adapter, AA batteries, or an optional car adapter.

Tip

Just like any other personal care item—such as a toothbrush—breast pumps should not be shared with other users. The FDA considers all personal breast pumps to be "single-user devices" to be used by only one woman.

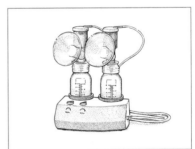

A portable, double electric daily-use breast pump

Hospital-Grade, Rental Double Pumps. The most effective, efficient, and comfortable breast pumps available are the larger hospital-grade, rental electric pumps equipped with a double collection system for draining both breasts at once.

These full-size, durable pumps mimic your baby's natural nursing rhythm and suction and are remarkably effective in maintaining, and even increasing, your milk supply. Like the daily-use pumps, you can customize the rate at which the pump cycles, as well as the strength of the vacuum, to find the setting that is most comfortable and effective for you.

The Medela Symphony hospital-grade pump features a two-phase pumping action that mimics a baby's nursing rhythm and has been shown to generate more milk in less time. The first "stimulation" phase is a low-vacuum, high-speed setting that triggers milk letdown. The second "expression" phase is a higher-suction, lower-speed setting that simulates a baby's slow, long gulps when drinking milk rapidly. A hospital-grade, rental electric breast pump is strongly recommended for mothers who depend exclusively on pumping to bring in and maintain their milk supply (for example, if you're the mother of a premature infant).

Most hospital mother-baby units and Neonatal Intensive Care Units have a number of these pumps available for mothers to use during the postpartum period or when visiting their hospitalized newborn. A hospital-grade pump can be extremely helpful in relieving severe engorgement, increasing a low milk supply, healing sore nipples, or pumping during the workday. Unlike the daily-use pumps, hospital-grade pumps can safely be used interchangeably among mothers. Each woman attaches her own collection kit.

Tip

In many instances, the cost of the pump rental is covered by medical insurance, especially if your baby is in a Neonatal Intensive Care Unit. To locate an electric breast pump rental station near you, ask the lactation consultant at the hospital where you give birth, search in your local yellow pages or contact the manufacturers listed in the Resources. Hospital-grade pumps may be rented from private rental stations, maternity boutiques, lactation consultants, pharmacies, and physicians' offices. WIC clinics also can provide these pumps for eligible clients.

A rental, hospital-grade, double electric breast pump

Multi-tasking While You Pump

You can use a hands-free pumping bra (see Resources) to allow you to make a phone call, eat your lunch, use a computer, or read to your toddler while pumping without needing to hold your collection containers. Worn only when pumping, a hands-free pumping bra offers both added mobility and modesty. (See Chapter 9, page 252.) If you do not own a special pumping bra, you still can free up one hand by bracing your breastshield against your breast with your forearm on the same side and using your hand to secure the opposite breastshield.

PUMPING TIPS

Using your pump correctly will help you remove milk more efficiently and avoid discomfort. If you are having difficulty expressing milk, ask to meet with a lactation consultant who can watch how you assemble and use your pump and troubleshoot any problems. Like nursing your baby, effective milk expression is a learned art that becomes easier when you have confidence in your body's ability to make and release milk and when you use correct technique and have sources of expert help.

Breastshields or Breast Flanges. The breastshield, also known as a breast flange, is the part of your pump's collection system that fits over your nipple when you are expressing your milk. Since women's nipple sizes can vary from small to extremely large, it is important that your breastshield be properly fitted to your nipple. During the suction phase of pumping, your nipple is drawn into the tunnel of the breastshield. If the breastshield is too small for you, your nipple will rub against the sides of the tunnel instead of moving freely with each pumping cycle. This will cause tenderness on the outside of your nipple, and may leave a ring of skin flecks inside the tunnel. Also, a tight breastshield will press against the milk ducts inside your nipple, which may limit the amount of milk you are able to express. The resulting poor milk drainage can lead to plugged ducts, mastitis, and low milk supply.

The best way to know if your breastshield fits properly is to watch your nipple as it is drawn into the tunnel during pumping. For maximum comfort, center your nipple in the breastshield tunnel: You should see extra space around your nipple, which should move easily without rubbing against the sides of the tunnel. To maintain suction, your breastshield should not break contact with your breast. However, it should not be pressed so firmly against your breast that it blocks milk flow. You may need to try several flange sizes to find the one that is most comfortable and generates the most milk. Also, your flange size may change after a few weeks of pumping.

Triggering Letdown. You might have some difficulty getting your milk to let down when you are learning to use a pump, but

Tip

If you live in a dry climate, pumping may be more comfortable if you apply a thin coating of ultra-pure, medical grade lanolin (Lasinoh or PureLan) on your nipples to reduce friction during milk expression.

before long, you'll probably find that your milk ejection reflex is easily triggered. Even if you are comfortable using a pump, you may have trouble letting down under certain stressful situations—such as facing time constraints at work. To help condition your letdown when pumping, try to relax and visualize your milk flowing. Use all your senses: Gently massage your breasts or apply moist heat, using a warm, wet washcloth before using your pump. If you are pumping at work, it also helps to look at a favorite photo of your baby; play a recording of her laughing or cooing; or bring an unwashed article of her clothing to smell. You may find it soothing and relaxing to sip a cup of warm tea or cocoa. Calling your child-care provider to check on your baby may also help put you at ease and trigger milk flow.

In most women, the milk ejection reflex occurs multiple times during a feeding or pumping session. Breastfeeding mothers typically are aware of only the first letdown, while those who use a pump may notice that another letdown has occurred when their milk starts spraying again.

Vacuum Level. Start pumping at the lowest vacuum setting, combined with a rapid cycling rate, to trigger your letdown. Then switch to a slower cycling rate and gradually increase the suction level until you find the setting where your milk flows easily without causing discomfort. Using a higher, but painful, suction level will be counterproductive.

Pumping Routines

How often you should pump will depend on your reason for expressing milk. Your goal is very different if you are pumping to bring in and maintain your milk supply for a premature or sick newborn, pumping several times a day at the workplace when separated from your baby, or pumping simply to collect an occasional extra bottle of milk because you will be away from your baby for a few hours.

ESTABLISHING A GENEROUS MILK SUPPLY WHEN YOU ARE NOT NURSING

If you have a high-risk newborn who is unable to begin nursing or you have decided to pump all your milk and bottle feed, you will need to start pumping shortly after giving birth so that you can express your milk with the same frequency that a healthy newborn would breastfeed. The following strategies will help ensure that you bring in and

6

> **Tip**
>
> The best time to learn how to use your pump is when you are feeling calm and unhurried and when your breasts feel full or your milk is letting down. A good time to practice is after an early morning feeding, when your breasts are usually quite full. You may be able to express remaining milk easily after your baby nurses, especially from the second breast, which usually does not get drained as well as the first.

fastest, most comfortable, and most effective pumps available and will make it easier for you to pump as often as recommended. Your lactation consultant can refer you to a nearby pump rental station or, if you are eligible, WIC can loan you a rental-grade pump.

- For the first few weeks, try to pump at least eight, and preferably ten, times every twenty-four hours to bring in a generous milk supply. Until you are expressing a full milk supply (twenty-five or more ounces a day), don't go longer than five hours within a twenty-four-hour period without pumping. There's no precise time to pump. You might opt to pump at closer intervals during part of the day—especially in the morning when you have more milk—and go a little longer between pumping sessions at other times. Map out your daily routine to see where pumping can fit into your schedule.

maintain a generous supply of milk:

- Start pumping within six hours of delivery or as soon as possible. Pregnancy has prepared your breasts for lactation, and your body's hormone levels immediately after birth are ideal for making milk. The longer you delay getting started, the harder it may be to produce an abundant supply. In addition to pumping, hand expression of colostrum during the first three days after giving birth can help you establish a more plentiful milk supply.

- Whenever possible, use a hospital-grade, rental electric breast pump with a double collection kit. These are the

> **Tip**
>
> Schedule the single, longer interval between pumping sessions at night to cut down on sleep interruptions and get a decent night's sleep.

- Pump both breasts for approximately ten to fifteen minutes at each pumping session. If your milk stops flowing before ten minutes, continue for the full ten minutes to help stimulate further production. If your milk still is flowing steadily at fifteen minutes, you can pump a few minutes longer. Even if your milk keeps coming, it is best not to pump longer than twenty minutes at one session to avoid causing sore nipples.

- Massage your breasts or perform breast compressions while you pump—a technique known as "hands-on" pumping—to increase the amount of milk you are able to express.

- Keep a log of how often you pump and the amount of milk you express every twenty-four hours. The daily amount of milk you get should climb sharply throughout the first week of pumping and reach twenty-five to thirty-four ounces by ten to fourteen days. It is easier to maximize your milk supply in the early weeks and maintain this level of production than to try to increase a low supply later on. Gradually dwindling milk production is a common complaint among mothers of high-risk babies who may need to pump for many weeks. By bringing in a generous supply of milk right after delivery, you increase your chances of having enough milk when your baby goes home, even if your supply decreases over time. If you are not pumping at least sixteen ounces every twenty-four hours by the end of the first week, meet with a lactation consultant to explore ways to increase your milk supply.

> **Tip**
>
> At least once a week, add up the number of ounces of milk you produce each day to see if your supply is holding steady.

- Once you reach your target milk supply of at least twenty-five ounces daily, you may be able to decrease the number of times you pump each day. Begin by trying to lengthen your longest sleep period at night. Since your rate of milk production slows as your breasts become fuller, you need to be cautious as you extend your nighttime interval without pumping. Going too long without draining your breasts could cause them to become engorged and decrease your milk supply.

At your target milk supply, the average hourly rate of milk expression is about one ounce per hour, or more. For example, after a four-hour night interval, you should be able to pump at least four ounces. You can lengthen the time between pumping at night to five hours, provided you get at least five ounces when you pump. Similarly, you can wait six hours to pump, as long as you express at least six ounces. However, if you try sleeping seven hours without pumping, and you get less than seven ounces, you know that you have exceeded your maximum breast storage capacity. (See page 149.)

To maintain a generous supply of milk for the long term, keep pumping at least seven times daily until your baby begins breastfeeding. Remember, a generous milk supply is always preferable to a marginal or low milk supply. It will be easier for your baby to learn to nurse if your milk flows readily.

- Spend as much time as possible holding your baby skin-to-skin, since "kangaroo care" of your premature baby increases your milk production and promotes good health and long-term breastfeeding.

Tip

The strategies above also apply for mothers who do not desire direct breastfeeding and intend to pump all the milk for their baby's feedings.

PREVENTION OR INSURANCE PUMPING

For various medical reasons, some newborns don't remove very much milk when breastfeeding and may take several weeks to learn to nurse effectively. If this happens with your baby, you can still establish a generous milk supply by regularly removing extra milk after each breastfeeding. This routine, known as prevention pumping, or insurance pumping, is recommended to protect your milk supply until your baby is able to drain your breasts well. By keeping your supply abundant, your smaller or less vigorous baby can get more milk when she breastfeeds because she can "drink from a fire hydrant." Without this prevention pumping program to protect your milk supply, your production can decline if your newborn is unable to nurse well. The following strategies will help you preserve a generous supply and assure your at-risk newborn remains well nourished until she learns to breastfeed effectively:

- Allow your baby to nurse at both breasts. Depending on her condition, you may need to limit her nursing time to five to ten minutes on each side so that she doesn't get too tired.

- Use a hospital-grade or highly effective daily-use double electric pump to express the milk remaining in your breasts. Pump for about ten to fifteen minutes. It is important to pump as soon after breastfeeding as possible, so your breasts will be full for your baby's next feeding.

- Supplement with your expressed breastmilk. Until your supply is well established, your baby's doctor may prescribe additional formula or donor breastmilk, as required. Refrigerate or freeze any extra milk you express, depending on how soon you expect to use it. This regimen of breastfeeding, followed by pumping, and then supplementing with additional milk is commonly referred to as *triple feeding*. (See Chapter 8, pages 235–236.)

Tip

For your baby's welfare and to avoid becoming exhausted yourself, it is important to complete the triple feeding process within one hour.

• Ask your baby's doctor to monitor your infant's weight closely and to help you track her progress with breastfeeding so that you can gradually decrease the number of times you pump. Your lactation consultant can weigh your baby before and after breastfeeding to measure how much milk she drinks. (See Chapter 8, pages 227–228.)

PUMPING DURING REGULAR SEPARATIONS

If you plan on going back to work, you can begin early to collect and store the milk that remains after several feedings each

Pumping After Feedings to Increase a Low Milk Supply

Pumping immediately after breastfeeding is commonly recommended if you have a low milk supply. (See Chapter 8, page 229.) Insufficient milk often results when your baby has not been able to drain your breasts well. Pumping after nursing provides extra breast stimulation and removes additional milk, which increases your rate of milk production. As an added bonus, the milk remaining in your breasts after your baby nurses–the creamy, calorie-rich hindmilk–can be used as a supplement. The following additional pumping strategies may help increase a low milk supply:

•Just as "cluster feeding"–when your baby nurses at close intervals for several feedings or even several days–is thought to increase milk production, "cluster pumping" may boost your milk production. Place your pump in a convenient location and use it for ten minutes every hour for several consecutive hours. Or, cluster-pump during a single hour (perhaps during your favorite television show) by alternately pumping and resting every ten minutes.

•Try "power pumping" by devoting twenty-four to forty-eight hours to nursing and pumping as frequently as possible (so long as your nipples don't get tender), perhaps ten times a day. Some mothers report a surge in milk production after a day or two of intense breast stimulation and draining.

day—preferably in the morning, when your production is highest. This routine will get your breasts used to responding to a pump and allow you to start putting away supplies of breastmilk before you begin working. Many women begin collecting and freezing extra milk a few weeks before they start work. However, you will establish a much greater milk supply if you begin expressing several times each day as soon as your milk comes in after you give birth. Pumping after one or two morning feedings—or other times during the day when your breasts remain full after

Tip

Low milk supply is one of the main reasons moms who go back to work stop breastfeeding. Using a breast pump during your maternity leave to keep your supply super-abundant can help guard against low milk later on and help you continue breastfeeding as long as you desire.

Extra Pumping Tips for Working Moms

Before you return to work, count the number of times your baby typically nurses over the course of the day. This is the target number for you to try to maintain each day (by a combination of pumping and breastfeeding) after you start work.

Pump for at least ten minutes approximately every three hours while you are away from your baby–morning, lunchtime, and afternoon. You will save valuable time if you use an effective daily-use or hospital-grade electric pump with a double collection system.

Don't let your breasts get hard and lumpy by going too long without pumping, since overfull breasts will slow down your milk production.

Pumping to Relieve Breast Engorgement

Severe engorgement can make it difficult for your baby to attach to your breast correctly. In addition, the pressure in engorged breasts can limit milk flow and decrease your production. During engorgement, you may find it easier to get your milk flowing with hand expression. Removing some milk before attempting to latch your baby can soften your areola and make it easier for your baby to attach correctly. Pumping or hand expressing after your baby nurses can remove extra milk, reduce the pressure in your breasts, and improve milk flow through the ducts. Contrary to popular belief, removing extra milk will not worsen uncomfortable engorgement; rather, it will improve milk drainage. (See Chapter 4, pages 99-102.)

nursing—each day while you are on maternity leave will keep your supply generous and allow you to stockpile plenty of frozen milk before you return to work. In fact, many women who start pumping and collecting milk early on have enough frozen breastmilk to feed their babies for several weeks or even months after they stop breastfeeding. (Of course, you may need to purchase an extra freezer to hold all your milk!)

OCCASIONAL PUMPING

If your goal is to obtain an extra bottle of milk for an occasional missed feeding or to let your partner feed the baby, you can begin collecting milk the day before you expect to need it. Because your supply closely matches your baby's appetite, you may be able to pump only about an ounce or so (combined from both breasts) after nursing your baby—which means you will need to express after several feedings to get a three- to four-ounce bottle of milk for a full feeding.

Because more milk is produced in the morning than in the late afternoon and evening, you might make it a practice to express

---

Tip

Having some surplus milk on hand can ease your mind in the event you ever need to be separated from your baby unexpectedly.

---

regularly after a morning feeding to collect a little extra milk every day. Also, removing some extra milk each morning stimulates extra milk production later in the day—an added bonus.

Pumped Milk Quantities

The amount of milk you are able to pump at one session depends on many factors, including:

- **Baby's age**
  If you are trying to express colostrum on your baby's first day of life, you will probably collect more by expressing drops of milk by hand into a tiny collection tube or onto a plastic spoon than by using an electric pump. By day two, you may be able to express half an ounce total from both breasts every few hours. By seventy-two hours, when your milk is coming in, you can expect to remove a full ounce of milk at a feeding time. By the time your baby is four to five days old, you should be able to remove about two ounces every two and a half hours. By a week or so, you can expect to pump about three ounces every three hours.

- **Timing of pumping sessions**
  Ordinarily your breastmilk supply is closely linked to your baby's demand for milk. If you pump at a regular feeding time instead of nursing your baby, you may get as much—or even a little more—milk than she regularly

takes. On the other hand, if you pump immediately after your baby has just nursed well, you may get only about half an ounce or so from each breast. Usually you can remove more milk from the second breast nursed, which does not get drained as thoroughly as the first.

- **Baby's ability to suckle**
  You may get little milk if your vigorous thriving baby does a great job of draining your breasts. On the other hand, if you pump after your hospitalized premature infant has nursed very briefly on one side, you can expect your breasts to still be quite full.

- **Scheduling**
  If you pump two hours after feeding your baby or pumping, you will get less milk than if you wait three hours to express. If you wait too many hours to pump, however, you will get less milk. This is because milk production slows as your breasts become fuller. (See below.)

- **Breast storage capacity**
  Women vary greatly in how much milk their breasts can hold before the pressure in their breasts (and a chemical inhibitor in milk) signal the milk glands to produce less milk. Some women's breasts feel full very quickly and can store only about two ounces in each breast. These women can produce an ample milk supply but must nurse their baby or pump their breasts every few hours. At the other extreme, some mothers

are able to store six or more ounces in each breast. These moms might pump only once or twice during the work day and still maintain a generous supply. Their babies may be able to drink a large volume of milk every four hours, instead of nursing at closer intervals.

Tip

Because milk production slows down as your breasts become full, keeping your breasts well drained will increase your rate of milk production.

- **Time of day**
  Your breasts produce more milk during the night and in the morning than later in the day. Most mothers awaken with very full breasts in the morning and find their supply is lower in the late afternoon and early evening. Thus, you can expect to remove more milk when you pump in the morning than in the evening.

- **Milk ejection reflex**
  Milk letdown is essential for effective milk removal, whether you are breastfeeding or pumping. If you are intimidated by the idea of using a breast pump, face time pressures when pumping at work, or must express in a hospital setting for a sick or premature newborn, these kinds of stressors may inhibit your milk ejection reflex (letdown) and limit the amount of milk you are able to pump.

Breast Pump Maintenance

Before using your pump for the first time, carefully read the instruction manual to make sure you understand how to assemble and use your pump correctly. You also need to follow the manufacturer's instructions for taking apart and appropriately cleaning specific pump parts. If you obtain your pump from a lactation consultant, ask her to review its proper use and care with you before you take the pump home.

CLEANLINESS

First, always wash your hands thoroughly with soap and water—especially in the area around and under your fingernails—before and after pumping your breasts or manually expressing milk. If you

use bar soap, place it on a soap rack, since bacteria can grow when the bar is left in a pool of water in a dish. Before using your pump for the first time, take it apart and wash all the parts that will come in contact with your breast or your milk, and sanitize them by boiling them as instructed. Immediately after each use, rinse these parts with cold water to remove milk residue before it dries. Then, using a clean bowl (not the sink) of warm, soapy water, wash the collection bottles and all pump parts that come into contact with your milk. Rinse everything well in clear water. Allow the parts to air-dry on a clean paper towel or a drying rack. All parts that come in contact with milk may also be washed in the top rack of a dishwasher.

> **Tip**
>
> Inspect the pump tubing for condensation or milk after each use, since this can be a source of contamination. Run the pump with the tubing attached for several minutes after each use to eliminate condensation. If milk appears in the tubing, follow the manufacturer's instructions for cleaning and drying the tubing and affected pump parts.

> **Tip**
>
> If you don't have access to soap and water—or time to wash up after pumping—you can use special disinfectant wipes to clean your pump parts. This can be especially useful if you pump during your workday at the office. (See Resources.) If necessary, you can refrigerate your pump parts without washing them between pumping sessions and reuse them once. Some women buy more than one collection kit so they always have an extra clean one available.

Micro-steam bags, manufactured by Medela, allow you to disinfect your breast pump accessories, bottles, caps, nipples, and pacifiers in the microwave in about three minutes. (See Resources.) Microwave steam-cleaning kills 99.9 percent of most harmful bacteria and germs. Mothers of hospitalized infants may be advised to disinfect their pump parts after each use.

Collecting Milk

The appearance of milk varies depending on whether it is colostrum, transitional, or mature milk and when it was collected. Colostrum looks more yellowish and is often thicker than mature milk, which can be light bluish in color. The milk you express after your baby has nursed well will be higher in fat and look creamier than the milk you pump at the beginning of a feeding. The fat layer in milk separates and rises to the top of the container.

SAFE CONTAINERS FOR BREASTMILK

These guidelines will help you safely collect and store your pumped or expressed breastmilk:

- Pour milk into a clean plastic or glass container (typically a feeding bottle or breastmilk storage bag) and seal it tightly. Use an airtight cap—not a nipple—on a baby bottle. Specially designed, leakproof, breastmilk storage bags

resist splitting and cracking at freezing temperatures and take up less freezer space than storage bottles, making them more practical to use if you are accumulating a large stockpile of frozen milk. (See Resources.) Place multiple bags into a larger freezer storage bag for extra protection.

- To freeze your milk, fill the container only three-quarters full to allow for expansion during freezing.

- Ordinary plastic bottle bags are not meant to be frozen and can rupture easily, causing leakage and contamination of milk during thawing. If you use these bags, place one inside another to help prevent nicks and tears, and place multiple bags into a larger sealed storage bag meant for freezer use.

- Plastic sandwich bags are not suitable for storing breastmilk.

- Freeze your milk in small quantities of three to five ounces to avoid waste. Close communication with your child-care provider or your baby's hospital nurse will help you know approximately how much milk to pour into a single-feeding container.

- Use a non-toxic permanent marker or pen to label each container (use tape or adhesive labels for bottles) with your baby's name and the date the milk was expressed. Labels are included on commercial breastmilk storage bags. Labeling ensures that your baby will be fed your milk while she is in child care or at the hospital. If you are pumping milk for a sick newborn or premature infant, you may be asked to add additional information to each label, such as your current medications.

- If you are pumping for a healthy baby, it is fine to "layer" milk collected on the same day by adding milk from more than one pumping session to the same bottle, provided the milk is kept chilled. If you are adding freshly expressed milk to previously frozen breastmilk, chill it first in the refrigerator before adding it to the frozen portion. Avoid adding a greater amount of freshly expressed milk than the volume of frozen milk already in the container.

- If you are pumping for a sick newborn or preemie, do not re-open milk storage containers after they have been sealed.

Your expressed breastmilk can be safely stored in tightly sealed reusable baby bottles or in special disposable breastmilk storage bags.

Safe Storage Temperatures

Whenever your milk is expressed, some skin bacteria get mixed in with it. Fortunately the many immune properties in human milk help prevent these germs from multiplying. Refrigeration preserves most, if not all, of the nutritional and immune properties of your breastmilk. Although freezing destroys the white blood cells in your milk that help protect against illness, it preserves most of the other immune properties.

Ideally, freshly expressed breastmilk should be fed to your baby as soon as possible to have the maximum benefit. Generally the vitamin content of milk decreases the longer it is stored, while the growth of bacteria increases after a period of time. Still, properly collected and stored human milk is superior to any infant formula product.

The following guidelines for safely storing freshly expressed breastmilk for healthy infants are based on the limited research available, the opinion of numerous experts, and common practice.

INSULATED COOLER

If you don't have access to a refrigerator at work (or prefer to keep your milk nearby), you can safely store your expressed milk in an insulated cooler that contains freezer gel packs (at 59°F = 15°C).

Storage Method and Approximate Temperature	Approximate Storage Time
Room temperature* (66-78°F = 19-26°C)	4 hours (ideal) Up to 6 hours (acceptable)
Refrigerator (35-40°F = 1-4°C)	72 hours (ideal) Up to 5 days (acceptable)
Freezer compartment inside refrigerator (5°F = -15°C)	2 weeks
Refrigerator/freezer with separate doors (0°F = -18°C)	3-6 months
Chest or upright manual defrost deep freezer (-4°F = -20°C)	6 months (ideal) Up to 12 months (acceptable)

* It is always preferable to refrigerate expressed milk immediately, especially in climates warmer than 79°F (26°C).

REFRIGERATOR

There is no need to freeze your pumped milk if you will be feeding it to your baby within several days. For example, the milk you express at work on Friday can be kept refrigerated over the weekend and taken to your babysitter for feeding on Monday. (Freshly pumped milk, when available, is preferred for premature and other high-risk babies in Neonatal Intensive Care Units (NICUs), although frozen breastmilk also is commonly used.)

FREEZER

If you don't plan to use your milk within several days, freeze it as soon as possible after collecting it. Always place containers of breastmilk at least an inch from the freezer walls, to prevent them from defrosting and refreezing in a self-defrosting freezer, and not in the door of the freezer, where the temperature is less stable. Maintain a freezer temperature between −4 and 0° F. Placing breastmilk storage bags in a plastic bin or box will help you locate them easily, protect them from tearing open, and keep them upright.

When using frozen milk, feed your baby the oldest milk first to prevent it from exceeding storage duration guidelines. Many women who pump daily accumulate so much expressed milk that they need an extra deep freezer to store their huge stockpiles, and are able to continue feeding expressed milk to their babies for weeks or even months after they have stopped pumping or breastfeeding!

TRANSPORTING EXPRESSED MILK

When taking thawed or freshly expressed milk on an outing or to your child-care provider, use an insulated cooler bag or other insulated container. When taking frozen pumped milk to the hospital for your premature or sick newborn, use a cooler with frozen gel packs. Pack frozen milk tightly, filling any extra space with other containers of frozen milk or a clean towel, to ensure the milk stays frozen. Keep freshly pumped milk well chilled on ice while en route to the hospital.

THAWING FROZEN BREASTMILK

Several safe methods are suitable for thawing frozen breastmilk:

- Milk may be thawed slowly in the refrigerator—it takes several hours to thaw three or more ounces of milk.

- Milk may be thawed in a matter of minutes by holding the container under running warm (not hot) water or placing it in a clean bowl of warm water. Change the water when it cools. Be sure to keep the top of the milk container above the water at all times.

- Do not thaw milk by leaving it at room temperature. Immediately place thawed milk in the refrigerator where it can be kept for twenty-four hours—or feed it promptly to your baby.

- Do not leave thawed milk at room temperature.

- Do not refreeze thawed milk. The ability to inhibit the growth of bacteria is slightly diminished in previously frozen milk.

REUSING THAWED BREASTMILK

When your baby does not finish a bottle of expressed milk, you may be reluctant to throw it away, especially if your supply is low. However, most experts recommend discarding all milk leftover after a feeding because your baby's saliva enters the milk during feeding—adding bacteria.

Although formula left over from a feeding should always be discarded, it seems reasonable to

What's That Soapy Smell?

You may be surprised or distressed to notice that your refrigerated or frozen breastmilk has acquired an unpleasant taste or smell. Some moms describe the taste as soapy or metallic, while others report a fishy smell to their milk. This unpleasant taste and/or smell does not affect the nutritional quality of your milk—although some babies will not drink soapy-tasting milk. The taste of expressed breastmilk can be altered when it is stored, either frozen or refrigerated. Here's why: Breastmilk contains an enzyme—known as lipase—that breaks down the fat in milk into smaller globules so that babies can digest it easily. This breakdown of fat—which occurs more readily at cold temperatures and with freezing and thawing—is what sometimes gives stored breastmilk an unpleasant taste. Some women produce breastmilk with more lipase than others, causing the taste changes to be stronger and occur more rapidly.

Most babies, especially younger infants, will accept the unpleasant-tasting milk without objection. Other babies, especially those over three or four months, who are offered previously frozen milk for the first time when their mother returns to work, may reject the bad-tasting milk. You may be able to entice your baby to drink stored milk that has an unpleasant taste by mixing it with some freshly expressed milk. Better yet, if you want your baby to acquire a taste for stored breastmilk, begin offering it regularly (perhaps every other day), beginning around a month of age. Because the lipase enzyme is sensitive to heat, it can be inactivated by scalding (not boiling) your milk before storage. However, scalding your milk is not advised because it destroys many of the immune properties. Furthermore, scalding should not be necessary if you keep your baby familiar with the taste of stored breastmilk.

Milk collected under less than ideal hygienic conditions and contaminated with too many bacteria can become sour and clumpy, just like spoiled cow's milk. Discard this milk and make sure that all parts of your pump are clean before you use it again. Review good hygiene practices for expressing milk, pages 150-151.

reuse leftover breastmilk at the next feeding for a healthy baby, provided that the milk has not been at room temperature for more than an hour and is returned to the refrigerator.

A word of caution: Any milk remaining after a second feeding should be discarded.

Do not add fresh milk to a bottle that already has been used. Instead, let your baby finish the first bottle before offering a fresh bottle.

WARMING CHILLED MILK

Milk for young babies should be warmed to between room temperature and body temperature, and many older babies continue to prefer their milk warmed. Here are a few ways to ensure your baby isn't "crying over chilled milk":

- Run the bottle under warm water.

- Set the container in a cup or bowl of warm water.

- Use a commercial bottle warmer, taking care not to overheat the milk.

Tip

Since milk fat rises to the top during storage, gently swirl the bottle of warmed milk or squeeze the breastmilk storage bag to mix all the layers.

Do not use a microwave or stovetop to either thaw or warm expressed breastmilk. Unintentional overheating of milk occurs easily in a microwave, and infants have been burned accidentally. Heating breastmilk can destroy antibodies and other immune factors as well, depending upon how hot the milk gets.

Using Bottles and Artificial Nipples

In most cases, your baby will easily drink your expressed milk from a bottle. You can find an incredible variety of bottle and nipple combos on the market. In fact, the choices are so numerous, parents are often overwhelmed by the selection. How do you choose between traditional or angled bottles, disposable bottle bags, and nipples with diverse lengths, shapes, openings, flow

rates, and anti-vacuum features? Each of these product options has arguable merits for breastfed babies, and reports vary about how successfully babies switch back and forth from breast to bottle. One baby may feed well with a certain nipple, while another infant who uses the same nipple may obtain milk too rapidly or have difficulty taking her feeding in a reasonable length of time. What's a parent to do? Ask your pediatrician or lactation consultant for suggestions, and try a few options before letting your baby decide which she prefers.

Tip

Generally, a slower-flow nipple will work best for supplementing a breastfed baby, since you don't want bottle feeding to be so easy that your baby prefers it over breastfeeding.

BOTTLE FEEDING A BREASTFED BABY

When a baby breastfeeds, she coordinates her breathing with sucking and swallowing. During bottle feeding, however, she may need to hold her breath against the rapid flow of milk. While breastfed babies are used to controlling the flow of milk as they nurse, the flow of milk from a bottle largely depends on gravity and the size of the nipple opening. For these reasons, your breastfed baby may have trouble adjusting to the rapid flow of milk when attempting to bottle-feed. You can help your baby control the flow of milk from the bottle by using these techniques to pace her feeding:

- Instead of holding your baby in a semi-reclining position, hold her nearly upright on your lap, supporting her head and neck with your hand. Your baby should be able to see your face.

- Use a slow-flow nipple. A healthy, vigorous baby can take her

Tip

Your baby should be able to take her feeding by bottle within fifteen to twenty minutes. If she takes longer than twenty minutes, the nipple flow may be too slow. This will only frustrate her and cause her to work extra hard for her feeding.

Alert: Bisphenol-A in Baby Bottles

New scientific research shows that high levels of an industrial chemical called bisphenol-A (BPA) leaches into milk from clear, untinted, rigid plastic baby bottles made of polycarbonate plastic. Even tiny levels of this chemical produce adverse health effects in lab animals, including hyperactivity, impaired immune function, early onset of puberty, diabetes, obesity, decreased fertility, and some cancers. A recent (September 2008) study in humans found a link between higher BPA levels in adults and an increased risk for heart disease, diabetes, and abnormal liver tests. As a precaution, Canada announced its intention to ban bisphenol-A in baby bottles in October 2008. In the United States, the FDA is in the process of reviewing the safety of BPA. Until recently, most baby bottles in the United States were made from polycarbonate plastic and contained BPA. However, in March 2009, the six biggest manufacturers of baby bottles voluntarily agreed to sell only BPA-free bottles in North America, after major retailers began phasing out their BPA-containing baby bottles.

Polycarbonate clear plastic is also found in other food containers, such as reusable water bottles, sippy cups, and microwavable plastic dishes. Polycarbonate plastic usually can be identified by the #7 recycling code or the letters PC on the bottom of the container. Leaching of BPA is increased if a polycarbonate bottle or other food container is heated—for example, in a dishwasher—and especially if it is worn and scratched. You can reduce your family's exposure to BPA by washing polycarbonate food containers with warm soapy water and a sponge instead of putting them in the dishwasher or cleaning them with very hot water and a brush. Ideally, you should avoid using all polycarbonate plastic food containers. Discard your polycarbonate baby bottles and replace them with BPA-free bottles. Fortunately breastfeeding is one major way to reduce your baby's exposure to BPA.

feeding all too rapidly from a bottle, which can cause her to overeat or to begin to prefer bottle feeding over breastfeeding. A slower-flow nipple will give her more sucking time and allow her to pace the feeding at a more appropriate rate.

- Lightly stroke your baby's upper lip with the bottle nipple as you did when your baby was learning to attach correctly to your breast. When she opens her mouth, gently introduce the nipple and touch it against the midpoint of the roof of her mouth to stimulate sucking. If your baby resists accepting the bottle, see Chapter 9, pages 243–245

- Tip the bottom of the bottle upward so that milk fills the nipple. As the feeding progresses, gradually allow your baby to lean backward while keeping her head and neck aligned.

- If your baby begins to gulp milk, allow her to pause and rest, just as she does with breastfeeding. Twist and remove the nipple or tilt the bottle more horizontally so that less milk fills the nipple. Pause to burp her after each ounce or so of milk she drinks. Stay attuned to your baby throughout the feeding and allow her to set the pace for how rapidly she takes the milk.

A Final Vote for Breastfeeding

The widespread availability of modern, highly effective breast pumps has dramatically increased the options for breastfeeding women, allowing more mothers to continue breastfeeding longer. By preserving your milk supply when direct breastfeeding may not be possible or desired, breast pumps have demonstrated that, "Got Milk? Got Options!" On the other hand, it is important to remember that feeding breastmilk is distinctly different from breastfeeding. It is true that pumping your breasts with a double collection kit can be accomplished faster than nursing your baby—after all, your pump can drain both breasts at once. Having said that, you simply can't duplicate the intimate nursing relationship when you express milk mechanically and feed it to your baby from a bottle. While there is no "right way" to breastfeed, most women who express or pump their milk do so to provide their at-risk or premature baby with superior nutrition, extend the unique nursing relationship they enjoy with their baby, and offer sustenance to their baby when they can't be present to breastfeed.

You and Your Breastfed Baby

The time you spend breastfeeding your baby is a relatively brief and very special period in your life that you will remember with fondness and pride. Many breastfeeding mothers fear they will have to make drastic changes in their lifestyle to accommodate breastfeeding. They may have concerns about what they should eat or what family planning method to use. Perhaps you, too, are wondering how nursing your baby when he's older will differ from breastfeeding your newborn, or whether nursing will still be comfortable after your baby has teeth. This chapter will guide you in making healthy lifestyle choices to help ensure that you produce a generous supply of high-quality milk for your baby. You'll also learn how breastfed babies grow, how to introduce solid foods into your baby's diet, and how babies wean from breastfeeding.

A Healthy Diet

Many breastfeeding women believe that they must eat a "perfect" diet to make nutritious milk for their baby. They fear that skipping a meal, drinking soda, occasionally eating junk food, or disliking vegetables might adversely affect the quality of their milk. Yet women all over the world produce milk of amazingly uniform composition, while eating diets that vary widely. The different nutritional components in milk are taken or made from substances in your bloodstream. Whether the protein you eat at a meal comes from fish, eggs, beans and rice, cheese, peanut butter, or the most expensive steak, the milk your body makes contains the right amount of human milk protein.

If your diet is temporarily deficient in a certain nutrient, such as calcium or folic acid, you will continue to make nutritious breastmilk by depleting your own body stores, if necessary. If you have an eating disorder or eat a chronically poor diet, however, the amount and quality of milk you produce may be reduced.

In all likelihood, you've focused on eating a healthy diet during your pregnancy and already know a lot about good nutrition. If you gained at least twenty-five pounds during your pregnancy and delivered a baby weighing at least six and a half pounds, your diet is probably adequate. Keep up the good work! Continuing proper nutrition after your baby is born can help ensure an ample breastmilk supply. A healthy diet also improves your energy level, increases your resistance to illness, enhances your sense of well-being, and has a positive effect on your whole family.

NUTRITION TIPS FOR BREASTFEEDING MOMS

Eat approximately 500 additional calories each day above your normal pre-pregnancy food intake during the first six months that you breastfeed. (To get those extra 500 calories, for example, you might add as little as one glass of skim milk, an apple, and a turkey sandwich on whole wheat bread to your daily food intake.) In general, it is recommended that you eat about 2,500 calories a day while you're breastfeeding.

Daily calorie requirements can vary widely, though, depending on your height, normal weight, and level of activity. As a nursing mother, you can expect to lose weight gradually during the course of breastfeeding because lactation—the process of making milk—burns up additional calories each day from the extra fat your body stored during pregnancy. From seven to nine months, the additional daily calorie requirement for lactation decreases to 400 calories. Consider the

Tip

Contrary to popular belief, consuming excessive quantities of liquids offers no advantage over drinking to satisfy your thirst. In fact, forcing fluids may actually decrease your milk production.

following advice when planning a breastfeeding-friendly diet:

- Eat three balanced meals a day and nutritious snacks. Eat a variety of foods in as natural or raw a form as possible to obtain the calories, protein, vitamins, minerals, and fiber you need while breastfeeding. Eat plenty of fruits, vegetables, and grains. Choose a variety of fruit over fruit juices; choose whole-grain over refined breads and cereals; and eat more dark green and orange vegetables. Add dry beans and peas to your diet. Choose low-fat or fat-free dairy products and lean meat, fish, and poultry. Limit your intake of "extras," like sugar,

Tip

Many women today are deficient in vitamin D, in part because reduced sunlight exposure prevents adequate vitamin D from being made in the skin. Also, because adolescents and women drink less milk and more soda, dietary intakes of vitamin D have dropped. The vitamin D in breastmilk—which reflects the mother's vitamin D level—often is low. For this reason, the AAP recommends that breastfed infants be supplemented with vitamin D. (See pages 174–175.)

salt, fatty meats, soft drinks, candies, fried foods, whole-milk dairy products, and highly processed foods. Keep nutritious snacks on hand and stop eating when you're full, rather than cleaning your plate or habitually snacking.

- Drink plenty of liquids each day, since milk production requires water. Pour yourself a glass of water each time you sit down to nurse. Pay attention to your body's thirst cues, since thirst is an early sign of dehydration. Not drinking enough can diminish your milk supply or contribute to constipation.

- Continue to take the prenatal supplements prescribed for you during pregnancy to ensure that you get the right balance of vitamins and minerals you need. Generally your breastmilk contains enough vitamins if you eat a typical diet. However, the amounts of vitamins—especially A, D, B_6, or B_{12}—can be low in your breastmilk if you are malnourished or have a vitamin deficiency.

- As a nursing mother you will continue to require 1,000 mg of calcium daily. You can meet this requirement by eating three dairy servings—milk, cheese, or yogurt—each day. Other good sources of calcium include sardines (canned with the bones), turnip greens, dried beans, calcium-fortified tofu, and fortified soy beverages.

- Each week eat two to three meals of a variety of seafood (twelve ounces total per week). Fish is low in saturated fat and rich in many nutrients, including healthy omega-3 fatty acids (DHA) that reduce your risk of heart disease and are important for your baby's brain and eye development. Do not eat shark, swordfish, king mackerel, or tilefish, as these contain high levels of mercury, which can

Tip

If you are a strict vegetarian you will need a vitamin B_{12} supplement. Other nutrients important for vegetarians include protein, calcium, iron, and zinc. The U.S. Department of Agriculture offers tips and resources on vegetarian diets at www.mypyramid.gov/tips_resources/vegetarian_diets.html.

Tip

To check local advisories about the safety of eating seafood from your local lakes, rivers, and coastal areas, contact your state or local health department or the Environmental Protection Agency's Fish Advisory Web site (www.epa.gov/ost/fish).

damage your baby's developing brain. Popular low-mercury seafood options include canned light tuna, salmon, catfish, tilapia, sardines, cod, pollack, shrimp, crab, scallops, and clams. Eat a variety of seafood, and don't eat the same type more than once a week.

> **Tip**
>
> Other foods rich in omega-3 fatty acids include flaxseed, walnuts, and eggs fortified with omega-3s.

- In general, you do not have to restrict the kinds of foods you eat while you are nursing. One popular myth related to breastfeeding is that nursing mothers must refrain from eating spicy foods, chocolate, beans, onions, and a host of other foods that could upset their infant's digestion and make their baby fussy. In fact, women all over the world

> **Tip**
>
> If you eliminate a major food group such as dairy from your diet or eat very little from a particular food group, talk to your doctor or a registered dietitian first to make sure you replace any missing nutrients.

breastfeed their babies while eating a diversity of foods, including curried and spicy foods and other fare that nursing mothers in America are often cautioned to avoid. "Everything in moderation" is a good rule of thumb. If a particular food or beverage seems to upset your baby, avoid it for at least a week and then try a small amount of the offending food again to see if it truly affects your baby.

- Seek advice if you have a family history of allergies. Certain dietary restrictions may be recommended if you, your partner, or any of your children suffers from food allergies, eczema, asthma, hay fever, or other allergic disease. The most common foods that provoke allergic reactions include milk and other dairy products, wheat, eggs, peanuts and tree nuts, fish and shellfish, and soy.

> **Tip**
>
> If you have a strong family history of allergies or believe your baby is allergic (as evidenced by skin rashes, red cheeks, vomiting, diarrhea, runny nose, cough or congestion, fussiness, or "colicky" behavior), notify your baby's doctor, who may refer you to a pediatric allergist. (See Chapter 8, pages 218–221.)

Getting Back to Your Pre-Pregnancy Weight

Immediately following delivery, you can expect to lose about twelve pounds—the combined weight of your baby, the placenta, amniotic fluid, and blood. In the following weeks, you'll shed about five more pounds when you lose excess water. After that you can expect to lose about one to two pounds each month for the first four to six months. On average, breastfeeding women return to their pre-pregnancy weight five months after giving birth.

Breastfeeding decreases body fat, particularly in the thighs and hips. Trying to return too quickly to your pre-pregnancy weight, however, by sharply reducing your calorie intake to fewer than 1,800 calories daily, is likely to make you feel tired and decrease your milk supply. If you increase your physical activity through moderate exercise and stick to a healthy diet, the result will be steady—and more permanent—weight loss without compromising your breastfeeding goals. Include at least thirty minutes of physical activity on most days, and preferably every day. You can break your thirty-minute exercise regimen into shorter periods of ten minutes each, if it's more convenient for you.

MyPyramid

In 2005, the USDA replaced and updated the former U.S. Food Guide Pyramid with MyPyramid, the new icon to educate consumers about healthy eating and activity consistent with the latest Dietary Guidelines for Americans. The MyPyramid logo depicts a person climbing steps on the side of the pyramid, as a way to emphasize the importance of physical activity.

The interactive www.MyPyramid.gov Web site individualizes nutrition education based on your age, gender, and activity level. You can enter a day's worth of dietary and exercise information and receive an evaluation of your food intake and physical activity.

Recommendations are given in easy-to-understand cup and ounce measurements, rather than serving sizes. The different widths of the six food group bands suggest the relative amount you should eat among the five food groups (and oils). There are new interactive Web pages at the MyPyramid site called MyPyramid for Moms, which provide individualized nutrition guidance to meet the special nutritional needs of pregnant and breastfeeding women. Three fact sheets offer nutrition tips for pregnant and lactating moms, and the interactive site enables you to choose the right amount of food from each food group.

Rethinking Personal Habits

The positive lifestyle changes you made while carrying your baby have undoubtedly had a significant influence on your own well-being—and now that you're nursing your baby, you may have some questions about the effects of using an herbal remedy, drinking coffee, having the occasional glass of wine, or even smoking. The information below on the effects of such substances addresses those concerns.

Coffee. Breastfeeding moms can drink caffeinated beverages in moderation. The amount transferred in milk is less than 1 percent of what you consume. However, caffeine can accumulate in young infants, and drinking five or more caffeinated beverages in a day can overstimulate your breastfed baby, causing him to be wakeful or disrupting his sleep. You can probably drink two or three caffeinated beverages daily while you breastfeed without it bothering your baby. A cup of coffee has more caffeine than tea, caffeinated soft drinks, or hot chocolate.

Herbal Products. Many people assume that "natural" products are always safe, but this is not necessarily the case. In the United States, herbal products are *not* regulated by the FDA the way medicines are. Herbal products can be marketed without being tested for safety or effectiveness, and their product labels may not accurately reflect the amount or concentration of the ingredients. Imported products may be contaminated with pesticides, animal wastes, or the wrong herb. Use herbal products with caution, if you use them at all, in children under two years of age—and avoid them altogether when you are pregnant or breastfeeding. To be on the safe side, always talk to your doctor before taking—or giving your child—any herbal remedy or product.

Cigarettes. While women who smoke can still breastfeed their babies, it is far preferable for you to quit, or at least reduce your smoking habit. In addition to the considerable risks of passive smoking, you are exposing your breastfed baby to the by-products of nicotine and pesticides used on tobacco plants that pass into your milk. Some studies show that women who smoke produce less milk than non-smokers, and babies of smokers sleep less. Nevertheless, breastfeeding is preferable to formula feeding for babies of moderate or infrequent smokers. The protective effects of breastfeeding against wheezing, ear infections, pneumonia, and upper respiratory illness can help reduce the adverse effects of secondhand smoke. Limit your smoking to immediately after breastfeeding to minimize the amount of nicotine in your milk at the next feeding. The nicotine patch can be used, provided you do not smoke *and* use the patch. Remove the patch at night to reduce your blood and milk levels of nicotine. If you use nicotine gum, chew it after breastfeeding. Check with your doctor about the dose and frequency of the nicotine patch and gum. Never smoke around your baby, and make sure your home and car are smoke free.

Alcohol. After abstaining from alcohol during pregnancy, many women wonder whether they can safely drink any alcoholic beverages while breastfeeding. Alcohol passes readily into human milk, and consumption of large quantities can cause potentially dangerous sedation of a nursing infant. However, it is not yet clear whether drinking small to moderate amounts of alcohol has a harmful effect on breastfed infants. One study found a slight delay in motor development at one year of age in breastfed infants whose mothers drank at least one alcoholic beverage daily, when compared to infants of mothers who drank less alcohol. Contrary to the once popular belief that drinking alcohol enhances lactation, alcohol may actually inhibit the letdown reflex and reduce the amount of milk your baby drinks. Infants sleep for a shorter time immediately after consuming breastmilk that contains alcohol. For these reasons, the American Academy of Pediatrics (AAP) recommends that breastfeeding mothers avoid the use of alcoholic beverages. An occasional, single, small alcoholic drink is acceptable, but breastfeeding should be avoided for two hours after the drink to allow most of the alcohol to clear from your body and your milk. You should limit your consumption of alcoholic beverages to two drinks per week. To minimize the amount of alcohol your baby receives, drink immediately after nursing—not beforehand—and don't drink on an empty stomach. If you drink more than one alcoholic beverage, wait at least two hours per drink before breastfeeding again. You may need to pump and dump your milk during this time to avoid uncomfortable engorgement or a decrease in milk production. However, pumping does not eliminate alcohol from your breastmilk any faster. As your blood level of alcohol falls, the alcohol in your milk does too. Seek help if you are concerned about alcohol use.

> **Tip**
>
> One standard alcoholic drink contains ten grams of alcohol. This is the amount contained in twelve ounces (one can or bottle) of regular beer, five ounces (one small glass) of wine, or one and a half ounces (one shot glass) of eighty-proof hard liquor.

Recreational Drugs. No level of recreational drugs in human milk is considered safe for breastfed infants. The AAP strongly insists that *no* illicit drugs—including methamphetamine, cocaine, LSD, heroin, marijuana, and PCP—should be taken by nursing mothers. Substance abuse is incompatible with breastfeeding! In addition to posing a serious hazard to nursing infants, a mother who uses drugs is emotionally unavailable to her baby and incapable of meeting her infant's emotional and physical needs. On the other hand, if you are a former substance abuser, you can nurse your baby as long as you remain drug-free, are enrolled in a drug treatment program, receive close follow-up with regular postpartum urine drug screening, and test negative for human immunodeficiency virus (HIV). Discuss your situation with both your own and your baby's doctors.

Exercise

Being physically active is an important aspect of a healthy lifestyle and helps create a positive outlook on life. Research has shown that moderate aerobic exercise has no adverse effect on lactation, and it significantly improves the cardiovascular fitness of mothers. On the other hand, some breastfeeding women report a fussier baby who may even refuse to nurse after they've exercised. One study has shown that babies prefer pre-exercise milk to the milk produced after strenuous physical activity. Presumably the babies in the study were temporarily turned off by the increased levels of sour-tasting lactic acid, which is produced during exercise, in their mother's milk after they worked out! Plan to nurse your baby just before you exercise, since lactic acid remains elevated in milk for approximately ninety minutes afterward. You also should wear a well-fitting athletic bra that provides good support, since vigorous jostling of full breasts can predispose you to a breast infection (or mastitis; see Chapter 8, pages 206–209). If you experience one or more bouts of mastitis that occur within a day or so after vigorous upper-body exercise, consider switching to a lower-impact activity.

Hygiene

A daily shower or bath provides sufficient cleansing of your breasts and nipples. You should also wear a clean nursing bra every day as long as you are leaking milk. If you wear breast pads, change them frequently, because moist pads can irritate nipple skin and harbor germs.

Wash your hands before meal preparation or eating, and after using the bathroom. If you have grown lax in this area, now is a good time to begin reinforcing sound hygiene. For a breastfeeding mother, this also means washing your hands before you nurse your baby or express your milk and after all diaper changes. Frequent hand washing is one of the best ways to reduce infections in your family. Don't be shy about telling relatives and guests that your pediatrician insists they wash their hands before holding the new baby and after changing his diaper. This is especially true if your baby is a preemie.

Breastfeeding and Family Planning

Spacing children at least two or three years apart has several advantages: Your baby can enjoy the luxury of your undivided attention throughout his babyhood before having to share you with a new brother or sister, and sibling adjustments are usually easier when your older child has acquired sufficient language skills to communicate his natural ambivalence about a new baby in the family. Allowing a period of two or three years between births gives you and your partner ample time to renew your relationship as a couple before the family dynamics shift once again. And spacing pregnancies gives you time to recharge your batteries. Most new parents agree that family planning gives them the peace of mind to thoroughly enjoy their new role before contemplating another pregnancy.

The Return of Your Period

Most formula-feeding mothers will get their period by the third month postpartum while, if you're a fully breastfeeding mom, you may go many months—sometimes a year or more—before your menstrual period returns. The duration of amenorrhea (the length of time when you are not menstruating) is related to unrestricted breastfeeding. In other words, amenorrhea is shorter for women who wean early or breastfeed in a token fashion, but is longer for those who breastfeed their baby on demand around the clock and delay the introduction of solid foods for about six months.

Typically menstrual periods resume within a month or so of interrupting round-the-clock, unrestricted breastfeeding (that is, when your baby starts sleeping through the night or you start replacing breastfeedings with formula supplementation). Nursing mothers often notice that their milk supply diminishes just before and for a few days after their period starts, and that they have more milk at other times in their cycle.

Because the return of menstruation is linked to a decline in their level of the hormone prolactin, many women unfortunately continue to produce less milk after resuming menstruation.

> **Tip**
>
> The return of your menstrual period does not mean you need to wean your baby. However, you should assume that you are fertile and could conceive, even if your baby is under six months of age. You may also need to supplement your baby if your milk supply remains low.

Nursing in Public

In some countries, breastfeeding is considered so natural that people scarcely take notice of it. In the United States, however, even though the large majority of women begin breastfeeding their newborns, many discontinue nursing within a few weeks or months, and relatively few manage to breastfeed the whole first year or more. Parents don't think twice about bottle feeding their babies in virtually any setting, but few American mothers are willing to nurse in front of others, and even fewer of their partners are comfortable with public nursing.

(continued on page 173)

Contraception Choices and Breastfeeding

The following information should help you select a contraceptive method that is most suited to your needs.

NON-HORMONAL METHODS

Non-hormonal methods of contraception don't affect breastfeeding or pose any risk to your baby. Breastfeeding inhibits ovulation and fertility after childbirth. As long as you are fully breastfeeding, your estrogen levels remain low and your prolactin levels high. This combination usually prevents your periods from returning for many months. In addition to decreasing your chances of conceiving, not having periods (amenorrhea) postpones menstrual blood loss, which helps you rebuild iron stores that have been depleted by pregnancy and delivery.

Extensive research has documented that women who continue to fully breastfeed their infants, and who have no vaginal bleeding after fifty-six days postpartum (i.e., menstrual periods have not yet returned) have less than a 2 percent risk of pregnancy during the first six months postpartum. The delay in both ovulation and return of menstrual periods after childbirth that is attributed to breastfeeding has been called "lactation amenorrhea," and its use as contraception after childbirth is known as the Lactation Amenorrhea Method (LAM). LAM is now recognized as a highly effective temporary family planning method for breastfeeding women in the early months after delivery. By providing natural protection against pregnancy for up to six months postpartum, LAM gives you time to choose a more permanent method of contraception with which you are comfortable.

Important note: It is critical that you meet all three criteria for LAM before using it as protection against pregnancy: (1) You must be less than six months postpartum, (2) Your periods must not have returned yet, and (3) You must be fully breastfeeding. Your chances of becoming fertile (and getting pregnant) increase if you supplement with formula more often than once every ten feedings or go longer than four hours between feedings during the day, or longer than six hours at night. When any one of the above three conditions changes, you need to begin using an additional family planning method to protect against pregnancy. You should also use another family planning method if you are unwilling to accept even a remote risk of pregnancy.

Other Non-Hormonal Methods. In addition to LAM, the use of condoms, diaphragms, cervical caps, spermicides, IUDs (copper intrauterine devices), and natural family planning are other non-hormonal methods of preventing pregnancy. Permanent options include tubal ligation or vasectomy. You will want to discuss the respective pros and cons of these options in greater detail with your health-care provider and your partner.

HORMONAL METHODS

Hormonal contraceptive methods include two main categories: those that contain both estrogen and progestin (synthetic progesterone), and those that contain progestin only. Although some of the hormones pass into breastmilk, no immediate or long-term negative effects on infants have been proven.

Little research is available concerning the effect of hormonal contraceptives on breastfeeding. However, some studies suggest that combination hormonal methods, containing both estrogen and progestin, may decrease your breastmilk supply. Although progestin-only contraceptives are less likely to affect breastfeeding, some women who use progestin-only methods notice a decrease in their milk supply. Consequently early use of hormonal family planning methods is not recommended if your milk supply is marginal or if you're feeding multiple babies.

Progestin-Only Hormonal Methods. The preferred hormonal contraceptive for nursing mothers is a progestin-only method that is started after you have established a full milk supply and your baby is gaining weight well. These options include oral contraceptives (the "mini-pill"); progestin shots (such as Depo-Provera); progestin implants inserted under the skin (such as Norplant); and the progestin IUD (such as Mirena). While implants provide up to five years of protection, the injections last only about three months.

The American College of Obstetricians and Gynecologists (ACOG) recommends waiting two to three weeks postpartum before taking the mini-pill and six weeks before starting to use an injectable or implantable progestin method of contraception. However, many physicians prescribe progestin-only contraceptives earlier than recommended, sometimes even before hospital discharge. Before using one of the more permanent progestin contraceptives, you would be wise to try the mini-pill first for a month or two to see whether it affects your milk supply. If you notice a decrease in production, you may choose to stop taking the mini-pill and see if your supply increases when you switch to a non-hormonal contraceptive method. Talk to your doctor or midwife about your concerns and your options.

Combined Estrogen-Progestin Methods. Combination hormonal contraceptives contain both estrogen and progestin. Options include the pill, the patch (applied weekly for three weeks each month), the vaginal ring (a thin, flexible ring inserted into the vagina each month and left for three weeks), and a monthly shot. Because estrogen may decrease your milk supply, combination therapies usually are not recommended as a first choice for breastfeeding women. If you use a combination hormonal contraceptive, take the lowest dose possible and wait at least six weeks—preferably six months—after the birth of your baby to minimize the risk of decreasing your milk production. Try to avoid other situations that contribute to low milk, such as prolonged separation from your baby, skipped breastfeedings, and long intervals without draining your breasts.

Tip

The "morning-after pill," or emergency contraception, can be safely used by breastfeeding women.

(continued from page 169)

If you do nurse in a highly trafficked area, like a mall or a restaurant, you may risk feeling self-conscious or becoming the recipient of judgmental glances. The topic has come into the spotlight on a number of recent occasions when breastfeeding mothers have been asked to leave public places because exposing their breasts to nurse might offend other patrons.

Almost every state has passed legislation that permits nursing mothers to breastfeed their infants in any public or private location. To check whether your state has a law protecting public breastfeeding, visit the Web site of the National Conference of State Legislatures at www.ncsl.org/programs/health/breast50.htm. The more mothers who venture to nurse in public, the more visibility breastfeeding receives in our society. Yet, even if you know you have the *right* to nurse in a public place, you may not feel comfortable doing so unless you know how to breastfeed discreetly.

BREASTFEEDING DISCREETLY

As you first learn how to breastfeed, it is only natural to feel self-conscious about having your breasts partially exposed and to worry whether you will ever be able to breastfeed discreetly in a public place. Rest assured that, before long, you'll probably feel comfortable and confident nursing anywhere. While you don't need special clothes to breastfeed, many maternity shops and specialty catalogs sell clothing that has been altered specifically for breastfeeding women, including casual, professional, and even formal wear. Breastfeeding garments have Velcro flaps and other discreet modifications that make it convenient for you to nurse. A wide selection of breastfeeding apparel is available from the member companies of the Association for Breastfeeding Fashions. (See Resources.)

Even if you don't own any special breastfeeding garments, you can easily put together outfits that let you breastfeed with modesty and confidence in any setting. You will want to dress in two-piece outfits that make breastfeeding convenient, like skirts and/or pants and a top, and choose a bra with a release mechanism that is easy to manipulate with a single hand. Wearing a vest or outer blouse over your top is a convenient way to keep your midriff covered when you lift your shirt or unbutton it from the bottom to nurse. Many of the infant slings that are so popular today allow your baby to breastfeed unnoticed while being carried. A simple receiving blanket or shawl thrown over your shoulder can allow you to see your infant while nursing discreetly. Practice latching your baby in front of a mirror to reassure yourself that you can breastfeed with complete modesty before you venture to nurse in public.

You also can choose where to nurse your baby when you are on the go. For example, you might want to breastfeed in your car in the parking lot before entering a store. Many women's lounges in department stores have facilities designed to permit comfortable breastfeeding, or you can use a dressing room. When visiting friends or relatives, you can choose to nurse in their presence or go into another room if it makes you feel more comfortable.

How Your Baby Grows

Breastfed babies grow rapidly in the early weeks and months of life, putting on weight at least as fast as formula-fed babies. Once your milk comes in, your breastfed baby should start gaining about one ounce each day, or one and a half to two pounds each month, for approximately the first three to four months. Most babies double their birth weight at about four and a half months of age. This rapid weight gain occurs without a steady increase in your milk supply because babies grow on fewer calories per pound as they get older. In most cases, the supply you bring in by two weeks postpartum is close to the amount you'll continue to produce for the first six months.

Your baby's early pattern of rapid weight gain will gradually taper to about a half ounce per day (or a pound each month), beginning around four months of age. He won't triple his birth weight until he's about a year old, and his weight will quadruple at around age two. Beginning between four and six months, it's normal for your breastfed baby to gain weight less rapidly than a formula-fed baby during the remainder of the first year.

GROWTH CHARTS

Weighing and measuring your baby and plotting the results on a standardized growth chart is one of the most helpful methods health professionals use to track your baby's physical growth—in relation to other infants the same age—and tell whether it's on track. Measurements of your baby's length, weight, and head circumference are a part of every routine physical examination and provide a valuable clue to your baby's overall well-being. Separate charts are used for boys and girls since boys are slightly longer and heavier than girls, even in infancy.

Just as adults vary widely in height and weight, babies come in all sizes. This variation in size is based on inherited tendencies, as well as a baby's diet, health, and activity level. Plotting your baby's measurements at each pediatric visit reveals her pattern of growth over time.

The current U.S. growth charts developed by the Centers for Disease Control and Prevention are based on both breastfed and formula-fed babies. In 2006, the World Health Organization (WHO) published new international growth charts based solely on healthy breastfed babies. These new growth charts more accurately reflect the normal growth of breastfed babies, and represent the "ideal" standard for how children *should* grow. They are available from the WHO Web site (www.who. int/childgrowth/) and increasingly are being used in doctors' offices and clinics around the world.

Head circumference, or

occipitofrontal circumference (OFC), is one of the most important measurements in infancy, since it reflects brain growth. Head size increases dramatically during the first two years of life, when the brain is growing most rapidly. In fact, a child's brain completes half of its postnatal growth by the end of the first year. Both an unusually large head and an unusually small head may be reasons for concern.

Vitamin and Mineral Supplements

For healthy, full-term breastfed infants, supplementation with vitamin D, iron, and fluoride is recommended, as follows:

VITAMIN D

Vitamin D helps your baby build strong bones and may also have lifelong health benefits for his immune system. An adequate amount of vitamin D is made in

> **Tip**
>
> The OFC measurement can be misleading if your baby's head has an unusual shape. In fact, errors in measuring head circumference can easily occur if the tape is not positioned correctly or if your child has thick hair. Like your baby's length and weight, a series of measurements provide much more information than a single number.

your skin during sunlight exposure. If you have dark skin, you require more sunlight exposure than if you are light-skinned. These days, however, sunlight exposure is reduced by the routine use of sunscreen to prevent skin cancer. Furthermore, infants younger than six months should be kept out of direct sunlight. A deficiency of vitamin D can cause rickets (softening of the bones, producing bowing of the legs and other bone deformities). Because

Making Sense of the Percentiles

When a baby's weight falls at the fiftieth percentile for age, this means that half of same-sex infants the same age are heavier, while the other half weigh less. A baby girl whose weight is at the twenty-fifth percentile will be smaller than most female infants her age (75 percent of infants are heavier, and 25 percent weigh less than she does). A baby boy whose weight is at the ninetieth percentile will be heavier than most male infants his age. Ask to see your baby's growth curve at each pediatric visit and inquire whether his weight and length are proportionate and whether any changes have occurred in his pattern of growth over time.

the breastmilk of many mothers does not contain enough vitamin D to prevent rickets or vitamin D deficiency, the American Academy of Pediatrics now recommends that all breastfed and partially breastfed infants be supplemented daily with 400 IU of vitamin D. You can easily give the supplement as liquid vitamin drops, either as vitamin D alone or in combination with vitamins A and C. Continue to give your baby the vitamin D supplement until he is weaned to at least one quart every day of vitamin D–fortified formula or whole milk (if he is over one year). See page 162 for more about the causes of vitamin D deficiency.

IRON

Iron is an important mineral, necessary for making red blood cells that carry oxygen to all parts of the body. If your baby doesn't get enough iron in his diet, iron deficiency and anemia can occur and may cause impaired development. Although your milk contains a low amount of iron, it is sufficient for young infants and is exceptionally well absorbed by your breastfed baby. After about

> **Tip**
>
> Premature and low-birth-weight babies, infants born with low red blood cell counts, and babies with other special health needs might require supplemental iron on an individual basis.

six months of a diet of breastmilk exclusively, however, your baby's iron stores become depleted and he requires additional sources of iron to prevent iron deficiency and anemia. Once semisolid foods are started, iron-fortified infant cereal and pureed meats are usually an adequate source of the extra iron needed by your breastfed baby. Ordinarily iron drops are not prescribed for healthy, breastfed infants.

FLUORIDE

Fluoride in drinking water or taken as supplements is incorporated into the enamel of your baby's teeth and makes them more resistant to developing cavities. If your community water supply is not fluoridated or your well water does not have an ideal amount of naturally occurring fluoride, your baby's dentist or doctor can prescribe a fluoride supplement, beginning at six months of age.

> **Tip**
>
> Human milk is about 87 percent water. A baby who drinks enough milk to meet his other nutritional needs ordinarily will receive sufficient water. When you find yourself thirsty on a hot day, be sure to nurse your baby more often to provide him with extra fluids.

Appetite (Growth) Spurts

Following a successful start with breastfeeding, you may mistakenly assume that your breasts no longer are making enough milk if your baby suddenly wants to nurse more often. Appetite spurts, also known as growth spurts or frequency days, are normal occurrences in breastfed babies. This sudden pattern of frequent nursing is not a sign that it's time to introduce supplements or wean your baby. If you're not forewarned about these predictable episodes, however, you might begin giving your apparently hungry baby regular supplements of formula, which can undermine your own milk supply and lead to early weaning. Although appetite or growth spurts can happen at any time during the course of breastfeeding, they typically occur at four key times: ten days, three weeks, six weeks, and three months of age. It is not known whether an appetite spurt is caused by a temporary decrease in your milk production—perhaps as the result of over-activity and fatigue—or is due to other explanations.

STRATEGIES FOR DEALING WITH AN APPETITE SPURT

Your best response to an appetite spurt is to remember the breastfeeding law of supply and demand: If your baby acts hungry more often than usual, simply nurse him more frequently to stimulate additional milk production. You may need to breastfeed every two hours or so for a couple of days until your supply readjusts to your baby's increased requirement and he returns to his former feeding routines.

When your baby's sucking slows down during a feeding, begin breast compressions to keep him nursing longer. (See Chapter 4, page 96.) You can also try switch nursing during a feeding to help your baby take more milk. (See Chapter 4, page 95.)

Stay at home with your baby as much as possible during this time; curtail your other activities; get extra rest; and nurse as often as necessary to satisfy your baby. If you anticipate these intermittent frequency days, your confidence

Tip

Beginning at around four to six weeks of age, the number of daily bowel movements your baby passes may start to decrease. By a couple of months of age, an exclusively breastfed infant may go for days—even a week or more—without having a bowel movement. This pattern is not considered constipation because, when a stool finally is passed, it is loose, not hard. It may be quite large—indeed, a mudslide!

Changing Nursing Patterns

While your newborn took up to forty minutes to complete a feeding, by the time your baby is a few months old, he will be so proficient at breastfeeding that he may nurse only ten to fifteen minutes at a feeding. He may be content to nurse from one breast at some feedings and take both sides at others. Once your baby latches without assistance, breastfeeding is so easy and natural that you feel more comfortable nursing around other people. As your baby gets older, however, he is distracted more easily while nursing. Your six-month-old may pull off the breast to check something out across the room, or turn his head with your nipple in his mouth. He may develop precious habits, like touching your breast as he nurses or looking up at you and smiling in the middle of nursing. He may frequently want to nurse for comfort—when he is frustrated or tired—not just when he is hungry.

Keeping a Plentiful Milk Supply

Two of the most common reasons that women give for discontinuing breastfeeding before their baby is a year old are: "I didn't have enough milk" and "Breastmilk alone did not satisfy my baby." An insufficient milk supply is a common breastfeeding problem that prevents many women from reaching their breastfeeding goals. The following strategies can help keep your milk supply plentiful throughout your baby's first year, and make continued breastfeeding mutually enjoyable:

- **Keep your baby with you as much as possible.**
  Allow him to nurse whenever he wants. Avoid supplementing with formula (unless there is a medical reason) or skipping feedings due to long separations.

- **If your baby starts sleeping seven or more hours at night, avoid letting your breasts become overly full so that your rate of milk production doesn't decrease.**
  Many women soon notice a reduction in their previously ample milk supply once their baby starts sleeping a long stretch at night. To shorten the long periods between draining your breasts, you can express milk just before you go to bed. It's also a good idea to pump after your first morning feeding to ensure that both breasts get well drained after a long night.

- **To reduce the risk of SIDS, use a pacifier when putting your baby to sleep.**
  Use it sparingly at other times. If your baby uses a pacifier frequently, he may nurse less often.

- **If you plan to return to work, begin early to express extra milk after several feedings each day, especially in the morning when your milk production is higher.**
  Removing extra milk will not only keep your supply plentiful, it will allow you to accumulate frozen stores of milk to use later, if needed.

won't be shaken when your baby temporarily acts hungrier than usual.

If your baby still acts hungry after seventy-two hours of nursing more often, your milk supply may be low. You should arrange to have your baby weighed, and preferably to have infant feeding test weights performed to measure how much milk your baby takes when breastfeeding. (See Chapter 8, pages 227–228.)

An apparent appetite spurt that occurs around six months probably signals your baby's readiness for solid foods.

Baby Teeth

Although a baby's first tooth usually appears around six months, many babies will have a tooth by four months while others don't get one until twelve months. The age at which teeth erupt can vary widely, but the sequence in which teeth appear tends to be fairly predictable. The two lower central teeth are usually first, followed by the upper matching pair. These are followed by the upper teeth on either side of the central ones, so that at around one year of age your baby has six teeth. The lower teeth next to the central ones come in next, followed by the first molars. Then the pointed canines erupt next to the central group. The last baby teeth to appear are the second molars, which come in behind the first ones, between two and two and a half years of age.

TEETHING

The eruption of teeth through the gums is called *teething*, and the process may cause increased saliva, drooling, and a desire to chew on things. However, teething generally is painless, or at most, causes a little soreness that can make your baby slightly fussy. There is no evidence that teething causes fever, rash, diarrhea, marked irritability, or other signs of illness. Although parents tend to blame teething for such symptoms, an unrecognized illness is probably the cause.

If your baby's gum is swollen or irritated where a tooth is erupting, you can massage it with your finger for a minute or two or allow your baby to chew on a wet washcloth or a smooth, hard object, like a chilled teething ring. Don't use frozen objects, like Popsicles, because these can cause frostbite. Also, you should not offer hard foods that can cause choking, like raw carrots. While acetaminophen may rarely be required, you should use it only as directed by your doctor. You should also avoid teething gels containing a topical anesthetic, since your baby may have an allergic reaction to these.

BITING

A common myth persists among both parents and professionals that breastfeeding is uncomfortable for the mother once a baby's teeth start to erupt. Although nursing a toothless newborn seems innocuous enough, a toddler with a full set of choppers can make breastfeeding look perilous.

However, countless women throughout the world continue to nurse their babies well beyond the time that all twenty primary teeth have erupted. While a teething infant may indeed bite his mother's nipple, nearly all breastfed babies quickly learn the unacceptability of biting. The shock and pain of being nipped immediately evokes a big reaction in the mother that startles and upsets her baby. A mother's involuntary, alarming response and perhaps the abrupt ending of the feeding usually prove effective in curbing further biting.

Biting does not occur while your baby is actively nursing because his tongue covers his lower teeth. Instead, biting tends to happen toward the end of the feeding, when the flow of milk has tapered and your baby is restless or playful.

Once his "no-nonsense" sucking has stopped, do not let your baby linger at the breast. Switch to the other side or end the feeding before your baby has a chance to bite. If your baby does bite, sternly say "no," remove your breast, and make sure you don't crack a smile at his antics! Remember that a human bite can become infected easily. If your baby's teeth break the skin on your nipple, contact your doctor, who may want to prescribe an antibiotic to prevent you from getting mastitis. (See Chapter 8, pages 206–209.)

CAVITIES

Our understanding of how dental caries (cavities) develop has been greatly clarified recently. The cause of cavities involves more than diet, oral hygiene, and fluoride. For cavities to develop, several things must be present: (1) a caries-causing strain of bacteria (mainly *Streptococcus mutans*) present in tooth plaque, (2) dietary sugars that adhere to teeth and are digested by bacteria to produce acids, and (3) a susceptible tooth surface. We now know that an overgrowth of certain bacteria that occur normally in people's mouths cause the production of much higher levels of acid in some individuals. This high acid level dissolves the enamel coating on the teeth, which is only half the thickness of an eggshell in babies. Based on this understanding, caries is now recognized to be a contagious infectious disease that is also influenced by diet.

Babies can acquire the *Strep mutans* bacteria that cause cavities between six and thirty months of age, beginning shortly after their first tooth erupts. It is usually passed by their mother's saliva, especially when her own *Strep mutans* bacterial count is high. The earlier a child acquires these bacteria and the greater the number of them in his mouth, the more caries he will have. To prevent transmitting these bacteria to your baby, avoid letting your saliva enter your baby's mouth by sharing eating utensils or a toothbrush or placing your baby's pacifier in your mouth.

Diet also plays a role in dental caries, since prolonged exposure to dietary sugars—including the carbohydrates in breastmilk, formula, juice, and other beverages—increases the level of caries-causing bacteria. Regular effective brushing is important to reduce the amount of sugars and acid-containing plaque—the off-white, soft, sticky film that grows along the gum line of the teeth. Visible plaque on the front teeth of a toddler is highly predictive of the development of cavities by the age of three years. While most breastfed babies enjoy good dental health, decay can occur in breastfed infants, especially when there is a strong family history of cavities and when infants nurse for prolonged periods both day and night.

CARING FOR BABY TEETH

To protect your baby from developing cavities, ideally you should begin at birth to clean your baby's gums with a clean damp washcloth after feedings and at bedtime. Once your baby's first tooth erupts, you should begin brushing his teeth morning and evening with a soft, small-bristled infant toothbrush. Do not use a fluoride toothpaste, however, until your baby is about three years old because younger children tend to swallow toothpaste and may consume too much fluoride. Start flossing your child's teeth as soon as the teeth touch one another. When oral hygiene is a regular practice, even babies learn to accept it as a daily routine. And healthy habits that are established early in life are apt to be continued. The American Academy of Pediatric Dentistry recommends that the first dental visit occur as soon as the first tooth erupts, or no later than your baby's first birthday.

Starting Solid Foods

Starting solids is one of the most memorable transitions in your baby's first year of life. Not only does the introduction of solids add essential nutrients to your baby's diet of breastmilk, it allows him to use his emerging fine motor skills and brand-new teeth to begin—and enjoy—a varied diet. Because your breastfed baby has been exposed to the flavors of your family's diet through your milk, you may be surprised by how readily he accepts new foods when you introduce them.

WHEN TO START

Most babies are ready to start solids between four and seven months of age. Introducing solids too early—a common practice decades ago—can be an exercise in frustration, since young babies reflexively push food out of their mouths. And, by introducing solids to your baby before he needs additional food, you risk displacing breastmilk in his diet and diminishing your milk supply,

> **Tip**
>
> Studies have failed to support the popular belief that feeding your baby solids at bedtime will make him sleep longer at night.

as well as exposing your baby to potentially allergenic foods.

SIGNS OF READINESS

Your baby will display certain cues that let you know he is ready for solid foods, usually between five and six months. Some babies show signs of readiness as early as four months, while a few will not need or be interested in solid food until seven months or so. Your baby may start acting hungry after nursing from both breasts, especially in the evenings when your milk supply is lower. He may show an interest in the food you eat, for example, watching you take food from your plate to your mouth or even trying to grab it. He will demonstrate the ability to bring objects to his mouth and lose the tongue-thrust reflex— the reflexive thrusting action of a baby's tongue that helps keep foreign substances out of his mouth.

WHAT, WHERE, AND HOW

Solid foods provide your baby with additional calories, protein, vitamins, iron, other minerals and nutrients, and new tastes and textures. By the time your baby is ready to start solids, he should be able to sit with support and either can be held on your lap, seated in an infant carrier, or secured in a high chair.

Traditionally, iron-fortified, single-grain infant cereal, such as rice cereal, has been offered as the first food, since it is easily digested, relatively hypoallergenic, and helps

> **Tip**
>
> Always buckle the safety strap when your child is in his high chair and stay nearby.

meet your baby's requirement for extra iron. Infant cereal can be mixed with your expressed breastmilk. Begin mixing the cereal very thin so it is easy for your baby to swallow. You can thicken the texture gradually, as your baby gets used to having solid foods in his mouth.

Start one new food at a time and feed it to your baby for several days to be sure he tolerates it well, before you introduce another food. Typically parents have introduced pureed vegetables and fruits after infant cereal and before meat, but there is no scientific basis for introducing foods in a specific order. In fact, it makes good sense to give pureed meat as an early food, since strained meats are the most nutrient-dense commercial

> **Tip**
>
> As soon as possible, let your baby share family mealtime experiences in his high chair so he can interact with family members and learn from your healthy eating habits.

baby foods—providing the extra protein, iron, and zinc that breastfed babies need at around six months of age. Once pureed fruits are introduced, infant cereal can be mixed with fruits, such as applesauce, bananas, pears, or peaches. Fruits increase iron absorption from infant cereal. Popular choices for first pureed vegetables are carrots, sweet potatoes, squash, and peas. Select predominantly nutritious, single-item baby foods, rather than combination dinners and desserts that contain starches. Start with finely pureed foods and then gradually progress to more textured foods as your baby gets older.

While most parents rely, at least partially, on commercial baby foods, you also can cook and mash the simple foods you are preparing for the rest of your family—carrots, potatoes, or bananas, for example—or use a manual food mill to grind up foods for your baby. Remember not to add sugar or salt to his food and always use food safety precautions, including washing your hands thoroughly, when preparing food for your baby.

OTHER FEEDING TIPS

- Feeding solids allows Dad to have a role in feeding your baby. Most breastfeeding mothers have a greater milk supply in the morning, so it makes sense to begin offering solids after a nursing later in the day, when your baby is hungrier and his father is more likely to be home.

- A small, long-handled, rubber-tipped spoon works best for your baby's first feedings. Place a small amount of jarred baby food into a bowl. If you feed directly from the jar, bacteria from your baby's mouth will be introduced into the container. Also, you may find that foods with a lot of starch—like combination dinners—are partially liquefied when you reopen the jar to use it again. This is because salivary enzymes from your baby's mouth get introduced into the jar during feeding and begin digesting the starches in the baby food.

- Always check the lid on a baby food jar. It should be indented a little in the center and should pop out when you open it. Once a jar has been opened and some food removed, it should be stored in the refrigerator right away.

- At first you will want to purchase the smallest jars of baby food because your baby will start out eating very small amounts, and you need to discard unused food after forty-eight hours in the refrigerator.

- If you decide to take the chill off refrigerated food by warming it in the microwave, do so for only a few seconds on a reduced power setting, stir it well after heating to avoid "hot spots," and test the temperature before feeding your baby so you won't burn his mouth.

- Accept the fact that feeding a baby is a messy activity. Experimenting with food by testing its texture, taste, adherence to fingers, and response to the law of gravity is as important in the feeding process as consuming nutrients. Relax and enjoy the experience! You may need to place a plastic sheet under your baby's high chair to catch dropped food. Use a large plastic or cloth bib and wash it after meals to remove all food.

- Let your baby set the pace for his meal, and feed him as slowly or as quickly as he likes. Remember that it is natural for his appetite to vary from one meal to another.

- Once your baby starts reaching for the spoon, you can offer to let him hold his own spoon, preferably a plastic one with a short, wide handle. He can begin learning to manipulate his own spoon while taking most of his meal from you.

- Between seven and nine months, your baby will become more eager to try to feed himself. Safe foods that will let him practice his emerging pincer grasp include non-sugared dry oat cereal such as Cheerios, baby crackers that dissolve easily, cooked carrot slices or peas, and mashed bananas.

> **Tip**
>
> Remember that your job is to offer your baby a variety of healthy foods, and he is in charge of which foods he will eat and how much.

Neophobia

When first tasting a new food, your baby might contort his face, grimace, and give the appearance of disliking the food. However, this natural reaction to a new experience—known as *neophobia*, or fear of the new—is very common and should not be interpreted as your baby's rejection of the new food. Studies have shown that it can take ten to fifteen tries before a baby learns to accept a new food and begins to enjoy it. Yet more than half of mothers give up after three or fewer tries. Many parents conclude that, "Baby doesn't like peas," and make the mistake of eliminating foods from his diet simply because he puckered up his face or spit the food out. If a child is labeled as disliking many foods, he will be at risk for consuming a limited and unhealthy diet, rather than learning to enjoy a varied and healthful diet. It is important for babies to gain exposure to many different tastes and textures between the ages of six and eighteen months to increase the chances that they will try new foods later in life.

SIGNS OF FULLNESS

Offer small serving sizes and let your baby ask for more. When he is eager for food, he may move his arms and legs in an excited manner, open his mouth and move forward as the spoon approaches, or coo at you. Just as you correctly interpret these hunger cues, it is important to honor your baby's signs of being full. He may be trying to tell you he has had enough when he purses his lips, leans back, slows his pace of eating, turns his head away,

---

Tip

Do not try to entice your baby to take "just one more bite" or finish what's in the bowl or jar. Although babies have the natural ability to regulate their food intake based on their appetite, many parents make the mistake of teaching young children to keep eating after they are full just because the food is there. Eventually they stop paying attention to their own appetite control signals, which makes them prone to overeating and becoming overweight.

Fruit Juice and Cow's Milk

Juice should not be offered to your baby before six months of age and should be given only by cup to avoid feeding him excessive quantities. Don't let your baby carry his juice cup around with him, since this can cause his teeth to be bathed in a sugary solution for long periods and lead to tooth decay. Restrict your baby's daily juice intake to four to six ounces of 100 percent pasteurized juice such as apple, white grape, or pear. You can give him "baby" fruit juices or regular "adult" juices that have been diluted with equal parts of water. Excessive juice consumption can limit your baby's intake of breastmilk, in addition to causing gas and diarrhea. Encourage him to eat fruit rather than drink fruit juice.

Breastfeed as long as you and your baby enjoy nursing—since breastmilk continues to benefit your baby well past the first year. If he weans or requires supplemental milk before twelve months, use iron-fortified infant formula. Do not introduce cow's milk until one year of age. Some of the nutrients in cow's milk are excessive for an infant's requirements, while others are deficient. Use whole milk between one and two years, and do not try to restrict the fat in your baby's diet before two years of age, since fat is essential for his developing brain and rapid growth. After twenty-four months, you can offer him reduced-fat milk. In some instances however, It may be appropriate to feed your baby reduced-fat milk between twelve months and two years of age if he is overweight or if you have a family history of obesity, abnormal cholesterol levels, or heart disease.

stops opening his mouth when the spoon is offered, starts to spit food out, or bats the spoon away.

Food Allergies

Allergic disease, including food allergies, is on the rise. Most food allergies develop in the first two years of life, and approximately 6 to 8 percent of babies have a food allergy at one year of age. Fortunately many early food allergies—especially allergies to soy, wheat, milk, and eggs—are outgrown during childhood, while allergies to peanuts, tree nuts, fish, and shellfish tend to persist. Allergic components of foods eaten by breastfeeding mothers can appear in breastmilk and trigger an allergic reaction in their nursing babies. (See Chapter 8 pages 218–221.) Strictly avoiding the offending food is believed to improve a child's chances of outgrowing a food allergy.

Common symptoms of a food allergy in infants include vomiting and diarrhea, runny nose, sneezing, wheezing, and skin rashes, including itching hives. Symptoms usually appear within minutes to two hours after eating. Rarely, a life-threatening reaction, known as anaphylaxis, occurs. (See Chapter 8 pages 219–220.)

If your baby develops swelling of his face or lips or has trouble breathing after eating, call 911. If you suspect that your baby

Tip

The Food Allergy and Anaphylaxis Network (FAAN) at www. foodallergy.org is an excellent source of information, advocacy, and support for parents of children with food allergies.

Food Safety

When your baby begins eating solids, it is important to avoid foods that can pose a choking hazard. Do not offer your baby nuts, popcorn, raisins, pieces of raw carrot or other raw vegetables, fruits with pits or seeds, hot dogs, large pieces of meat, grapes, cherry tomatoes, or hard candies, including jellybeans.

Toddlers may eat grapes, cherry tomatoes, and hot dog slices if they are cut into quarters.

To avoid choking, always supervise your baby while he is eating; make sure foods are soft and cooked well if he has only a few teeth; do not let older children share their food with the baby; don't let your baby eat in the car (where it would be hard for you to reach him quickly) or while playing. Do not let your baby "pocket" food in his mouth. Wait until he chews and swallows each bite before putting more food into his mouth. Do not feed honey to a baby younger than eighteen months of age because honey has been linked with botulism in infants.

has a food allergy, notify your pediatrician. He or she may refer your baby to a pediatric allergist, who can perform allergy testing to pinpoint the food(s) causing the problem and can develop an action plan in case your baby ingests the offending food again by accident.

Nursing Your Older Baby

The American Academy of Pediatrics (AAP) recommends that infants be breastfed for at least twelve months and as long beyond one year as mother and baby desire. According to the AAP, "there is no upper limit to the duration of breastfeeding." Yet less than 25 percent of all infants in the United States are still nursing by their first birthday. Most Americans are comfortable with the image of a tiny, helpless newborn nursing at his mother's breast. It's an entirely different matter when an active toddler scrambles onto his mother's lap, pulls at her buttons or lifts her blouse, and cheerily

Prevention of Food Allergies

Until recently, physicians traditionally have recommended that parents delay the introduction of common allergenic foods until their baby is at least a year old. For babies at high risk for allergic disease (those with a sibling or parent with allergies), parents have been advised to delay cow's milk, soy, and wheat until one year; egg whites until two years; and seafood, peanuts, and tree nut products until three years or later. (Children cannot safely chew nuts until four years of age.) The AAP recently has summarized the available scientific research concerning early infant feeding and the development of allergic disease, as follows:

• The best prevention against allergic disease in high-risk infants is exclusive breastfeeding for four to six months to reduce the risk of eczema, cow's-milk allergy, and wheezing in early childhood.

• When an infant at risk for allergic disease does not breastfeed or weans before one year, he should be fed a special hypo-allergenic formula that does not contain intact cow's-milk protein. There is no strong evidence to support the use of soy formula as a way to prevent allergic disease.

• Convincing evidence is lacking to show that infant food allergies can be reduced by having mothers avoid highly allergic foods during pregnancy or while breastfeeding.

• Although solid foods should not be introduced before four to six months of age, conclusive evidence is lacking to confirm a significant protective effect of delaying solids—even highly allergenic foods, including cow's milk, eggs, peanut products, and fish—beyond this period. It is not clear whether any dietary modifications after four to six months of age will prevent allergic disease.

announces, "Nummie, nummie." The few women who manage to breastfeed a year or more often endure judgmental barbs from uninformed friends and relatives: "Are you *still* nursing?" "Don't you think he is too old for that?" In fact, the full natural course of breastfeeding—when a baby gives up nursing at his own pace—often extends into toddlerhood and beyond. Breastfeeding continues to meet your baby's changing nutritional and emotional needs as he grows and develops, providing solace, security, and a nurturing relationship, in addition to nutrition. Even though late nursing is perfectly natural and normal, some mothers resort to "closet nursing" their older babies to avoid critical comments. They may teach their toddlers to use a code word for nursing or not to ask for "milky" in certain settings. As a result, late nursing not only is uncommon, when it does occur, it is largely hidden from public view. Mothers who do manage to nurse for a year or longer should be congratulated

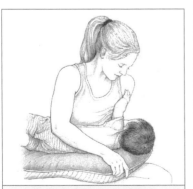

Throughout your baby's first year and beyond, breastfeeding provides a nurturing relationship, as well as nutrition.

and affirmed, and encouraged to talk about their experience with confidence.

Weaning 101

In the broadest sense, weaning begins as soon as your baby starts consuming any foods in addition to breastmilk. A two-week-old baby who is given a daily bottle of formula, for example, has already begun the weaning process, while an exclusively breastfed baby may not start to wean until solids are introduced around six months of age. Weaning can refer to breastfeeding that ends rather abruptly at an early age. Or, it also can describe a prolonged, gradual process that extends into a baby's second or third year, or longer. Whenever it occurs, the process of weaning from the breast is one of your baby's first significant developmental transitions of childhood.

Untimely weaning refers to the discontinuation of breastfeeding before a woman wants to stop nursing. It is difficult for someone who has not breastfed her own baby to fully appreciate the enormous sense of disappointment that can accompany a woman's loss of her anticipated breastfeeding experience. Weaning before you're ready to stop breastfeeding is not a trivial matter. It is a real and legitimate loss for many women who, rightfully, feel cheated out of an expected and longed-for experience. With time, however, the pain of untimely weaning can be offset by the sweet memory and the celebration of the breastfeeding experience you were able to enjoy.

MOTHER-LED WEANING

In our society, weaning commonly is structured around the mother's plans, desires, or needs. There are lots of reasons why women choose to initiate the weaning process. For example, many women wean their babies prior to returning to work because they doubt they can combine breastfeeding and employment. (See Chapter 9, pages 247–259.) Women may commit to breastfeeding for an arbitrary length of time, such as six months, and then stop nursing when they reach their predetermined goal. Others say they feel tied down by breastfeeding, and decide to wean to share responsibility for feedings with their partner. Sometimes the father of a breastfed baby urges the mother to give up breastfeeding, often in a misguided attempt to gain more of his partner's time and attention. Occasionally older mothers who started their families late decide to wean to increase their chances of conceiving another child. A few women must wean their babies due to compelling health issues, such as breast cancer, that leave them no choice. And countless women who originally intended to nurse longer resign themselves to weaning early due to unresolved lactation difficulties. Whether the decision is based on personal desire or pressing need, the fact is that mothers often determine when breastfeeding stops.

BABY-LED WEANING

Traditional weaning is a slow, baby-led process, geared to the baby's developmental needs. Among dozens of societies and cultures studied, breastfeeding extends into the third year, with the average age of weaning being around two and a half. In many cultures, breastfeeding may continue even longer. The gradual nature of the baby-led weaning process is captured by the expression, "You never know when the last nursing has occurred." Toward the end of the transition, days or even weeks may elapse between nursings. By this stage, the volume of milk a child gets is usually minimal. A nursing may last only a moment, as a youngster is reassured of his mother's presence and love. What starts out as principally a method of feeding a newborn gradually evolves into principally a method of providing comfort and security for an increasingly independent toddler or preschooler. Although weaning ideally is a gradual process, an abrupt end to breastfeeding is sometimes necessary. This is especially difficult for both mother and child when an exclusively breastfed baby must be weaned suddenly.

DECIDING WHEN AND HOW TO WEAN

If you are wondering when to wean your baby, the best advice is *not* to decide in advance. Instead, just take one day at a time, and savor the breastfeeding experience. After all, it is such a short and precious time in your life. Leave your options open and don't insist that you "could never nurse past a year." Few new mothers plan to be nursing two years later—it just happens, as successful breastfeeding takes its natural course.

Here are a few suggestions to guide you through the process:

- **Children vary widely in how they tolerate the weaning process.**
  Some adjust easily to decreasing breastfeeding, while others are extremely reluctant to nurse less often. What works for one baby may not for another. Be sensitive to your baby's needs and be as flexible as possible.

- **Consider the timing of weaning.**
  Some babies are easily distracted from nursing by nine months of age. If you haven't weaned by twelve to fifteen months, be aware that toddlers can become very attached to the breast as a security object, making weaning harder than it would have been earlier. Avoid weaning during times of family stress or turmoil in a baby's life, such as a divorce, a move, hospitalization, or starting day care.

- **Whenever possible, plan to wean gradually rather than abruptly.**
  Gradual weaning is easier on both you and your baby. Requiring him to abruptly give up both his method of feeding

and his principal source of comfort and security can be emotionally distressing. Begin by eliminating a midday nursing, substituting a bottle feeding with formula. Babies over seven or eight months of age may be able to wean directly to cup feedings. A week or two later (depending on how rapidly you plan to wean), you can replace a second nursing with a bottle feeding. Women who use a breast pump, including working mothers, may have stores of frozen milk. In this case, your baby can drink your expressed breastmilk by bottle as you decrease breastfeeding. Babies over one year can drink whole cow's milk.

- **Begin by eliminating the nursings that hold the least interest for your child.**
  You might choose to omit an evening nursing, especially if your supply is noticeably lower in the evenings, or if a substitute caretaker is available to take over. Allow your baby to continue enjoying those breastfeeding sessions that have special significance for him. Perhaps you have been bringing your baby into your bed first thing in the morning and the two of you start the day with a leisurely nursing. Or maybe you always nurse your baby to sleep for naps or at bedtime. Recognize that these feedings will be hardest for him to give up.

Weaning Toddlers and Older Children from Breastfeeding

Weaning your child from breastfeeding can be challenging for both you and him. Call to mind some of these suggestions as you navigate the process together:

•**Focus on your child's increasing independence.**
Emphasize what a big boy he is becoming and the new privileges he enjoys, like going to preschool, becoming potty-trained, and staying overnight at Grandma's house. You can acknowledge how special nursing is for little babies and reminisce about his babyhood.

•**Wear inaccessible clothing.**
Try wearing clothing that is inaccessible for nursing, such as a one-piece dress that pulls over your head or zips up the back. Explain in a matter-of-fact tone that you are not able to nurse right now because of what you are wearing. Although toddlers and preschoolers have a limited capacity to reason, your explanation may postpone your little one's desire to nurse, especially if you can distract him with an interesting activity or offer some cuddling and extra hugs.

•**Change your routine and avoid situations where you normally would nurse.**
If you have a favorite rocker where you often nurse, move it out of sight for a while. If you normally nurse while viewing television, do not watch any programs while your child is awake. If you want to eliminate early-morning or bedtime nursing, ask Dad to wake him in the morning or tuck him in at night.

•**Use a timer to limit the length of nursing sessions.**
In addition to eliminating the number of breastfeedings, you can also structure the weaning process by limiting the length of nursings. If you try to end a nursing before your youngster is ready, it can feel like rejection to him. Instead, use a timer to monitor the length and gently explain to your child that when the timer buzzes, he will have to stop nursing.

•**Let your child know that you have needs, too.**
When your child requests to nurse while you are doing something else, ask him to wait a few minutes until you are done. You might even say, as one mother told her two-year-old, that your breasts are getting tired of making milk and want to rest now.

•**Keep your sense of humor.**
On those days when you wonder whether your breasts will ever belong to you again, or when you're lamenting the end of a nurturing routine, remember that a sense of humor can help you maintain your perspective and a positive outlook. Every child does wean eventually, and your little one is sure to leave you with some funny anecdotes.

- **Substitute other forms of comfort, security, and intimacy for the close nursing relationship that your baby has enjoyed.**
Breastfeeding is such a highly effective method of soothing and quieting an upset child that it is easy to rely solely on nursing when other comforting measures might also be effective. There may be times when your child nurses simply out of boredom. Children may resist weaning if nursing is the principal one-on-one interaction they enjoy. As you decrease breastfeeding, substitute extra rocking, cuddling, stroking, singing, reading, or playing together. Between six and ten months is an ideal time to encourage your baby's attachment to a "lovey" item—such as a special stuffed animal, soft toy, or blanket—as a source of comfort.

- **Enlist the help of other caretakers.**
Encourage your child's dad, his grandparents, and babysitters to lavish extra love and affection on your child during the time he is tapering off nursing. They can help distract and entertain him, especially at former nursing times. Their close involvement will remind your child that other caring adults can be effective sources of comfort and love.

DRYING UP

If the weaning process is gradual, your milk will taper off slowly and you should not experience uncomfortable breast engorgement. (See Chapter 4, page 102.) The younger your baby is when you wean and the more abruptly you do it, the more likely it is that your breasts will become painfully full when your baby stops nursing. Abrupt weaning is uncomfortable, and the resulting engorgement could predispose you to a breast infection. (See Chapter 8, pages 206–209.) If you must stop nursing suddenly, you should use a breast pump to taper off your milk production. Gradually increase the length of time between pumping sessions, and do not fully drain your breasts when you pump.

As your milk production decreases, the milk becomes more like colostrum in composition. The sodium content increases and the milk tastes saltier. The low supply and less pleasant taste actually

> **Tip**
>
> Wearing a good support bra, applying cold compresses to your breasts, and taking ibuprofen as directed also will help relieve breast discomfort associated with rapid weaning.

help babies give up nursing. You may continue to produce a small amount of milk for many months after your baby is weaned. It is not uncommon for a woman who has breastfed to be able to express a few drops of milk even a year or more later. Frequent attempts to check if milk is still present and lovemaking involving nipple stimulation may contribute to continued milk production. Consult your doctor if you leak milk spontaneously or produce more than a few drops six months after weaning. Your breasts should return to your pre-pregnancy size several months after weaning.

MIXED EMOTIONS ABOUT WEANING

It's only natural to harbor mixed emotions about weaning your baby. Along with the increased freedom that weaning can bring comes the end of one of life's most unique and precious relationships. If you alternately feel relief and regret at saying good-bye to breastfeeding your baby, it might help to know you're not alone. You will soon discover that each transition in your parenting journey brings new joys and leaves sweet memories.

Common

Breastfeeding

Problems

ince breastfeeding is the natural way babies always have been fed, you might expect it to be trouble-free. Yet breastfeeding problems and concerns are not uncommon. Although most difficulties come up within the first few weeks of nursing your baby, a breastfeeding complaint can surface at any time. Fortunately, most problems can be prevented by getting a good start with breastfeeding in the hospital (see Chapter 3) and establishing regular and comfortable breastfeeding routines at home (see Chapter 4). If you do encounter a breastfeeding difficulty, it's always best to get help quickly from a lactation consultant, WIC, your doctor, or your baby's pediatrician. (See Chapter 4, pages 104–105, and Resources.) Since infrequent or ineffective milk removal is often at the root of a breastfeeding complaint, you can understand why problems often become complicated by a low milk supply. This chapter is dedicated to helping you troubleshoot common breastfeeding problems and concerns to help you continue nursing as long as you and your baby desire.

Sore Nipples

Like most women, you may experience mild nipple discomfort at the beginning of feedings during the first few days of nursing. This is completely normal. However, severe or persistent nipple pain is not a normal part of breastfeeding and is a major cause of early weaning. The last thing you want is to dread breastfeeding and miss opportunities to bond with your baby because of persistent pain.

Nipple pain usually occurs when your baby hasn't latched on correctly to your breast, which can limit how much milk she takes. Consequently your breasts are not well drained during feedings, and your milk production can decline. Your milk supply can also

> **Tip**
>
> Differences in skin sensitivity make some women more prone to nipple discomfort during breastfeeding. If you have very sensitive skin on other parts of your body, you may have more trouble with sore nipples. Seasonal and geographic differences also influence nipple pain, with more complaints occurring in the cold weather months when indoor air is drier.

be affected if pain causes you to skip, postpone, or limit the length of time you nurse. In addition, pain can inhibit your letdown reflex, which reduces milk flow during breastfeeding. These combined factors make diminished milk supply a common complication of chronic nipple pain.

PROBLEMS WITH INCORRECT LATCH-ON AND SUCKING

Here are some of the most important factors that can contribute to sore nipples:

- **In most cases, sore nipples beginning two to three days after your baby's birth are caused by a poor latch—typically a latch that is too shallow.**
  With a deep effective latch, your baby draws the most sensitive part of your nipple deep into her mouth. Her tongue extends over her lower gum to cushion your nipple as her jaw compresses your breast. With a shallow latch, on the other hand, your baby takes only the nipple and little surrounding areola into her mouth. She compresses her gums against the nipple, instead of the breast itself, causing nipple pain. When this happens, your nipple may look flattened on one side (like a new lipstick) when it comes out of your baby's mouth, and open cracks can occur at the tip or the base of the nipple.

- **Babies' mouths and sucking habits vary tremendously.**
  Some babies have a receded chin at birth, making it difficult for

them to grasp enough breast tissue next to their tongue and lower jaw to be able to compress the milk ducts beneath the areola. Other babies have a high-arched palate that affects the position of the nipple and areola in the baby's mouth. Some babies continue habits they practiced in the uterus—such as tongue sucking or sucking the lower lip—that can interfere with correct latch-on. When you consider the wide variety in women's nipples—long, flat, inverted, bulbous, large, and small—and the variations in infants' mouths, you can appreciate that helping babies learn to breastfeed correctly is a true art form! Fortunately, with time, growth, and increased maturity, infants can learn to nurse effectively, despite early nipple-mouth "mismatches."

- **Some newborns temporarily have an abnormal sucking pattern.**
  For example, your baby may tend to clench or bite instead of sucking, or perhaps she uses her tongue incorrectly. Babies may develop an abnormal sucking pattern to try to get more milk if the supply is low, or they may maintain a shallow latch to control excessive milk flow.

- **The tight attachment of a baby's tongue to the lower mouth, known as *ankyloglossia*, or tongue-tie, can prevent the tongue from protruding normally.**
  Tongue-tie affects about 5 percent of newborns and can

vary, from involving just the tip of the tongue to thick bands of tissue that hold the base of the tongue to the bottom of the mouth. The baby's tongue may not be able to extend beyond the gums or lips or may appear heart-shaped at the tip when extended. Although most tongue-tied babies are not bothered by the condition, tongue-tie sometimes causes a baby to have difficulty latching or breastfeeding correctly. Limited mobility of the tongue may prevent it from cushioning the breast against the lower gum during nursing, contributing to chronic sore nipples. When the tongue is tightly tethered to the bottom of the mouth, a baby may not be able to use it correctly to compress the milk ducts when nursing. A tight *frenulum* (the thin membrane that attaches the tongue to the bottom of the mouth) at birth may stretch over time. In some cases, however, uncorrected tongue-tie causes persistent breastfeeding difficulties and later speech problems. When tongue-tie causes an infant to have difficulty latching on and nursing effectively or contributes to sore nipples, clipping the tight frenulum typically results in rapid improvement in breastfeeding and relief of nipple pain. Clipping a tight frenulum usually is a simple office procedure that is performed without the need for anesthesia by a physician, dentist, otolaryngologist, or pediatric surgeon.

TREATMENT STRATEGIES FOR SORE NIPPLES

Fortunately there are many things you can do to improve your baby's latch, make breastfeeding more comfortable, and promote nipple healing. Try one or more of the following:

• **Try to trigger your letdown reflex before nursing and begin feeding on the less sore nipple.**
You can try simple measures to help condition your letdown reflex, such as breast stroking and massage, making a ritual of drinking a beverage or using relaxation breathing. Once milk has begun flowing and your baby has taken part of her feeding, she will be less hungry when offered the second, more painful breast. Breastfeeding will feel more comfortable once your letdown has been triggered.

> **Tip**
>
> As soon as possible, resume alternating the breast on which you begin feedings to prevent a lopsided milk supply.

• **Make sure your baby is positioned properly to nurse and latches on correctly.**
Carefully review the detailed guidelines in Chapter 3 for correct breastfeeding technique and the asymmetric latch. Don't hesitate to get expert help

from a lactation consultant, if necessary.

- **Frequent, shorter feedings are preferable to lengthy nursings spaced at wider intervals.**
Temporarily limit feedings to ten minutes per side if your nipples are very sore. Many women with sore nipples postpone feedings because they dread the pain associated with nursing. However, this can result in a ravenously hungry baby who causes more nipple damage when nursing. Also, the longer you delay feedings, the more engorged your breasts become, and the harder it is for your baby to latch on correctly. Finally, less frequent feedings can diminish your milk supply.

- **Gently pat your nipples dry with a clean cloth after nursing to remove surface wetness.**
Excessive moisture can delay healing and cause chapping. If you wear breast pads, change them as soon as they become wet. Some lactation consultants recommend expressing a few drops of milk after nursing, gently coating the nipples with it, and allowing the milk to dry on the nipples. However, a nursing mother's nipples are naturally bathed in milk throughout the day, offering the healing benefit of milk's anti-infective properties. Since wet-to-dry cycles (such as licking chapped lips) can cause excessive drying of skin, it makes sense to pat your nipples dry after feedings.

Tip

Don't go overboard with drying your nipples by leaving them open to the air for long periods or drying them with a hair dryer, since this can worsen the condition of your skin and further delay healing.

- **Keep your nipples covered with a soothing emollient between feedings to maintain internal moisture.**
Applying a soothing ointment to sore, cracked nipples will protect them from excessive drying and will speed healing, especially in dry climates. Most breastfeeding experts agree that USP Modified Lanolin (medical-grade) is the most effective and safest emollient to use on your nipples. (See Resources.) This ultra-pure grade of lanolin does not have to be removed before feedings. Wash your hands, then apply lanolin to your nipples after each feeding just as you would apply lip balm to chapped lips to maintain the normal skin moisture and promote healing.

- **Apply soft hydrogel pads to your nipples after feedings to help maintain a moist environment for healing and provide cool, soothing relief of nipple pain or trauma.**
Follow the manufacturer's instructions for how long to use the pads and how to care for the

specific product you choose. For extra comfort, you can chill hydrogel pads in the refrigerator before use.

- **Wear wide-based breast shells over your nipples between nursings.** Breast shells minimize discomfort from a crack or open sore and may speed healing by preventing direct contact with nursing pads or your bra. (See Resouces.) Without this protection, your bra or nursing pad might stick to cracked or irritated nipple skin, causing the wound to reopen when you remove the covering.

- **Consider using an ultra-thin, flexible silicone nipple shield to help protect sore nipples during breastfeeding.** Usually a nipple shield is used to overcome a latch-on problem, however, in some instances, feeding with a nipple shield proves to be more comfortable than direct nursing. Ask your lactation consultant whether trying a nipple shield might be appropriate in your case; work with her to ensure that you use the shield correctly and wean from it as soon as possible. (See Chapter 3, page 64.)

- **An over-supply of milk or an overly vigorous milk ejection reflex could be causing your baby to habitually latch on to the tip of your nipple.** If milk is flowing too fast for your baby to handle, she may clench the nipple tip to try to control the flow of milk. (See page 211.)

- **When nipple pain makes nursing intolerable, use a hospital-grade or daily-use double electric breast pump to express your milk comfortably.** Toe-curling pain during feedings is a warning sign that ongoing nipple trauma is preventing healing. Expressing with a highly effective, gentle electric pump breaks the pain cycle, maintains or even increases your milk production, and promotes nipple healing. Apply ultrapure lanolin to your tender nipples before pumping to protect nipple sores, reduce skin friction, and make milk expression more comfortable.

BACTERIAL INFECTIONS

Nipple cracks and sores can readily become infected with bacteria. When bacteria invade the broken skin barrier, the result can be worse pain, delayed healing, and the risk of breast infection. The germs that invade a break in the skin are usually those found in your baby's mouth, including *Staph* bacteria that cause skin infections. The infected area may have yellowish drainage and surrounding redness. Research shows that a bacterial nipple infection is likely to be present when: (1) nipple pain is severe, (2) a break in the nipple skin is present, and (3) your baby is less than one month old. A bacterial infection is also likely to result if your older nursing baby bites your nipple and breaks the skin. Your doctor can confirm a bacterial infection by taking a culture with a swab, or she might make a presumptive diagnosis from the appearance of the nipple. Untreated nipple sores infected with bacteria have a high risk of progressing to mastitis. (See pages 206–209.)

Treatments for Bacterial Infections

- A bacterial infection of the nipple should be treated with oral antibiotics to ensure complete healing and prevent mastitis (breast infection). In mild cases, a topical antibiotic ointment may be prescribed instead.

- As with any skin wound, wash sore nipples daily during bathing, using a moisturizing soap.

- In addition to treating the infection, you need to correct any problems with your baby's breastfeeding technique to prevent further nipple damage.

YEAST INFECTIONS (*CANDIDA*)

Persistent nipple pain sometimes results from a yeast infection of the nipples. Most women are familiar with vaginal yeast infections, and a new mother soon learns that her baby's persistent diaper rash can be caused by a yeast infection, too. Yeast, also known as *candida*, thrive in moist environments such as the mouth, vagina, diaper areas, and the nipples of a breastfeeding woman. Although yeast commonly

grow in these areas, they normally live in balance with bacteria and cause no symptoms.

> **Tip**
>
> Taking antibiotics for another condition may diminish the growth of normal bacteria and allow yeast to overgrow and produce symptoms.

Yeast is not likely to invade normal skin, but once the skin barrier has been broken, damaged skin is more susceptible to a yeast infection. For example, an ordinary diaper rash may develop when a wet/soiled diaper is left on too long. Once the rash has persisted for a few days, a yeast infection no doubt will be present and delay healing. Similarly, a nipple crack or other skin damage—perhaps caused by incorrect breastfeeding technique—may become infected by yeast. Because yeast is present in every baby's mouth, *candida* can easily be transferred to your nipples.

Diagnosing a Yeast Infection

The diagnosis of a yeast infection of the nipples is often based on circumstantial evidence. Proving that yeast is the culprit can be difficult, since culture results may be inconclusive. The following clues suggest that your nipple pain may be due to a yeast infection:

- **Timing and nature of the pain** The pain from yeast nipples typically starts *after* the first couple of weeks postpartum (although it can begin anytime). In a common scenario, early nipple tenderness is followed by a period of comfortable nursing before the mother experiences pain again. Women frequently describe their discomfort as burning, shooting, or stabbing pain that radiates from the nipple deep into the breast, both during and after feedings. However, pain of this nature also can be due to other causes. Nipple pain caused by a yeast infection can be chronic—sometimes lasting for many weeks.

- **Appearance of the nipples**
  It may be tricky to tell if your nipples have a yeast infection if there is little difference in their usual appearance. Occasionally the nipples will look pinkish, reddish, flaky, or shiny. Rarely the skin is inflamed with reddened bumps, similar to a yeast diaper rash. Any break in the skin—a crack, fissure, or other irritated area—can be invaded by yeast.

- **Recurring yeast infections**
  If you were prone to vaginal yeast infections before or during your pregnancy, you may be more susceptible to yeast infection of the nipples than women not "yeast-prone."

- **Recent treatment with antibiotics**
  Antibiotics promote an overgrowth of yeast by destroying the bacteria that live in balance with *candida*. If

you took antibiotics to treat a urinary tract infection, breast infection, or other illness just before your nipple pain began, the medication is most likely the culprit.

- **Yeast diaper rash or oral thrush**
  Your nipple pain may be due to a yeast infection if your baby has had thrush (a yeast infection in the mouth) or a yeast diaper rash. These infections often occur after a baby has been treated with antibiotics, perhaps for an ear infection. Oral thrush causes white patches on your baby's tongue (often assumed to be milk), and stringy white matter inside her lips or cheeks. A yeast diaper rash looks bright red (common in the thigh creases and between the buttocks), with red bumps at the margins.

- **Other risk factors for yeast**
  Diabetic women suffer more yeast infections than others, making them more prone to nipple yeast. Yeast infections are also more common among women taking birth control pills and those living in warm, moist climates.

Treatment for Yeast Infections

If you suspect that you have a yeast infection in one or both nipples, make an appointment with your obstetrician or family physician as soon as possible so that he or she can diagnose the problem and prescribe the right medication.

Although a lactation consultant may be more familiar with the problem, she may need to ask your doctor to write a prescription for you. Few studies have evaluated how to treat nipple yeast infections. However, several therapies are commonly prescribed, including a topical antifungal cream or ointment and/or oral antifungal medication, widely used to treat vaginal and other yeast infections. Sometimes a topical cortisone cream is also recommended to reduce inflammation. Alternatively, your pharmacist can prepare a special all-purpose nipple cream for you that combines three medications—an antibiotic, an antifungal, and a steroid.

Women vary tremendously in how rapidly and completely they respond to therapy. In some women whose symptoms do not improve with antifungal therapies there is another cause for their pain that mistakenly is attributed to yeast. Many nipple sores are infected with both *candida* and bacteria and need to be treated with both an antifungal medication and an antibiotic.

Tip

If you have a nipple yeast infection, your doctor may recommend treating your baby with cream or ointment (for a yeast diaper rash), or an oral medication (for thrush). Babies and their mothers often reinfect each other, so simultaneous treatment is best.

Other Strategies to Treat Nipple Yeast Infection

In addition to medication, these suggestions can help you combat a yeast infection of the nipples:

- **Arrange to see a lactation consultant to evaluate your baby's latch and nursing technique and your milk supply.**
  Babies can change their latch and sucking habits over time, especially in response to a low milk supply. Trauma to nipple skin during nursing may predispose you to a yeast infection. A lactation consultant can help you latch your baby more comfortably and increase your supply if necessary.

- **Keep your nipples free from surface moisture.**
  Remember, yeast thrive best in a moist environment. Change breast pads as soon as they become wet and allow your

---

Tip

It is popularly believed that dietary changes can help prevent and treat yeast infections. Try reducing your intake of sugary foods and eating more yogurt with acidophilus (harmless bacteria that keep yeast in check). Acidophilus is sold at health food stores and in the dairy section of some supermarkets.

---

nipples to air-dry for a few minutes after nursing.

- **Boil pacifiers and bottle nipples at least once daily.** They can harbor yeast and reintroduce it to your baby's mouth while you are trying to treat a yeast infection. If you use a breast pump, boil the breast shield and collection bottle(s) at least once a day.

- **If you have any signs of a vaginal yeast infection, ask your obstetrician or family physician to prescribe treatment for you.** Women with vaginal yeast infections are more prone to nipple yeast problems. One advantage of oral therapy over topical applications is that it can eliminate yeast from other sites while also healing your nipple infection.

- **Consider interrupting breastfeeding temporarily by using a hospital-grade or daily-use double electric breast pump.** If nursing is too painful, pumping can be a comfortable alternative that speeds your recovery from infection by breaking the mouth-nipple cycle of re-infection.

Nipple Blebs (or White Dots)

Some breastfeeding women develop a very painful, shiny white bleb (or dot) on the nipple tip. The spot looks like a tiny milk-filled blister that has formed at a nipple opening. Although the condition is not fully understood, it has been linked with trauma from a poor latch, a plugged nipple pore, or infection in a milk duct. Here are some treatment approaches that have helped resolve painful nipple blebs:

- Improve your baby's latch, if necessary, to reduce nipple trauma during nursing. Try using different nursing positions to find which is most comfortable.

- Use soothing warm compresses to provide comfort and to soften the bleb.

- Apply ultra-pure lanolin to keep the nipple tip moist and softened.

- If the nipple bleb is associated with a corresponding hard, blocked area of your breast, use the techniques described on the following pages to relieve a plugged duct.

- Some lactation consultants recommend trying to open what appears to be a milk blister and express the thickened milk. You can submerge your breast in a warm bath to soften the bleb and massage behind the areola to loosen the plug. Or, you can gently rub the bleb with a clean wet washcloth after first soaking your nipple in warm water.

- Some health professionals have tried opening the bleb with a sterile needle. Others have prescribed an antibiotic with favorable results.

Raynaud's Phenomenon

Intermittent nipple pain in breastfeeding women can be caused by Raynaud's phenomenon, a circulatory condition that causes a temporary (typically only a few minutes) decrease in blood flow, usually to the fingers, toes, ears, and nose, although the nipples can also be involved. Cold temperatures, emotional stress, fatigue, and other triggers, such as caffeine or certain medications, can cause temporary narrowing of small arteries supplying blood to the skin. Nipple trauma from incorrect nursing technique can trigger the response in nipple skin. The temporary lack of blood flow causes the affected area to turn white, and as blood flow returns, the area may become bluish, then red. If you experience painful nipples associated with skin color changes, get help from a lactation consultant and try the following strategies:

•Improve your baby's latch technique and seek treatment for sore or cracked nipples.

•Wear warm clothing and apply warm compresses to your nipples immediately after breastfeeding.

•Avoid caffeine and nicotine, including second-hand smoke, which can decrease blood flow to the skin.

Plugged Milk Ducts

A temporary blockage of one of your milk ducts causes a tender, hard knot, called a plugged duct. The surrounding area of your breast can become full and tender, and is known as "caked breast." Although any duct can be affected, the blockage often occurs in the outer areas of your breast nearest your armpits. The problem usually results when your breasts are not drained well (for example, if you go too long without nursing your baby). Some nursing moms, including women who have an overabundant milk supply, are more prone to developing plugged ducts than others. A plugged duct can be quite uncomfortable, and if

the blockage is not relieved quickly, it can progress to a breast infection (see pages 206–209).

STRATEGIES FOR RELIEVING A PLUGGED DUCT

Try one or more of these techniques to help alleviate a plugged duct:

• **Nurse, express, or pump more often.**
A plugged duct is the result of incomplete or irregular removal of milk. The best way to remedy it is to nurse more often to keep the breast well drained.

• **Gently massage the plugged area in a circular motion.**
Gentle pressure applied to

A Word of Caution

Cancerous breast lumps persisting for months have been mistakenly diagnosed as plugged ducts. True clogged ducts come on abruptly, are painful, and usually resolve within a day or two. Any lump that persists for days or weeks must be accurately diagnosed. It is not a plugged duct! Ask your physician to evaluate it thoroughly.

the tender knot in your breast will help milk to flow from the obstructed area while you nurse or pump. Keep your massage gentle, as overly rough breast manipulation increases the risk of mastitis.

- **To help drain the plugged side, start several feedings in a row on the affected breast.**
Your baby sucks more vigorously at the first breast she's offered. Be careful, however, not to let the second breast remain overly full or you might develop a blocked duct on that side or a decline in your milk supply. If either breast does not get well drained, use a pump to remove remaining milk.

- **Vary your nursing position to drain all areas of your breast well.**
In addition to the traditional cradle hold, try the cross-cradle hold, the football hold, and lying down to nurse to find which position works best to drain the plugged area. (See Chapter 3, pages 49–51.) Pointing your baby's chin toward the plugged duct may help to drain the affected area.

- **Take a warm shower or apply warm compresses to the**

plugged area, especially just before nursing, pumping, or performing breast massage.
Heat can help trigger your letdown reflex and improve milk flow.

- **Apply cold compresses between feedings to relieve discomfort and reduce inflammation.**
Hold an ice pack or frozen peas, covered with a thin towel, over the affected breast for fifteen to twenty minutes between feedings.

- **If your baby does not nurse well or you are separated from her during part of the day, you may need to use a breast pump to relieve a plugged duct.**
If you have an overabundant milk supply, you may need to express some surplus milk periodically to soften your overfull breasts to avoid plugged ducts.

- **Try to eliminate any risk factors you can identify, especially if you have a recurring problem with plugged ducts.**
In addition to an overabundant milk supply, other causes for a plugged duct include infrequent

nursing, infrequent pumping, wearing a poorly fitted bra or constrictive clothing, or chronic pressure against the breast from a diaper bag or handbag strap. Breast trauma, such as being bitten or kicked by your baby or massaging your breast too vigorously, can injure tissue and interfere with milk drainage. Some lactation consultants believe that a plugged duct is more likely to occur if you don't drink enough fluids. Because a low-grade breast infection can cause inflammation that impedes milk drainage, treatment with antibiotics may resolve recurrent plugged ducts.

Breast Infection (Mastitis)

Mastitis, the medical term for a breast infection, is a miserable flu-like illness that is accompanied by breast pain and redness. Up to 10 percent of nursing mothers will have a breast infection during the course of breastfeeding, and some will have multiple bouts. The condition seldom occurs in women who are not breastfeeding.

A breast infection is caused by bacteria—usually the same germs that are normally present on your nipple and in your baby's mouth. Two major risk factors for mastitis are: (1) a nipple crack or open sore that allows bacteria to enter your breast and (2) poor drainage (for example going too long without nursing or pumping or having a plugged duct). Mastitis can also

be caused by breast trauma, such as a poor latch, the wrong size breast flange or excessive breast pump suction, being bitten by your teething baby, or your older baby's stray kick or pinch. Exhaustion and sleep deprivation can also leave you vulnerable to mastitis (another reason for getting as much rest as possible, especially if you're trying to juggle work with taking care of your baby). Women who have had mastitis in the past are more prone to getting it again.

SYMPTOMS OF MASTITIS

Mastitis is most common during the early weeks after the birth of your baby, but it can occur at anytime during the course of breastfeeding. The illness causes both flu-like symptoms, as well as symptoms in the breast, including:

- **Fatigue, body aches, headache, nausea, vomiting, and other flu-like symptoms**
  If you are feeling ill you may not be aware that you have mastitis. In fact, you might call your doctor to request treatment for the flu or to ask whether your nursing baby might catch it from you, not knowing that you have mastitis.

- **Fever and chills**
  Mastitis usually causes a fever, although body aches, breast pain, and chills often come first. If you have other symptoms of mastitis, be sure to get treated, even if you don't have a fever.

- **Breast pain, redness, and firmness**
  Most women with mastitis will be able to pinpoint a warm, reddened, painful area in one or, rarely, both breasts. The skin over the tender area can be faintly pink to fiery red and typically is firmer than other areas of the breast. The discomfort can range from tenderness to severe pain. Often, an entire wedge-shaped area of the breast will be involved, starting at the nipple and extending toward the chest. In some cases, the entire breast becomes firm and swollen, due to inflammation and blocked milk flow.

- **Nipple or areolar pain**
  A breast infection can start when bacteria enter the milk ducts at the nipple openings. At first, the infection might be contained in one of the ducts near your nipple—causing a tender area on the areola—before affecting a larger portion of the breast.

TREATING MASTITIS

Call your doctor immediately if you have any symptoms of mastitis. The illness is treated with antibiotics, and the sooner you start treatment, the sooner you will feel better. Fortunately most antibiotics prescribed for mastitis are safe for breastfeeding. Take all doses of the medication your doctor prescribes for at least ten to fourteen days to fully treat the infection. A recurrence is possible

if an ineffective antibiotic is used, the infection is treated for less than ten days, or you don't take all the medication as prescribed.

Ibuprofen is a good choice for over-the-counter pain relief, because only minimal amounts pass into your milk. In addition, the anti-inflammatory effects of ibuprofen help reduce breast inflammation. Rarely, prescription pain medication is necessary for a day or two. Fortunately after twenty-four to forty-eight hours of antibiotic therapy, your symptoms, including breast discomfort, usually improve dramatically.

The following guidelines will help aid your recovery from mastitis.

- **Since most cases of mastitis are caused by germs from your own baby's nose and throat, you can continue to breastfeed her while the infection is treated.**
  Of course, whenever you or other members of your family are sick, your baby should be carefully observed for any signs of illness, such as poor feeding, irritability, listlessness, difficulty breathing, or fever. It is possible, though unlikely, for your baby to develop a serious infection from the same germs that have caused your mastitis.

- **Prepare to "pump and dump" if advised.**
  In a few instances—if you are the mother of a premature or sick newborn, for example— you may be advised to discard the milk expressed from the

infected breast until your symptoms clear up. Meanwhile, your baby can still drink your milk from the unaffected breast.

- **Rest as much as possible for a day or two.**
Mastitis can make you feel utterly miserable—and being run-down makes you more susceptible to this infection. Now is the time to pamper yourself so that you can get well before attempting to resume all your responsibilities. Enlist as much help as you can, and for at least two days, arrange to be relieved of all your duties except breastfeeding your baby and pumping (if necessary). It can take thirty-six to forty-eight hours before you notice significant improvement in breast pain and redness, fever, and body aches. Call your doctor if you are not feeling much better within two days.

- **Drink plenty of fluids, especially if you have a fever.**
Fever greatly increases your body's need for fluids and places you at risk for becoming dehydrated. Dehydration not only makes you feel worse, it also can reduce your milk supply.

- **Nurse more often, especially on the affected side, to keep your breast well drained.**
Leaving it full and engorged makes healing more difficult and increases the risk of breast abscess (see below). However, breast inflammation can interfere with milk flow, and the pain of mastitis can cause you

to postpone feedings or limit nursing on the infected side. Start feedings on the unaffected breast until your letdown reflex is triggered. Once milk is flowing, begin nursing on the infected breast and allow your baby to drain it well.

- **If nursing your baby on the infected breast is extremely painful, or if you are having trouble getting your milk to flow, use an electric breast pump for several days.**
Many mothers with mastitis find pumping with a hospital-grade or daily use electric pump to be more comfortable than nursing. You may want to remove milk regularly from the infected breast with a pump while continuing to nurse on the good side. Pumping will maintain your milk supply in the infected breast until you are able to tolerate direct breastfeeding again.

- **Contact your doctor if your symptoms are not dramatically improved within forty-eight hours of starting antibiotics.**
Persistent symptoms may mean that you need to take a different antibiotic, or in rare cases, a breast abscess (a very painful, walled-off pocket of pus that must be drained) may have formed. A breast abscess usually occurs when mastitis has not been treated promptly or when the antibiotic prescribed was ineffective. Ultrasound may help diagnose a breast abscess. While it is sometimes possible to continue

nursing from a breast after an abscess has been drained, many women choose to dry up the affected breast and continue breastfeeding on the other side.

- **To prevent getting a recurrence of mastitis, try to identify your own risk factors.**
Mastitis often follows some type of vigorous upper-body activity, such as high-impact exercise, scrubbing a floor, vacuuming, raking, mowing the lawn, rowing, or lifting and carrying heavy items. If you have had several bouts of mastitis after vigorous upper-body exercise, discontinuing these activities may help prevent a recurrence. If you're prone to mastitis, meet with a lactation consultant who can help you identify possible risk factors. You may need to take preventive antibiotics for several months to remain healthy. If you've had repeated bouts of mastitis in the same area of your breast, seek further evaluation from your doctor to make sure that there isn't an underlying abnormality.

Leaking Breasts

Most women notice milk leaking from their breasts during letdown, and milk usually drips from one breast while they're nursing on the other side. For most breastfeeding women, leaking milk represents little more than a minor inconvenience and many find it amusing to watch their milk spray during feedings or in the shower. But for others, leaking is an irritating and embarrassing problem that is seen as a drawback to breastfeeding. Women who experience excessive leaking complain of drenched clothing, soiled bedding, constant wetness; and for them, breastfeeding is more messy than it is convenient.

TREATING EXCESSIVE LEAKING

If leaking is a problem for you, try viewing it in a more positive light, and as an encouraging sign of successful breastfeeding. You can also feel gratified, knowing you have an abundant milk supply for your baby. It takes a week or two for the sensations and leaking associated with milk letdown to become noticeable. Leaking is usually most dramatic at two to six weeks postpartum. But hang on—within a few weeks you'll notice that less milk is leaking from your nipples, as the capacity of your milk ducts to contain milk increases. However, if you are bothered by excessive leaking perhaps the following suggestions will help you:

When you feel the familiar sensation of letdown, you can stop milk from leaking by putting pressure on your nipple openings.

To protect your clothing, wear washable or disposable breast pads inside your nursing bra to absorb any leaking milk. Change wet pads frequently to keep your nipples dry. You can make your own reusable pads from 100 percent cotton cloth. Wash reusable pads

Tip

To discreetly stop leaking milk, cross your arms in front of your chest and press your thumbs against your nipples.

and your nursing bra daily. Some breastfeeding mothers who've gone back to work wear breast shells to protect their clothing, since leaking on the job can prove especially embarrassing. (Do not save the milk that drips into breast shells.) Another option is to wear washable, re-usable, non-absorbent, soft silicone nursing pads that prevent leaking by adhering tightly to your breast. (See Resources.)

If your letdown is overactive and your baby is bothered by it, see suggestions below for overabundant milk supply.

Overabundant Milk Supply

Women vary widely in their capacity to produce milk. While many more women seek help for too little milk than for too much milk, an overabundant supply can be a frustrating problem for some women. Generally your milk supply is closely matched to your baby's need. It is a mystery why some women produce extra, unwanted milk, while others have difficulty producing enough. An exceptional production capacity, a brisk and well-conditioned milk ejection

reflex, and a super-efficient nursing baby all contribute to an overabundant supply.

YOUR BABY'S REACTIONS TO AN OVERABUNDANT MILK SUPPLY

If you have a superabundant milk supply, it can be just as frustrating for your baby as it is for you. Here are some of the distressing reactions your baby may have to an overabundance of breastmilk:

- Choking and sputtering when your milk lets down

- Excessive gas, apparent abdominal discomfort, excessive crying, and explosive watery stools from overeating

- Rapid weight gain

- Inability to enjoy "comfort nursing," since your baby obtains a rapid flow of milk even when trying to nurse to sleep

- Frustration with breastfeeding that leads to a nursing strike (abrupt refusal to nurse) or early weaning (see page 213)

Fortunately the problem of over-abundant milk usually improves with time. Your baby may "grow into" your milk supply as she gets a little older. In addition, your supply tends to gradually diminish by three months after the birth of your baby, since your over-full breasts do not get well drained. Milk production often decreases as your

Mothers' Complaints Due to Too Much Milk

Women with an over-abundant milk supply often have the following complaints:

•Breasts that easily become uncomfortably engorged

•Dramatic (sometimes painful) sensations of the milk ejection reflex

•Chronic leaking milk

•Repeatedly clogged ducts

•One or more breast infections

•Rapid weight loss due to the high metabolic demands of producing so much milk

•Chronic sore nipples because your baby uses a shallow latch to attempt to control the flow of milk

Lactose Overload

When a nursing mom's milk supply is superabundant, many lactation consultants attribute her baby's symptoms of overfeeding to undigested lactose. The theory goes like this: When drinking from over-full breasts, your baby takes a large feeding of relatively low-fat content milk, since she is unable to drain your breasts sufficiently to obtain high-fat hindmilk. Since fat in a meal slows digestion, it is believed that your baby's low-fat, large meal moves through the small bowel rapidly—too rapidly for all of the lactose to be digested by the enzyme lactase. Lactose that reaches the large intestine draws water into the gut and is fermented by bacteria to produce gas. The result is a build-up of gas and fluid that causes your baby to experience intestinal discomfort and cramps, irritability, excessive crying, and large, watery, sometimes green or explosive stools. The popular explanation is that a "foremilk-hindmilk imbalance" is what causes these symptoms. In fact, research shows that a breastfed baby's total fat intake is relatively stable from day to day, even though it may vary from one feeding to another. More likely, it is the large size of the feedings that causes an overfed baby's symptoms, whether she is breastfed or formula-fed. Instead of trying to manipulate your baby's intake of hindmilk—for example, by having her feed longer on one breast—focus on reading her cues during a feeding. When she is overwhelmed by the flow of milk, remove her from your breast, let her pause and rest, and allow her to set the pace for how much milk she takes, and how rapidly. When she appears satisfied, end the feeding.

baby starts sleeping longer at night, or if you return to work.

HANDLING AN OVER-ABUNDANT MILK SUPPLY

If you have too much milk, you can use nursing techniques to enhance your baby's comfort during breastfeeding, express your extra milk, and take measures to reduce your supply. Consider the following:

Enhancing Your Baby's Comfort

Position your baby so that her head and mouth are higher than your nipple. By nursing "uphill," she will be able to control the overly fast flow of milk better and enjoy nursing more. Use the football hold (see Chapter 3, page 50) and lean back to elevate her head. Or try the cradle hold, with your baby elevated higher than usual, while you lean back in a recliner.

If your letdown is causing your baby to choke or cry, temporarily interrupt the feeding until your milk stops spraying. Collect the letdown milk in a clean cup and freeze it for later use. Then allow your baby to resume feeding after the milk flow has slowed to a manageable level. The milk that leaks out will contain the least fat.

Pause often during feedings to burp your baby. Releasing some of the extra swallowed air may reduce symptoms of gassiness, and giving your baby periodic breaks may make feedings less stressful for her.

Try offering only one breast at each feeding, alternating the breast you use. After the initial rapid flow tapers, your baby may be able to comfortably handle the milk volume from a single breast. Or you can use the same breast for one or more consecutive feedings within three to four hours to drain it well before offering the other side for the next three to four hours. You may need to express enough milk from the unused breast to relieve some of the pressure and help you stay comfortable. Eventually your milk supply should decrease.

Expressing Your Extra Milk

Pump with a daily-use breast pump to soften your breasts whenever the need arises. Simply freeze your excess milk for later use—for example, if you plan to return to work.

Collect and donate your surplus milk to a milk bank. (See Resources.) Being able to provide milk for babies in need is a great way to turn a potentially negative situation into a positive one. You'll be providing an incredible service to other moms who are unable to produce enough milk.

Reducing Milk Production

You can remove less milk at each nursing or remove milk at less-frequent intervals. One option is to allow your baby to nurse from both breasts at each feeding, but avoid draining either side well. The first breast will be softer than the second, and neither will be thoroughly drained, so the rate of production will slow. If your breasts become uncomfortably full between feedings, express enough milk to relieve discomfort, but not enough to soften your breasts. Monitor your breasts carefully for signs of a plugged duct or mastitis.

Apply cool compresses to your breasts for about thirty minutes between feedings. Cold therapy not only helps relieve breast discomfort, it will reduce blood flow, which may help decrease milk production. You also can try cabbage leaf compresses that are recommended for postpartum breast engorgement. (See Chapter 4, page 102.)

A single sixty-milligram dose of pseudoephedrine (such as the brand name Sudafed) has been found to significantly reduce milk production. With your doctor's permission, you could take a sixty milligram dose once daily for a few days. Taking an estrogen-containing oral contraceptive also may reduce your milk production, perhaps by too much. (See Chapter 7, pages 170–171.)

> **Tip**
>
> Believe it or not, you can go from making too much milk to making too little milk in only a few days. Skipping nursings or inadvertently leaving your breasts engorged can rapidly decrease milk production.

Nursing Strike

Somewhere between your baby's fourth and seventh month, she may start refusing to nurse for no apparent reason. This sudden breastfeeding refusal—known as a nursing strike—can be upsetting for both you and your baby. Here's how it typically plays out: When you offer your breast, your baby cries, arches her back, pulls away, and refuses to nurse. She may latch on for a few seconds, but then quickly loses interest in breastfeeding. Meanwhile, she may contentedly take her feedings from a bottle. Faced with this curious turn of events, you may conclude that your baby has weaned herself and that it's time to give up breastfeeding. Your baby's breast refusal can feel like you're being rejected, and the thought of giving up nursing before you'd planned can be extremely disappointing. But hang on! Your baby's puzzling behavior is a clue that something is wrong. With a little detective work and a good deal of patient determination, chances are good that you can woo your little one back to nursing.

THE RUN-UP TO A NURSING STRIKE

At first glance, a nursing strike seems to come out of nowhere and without explanation. But if you look a little closer, you may notice that one or more of the following behaviors has come into play. A common theme for all of them is an unpleasant experience associated with breastfeeding.

Your baby may begin to refuse to nurse if she has an upper respiratory infection—when she has a bad cold, for example. A stuffy nose can create distress when she tries to breathe while nursing, and an ear infection can be more painful when she reclines to nurse. If your baby is teething, she may refuse your breast because sucking feels uncomfortable. Or your little one may have begun a nursing strike after she bit you by mistake. Your shriek of surprise and pain may have, in turn, startled and upset her.

You may have been away from home for a day or two; or perhaps you've been so busy that feedings have become a bit rushed—and your baby hasn't been able to nurse at a leisurely pace. Or perhaps there has been a change in family routine, such as a vacation or the arrival of houseguests.

If your milk supply has dwindled—perhaps as the result of giving supplemental feedings, nursing infrequently, or returning to work—your baby may begin refusing to nurse, preferring the steady, rapid flow of milk from a bottle.

Finally, as discussed in the previous section, an overabundant milk supply or an overactive milk ejection reflex might be frustrating your baby, making it difficult for her to nurse comfortably.

REVERSING A NURSING STRIKE

If your baby starts refusing your breast, seek help from a lactation consultant, and take your baby to her doctor to make sure that an illness is not the cause of her feeding problem. You'll also want to be sure that she continues to receive adequate nutrition while you're figuring out how to rekindle her interest in breastfeeding. With support from your partner, persistence on your part, and sensitivity to your baby, you should be able to reverse a nursing strike within several days. The following strategies can help.

- **Attempt to nurse while your baby is drowsy or even asleep.** Fortunately most babies will cooperate, although some stop nursing when they wake up at their mother's breast. Others may awaken and continue to nurse, without protesting.

> **Tip**
>
> You may find that your baby will keep nursing if you walk around with her.

- **If possible, avoid bottle feeding and pacifiers for a while.**
Try offering expressed milk by cup, spouted cup, or spoon. When regular bottle-feeding is inevitable, use a slow flow nipple, so she takes her milk less rapidly.

- **Eliminate any unpleasant associations with breastfeeding.**
If your baby has a cold, try nursing after clearing her nasal passages with a bulb syringe, and have her checked for a possible ear infection. If discomfort from teething may be contributing to her lack of

interest in nursing, soothe your baby's gums with a cold teething ring. Try nursing her in subdued, quiet surroundings to minimize distractions. Let her take all the time she wants, and give her your full attention as she nurses. Create "breast-friendly" time with your baby nestled skin-to-skin between your breasts.

- **Consider whether your milk supply might be low.** Breastfeeding may frustrate your baby because it does not satisfy her hunger. You may be able to entice her back to the breast by emphasizing the comforting aspects of breastfeeding. Give her just enough previously expressed breastmilk or formula to curb her appetite. Then let her nurse for "dessert," while she is calmed and soothed at your breast.

- **Maintain or increase your milk supply.** Even if your milk supply was plentiful prior to the nursing strike, it may start to decrease if your baby has been refusing to nurse. If the original problem becomes compounded by a low milk supply, it will be even harder to rekindle your baby's interest in breastfeeding. Unless your baby rapidly resumes her normal breastfeeding pattern, you will need to use an effective breast pump to maintain and increase your milk supply during a nursing strike. Pumping can create a potential dilemma, however, since you can't predict when your baby might be willing to

nurse. She may show an interest in breastfeeding just as you've finished pumping. On the other hand, if you leave your breasts full while waiting expectantly for your baby to nurse, your supply may be affected. Try offering your breast every few hours, preferably while your baby is asleep or drowsy. Then, immediately after nursing, pump both breasts to make sure they're well drained. (See page 229.)

Medications and Breastfeeding

If you take regular medications, or if a drug is prescribed for you while you're breastfeeding, it's natural to be concerned about the potential danger of passing medications along to your baby through your breastmilk. In fact, any drug you take while you are breastfeeding will appear in your milk to some degree. The amount depends on the drug dose and how often you take it, how the drug is taken (by mouth versus by injection), the physical and chemical properties of the drug, the amount of breastmilk your baby drinks, how often you nurse your baby, and the duration of treatment. Fortunately most medications are safe for your nursing baby because their presence in your breastmilk is usually minimal. Whenever your doctor prescribes a medicine for you, ask whether it is safe for breastfeeding. Notify your baby's doctor about medications you take, and observe your baby carefully for

Do Not Take These Drugs While Breastfeeding*

Some drugs are not safe for infants and babies at any level of use, and breastfeeding is not recommended if you must regularly take a medication that could pose a risk to your nursing infant. If you know in advance that you will temporarily need to take a drug that is incompatible with breastfeeding (such as any of those listed below), pump and save your surplus milk so that you can keep your baby well supplied during your course of drug therapy. Fortunately many breastfeeding mothers keep frozen stores of expressed breastmilk just in case they are needed.

- **Cancer chemotherapy**
  Even very small amounts of these drugs can be harmful to babies and suppress their immune system. You may be able to pump and dump your milk after each treatment until the drug has cleared.

- **Radioactive drugs used in diagnostic scans**
  You will need to pump and discard your milk until no radioactivity is present. The X-ray department can screen your milk for radioactivity until it is safe to resume breastfeeding.

- **Certain drugs that suppress the immune system**
  These drugs, including some medications used to treat autoimmune diseases, such as rheumatoid arthritis, decrease the body's defenses against infection. Little is known about their effect on breastfed babies, but they carry a risk of harm and are best avoided while you are breastfeeding.

* This list is not comprehensive.

Warning: Illegal drugs such as marijuana, cocaine, heroin, methamphetamine, ecstacy, phencyclidine, LSD, and others, pass readily into breastmilk and into your baby's brain. These drugs, as well as the overuse of prescription pain killers, are extremely dangerous to nursing infants and babies and should not be consumed under any circumstances during breastfeeding. It cannot be emphasized strongly enough that illicit drugs must *NOT* be taken by nursing women, because of the very real risk such drugs pose to a baby, as well as the danger that exists when a mother attempts to care for her infant while she is high. Several infant fatalities have occurred when babies drank tainted milk from their nursing mothers who used illicit drugs.

possible side effects that should be reported promptly to her doctor.

In the vast majority of cases, the benefits of breastfeeding outweigh temporary, minor effects of medication on a nursing baby (such as diarrhea, irritability, or drowsiness). Newborns—especially sick or premature babies—are at greatest risk of

Resources for your Doctor

If your physician prescribes a drug for you that might pose a risk to your nursing infant, ask whether a pharmacist could suggest an alternative medication that is safe for breastfed infants. Unfortunately lack of information about drugs passing into breastmilk frequently results in exaggerated concerns about the risks. For example, your doctor may advise you to wean your baby when the medication being prescribed for you actually is compatible with breastfeeding. Here are two up-to-date, comprehensive sources of information about medications and breastfeeding that your physician may appreciate knowing about: (1) *Medications and Mothers' Milk*, a popular reference for health professionals written by a clinical pharmacologist, Dr. Thomas Hale, containing the latest information on hundreds of drugs and their relative safety in breastfeeding mothers and infants; and (2) Lactmed, a free online government database, offering information on hundreds of drugs, including possible effects on breastfed infants and safer alternatives to consider. (See Resources.) Information about breastfeeding and medications also is available to health professionals at Dr. Hale's Web site, http://neonatal.ttuhsc.edu/lact/.

being affected, while older infants are able to handle medications more easily. In each instance, you and your health-care provider must weigh the compelling benefits of breastfeeding against the remote risks of a particular medication.

GUIDELINES FOR BREASTFEEDING WOMEN WHO NEED TO TAKE MEDICATIONS

- Take only medications that are necessary and clearly effective. Take the lowest effective dose for the shortest period of time. Avoid "sustained-release" or "long-acting" preparations that take longer to clear from your bloodstream and your milk.

- Opt for single-ingredient over-the-counter medications that target your major symptom(s), rather than drugs with multiple ingredients. Choose a nasal decongestant spray over an oral formulation to reduce the amount that gets into your milk. Use it only a few days.

- Generally, it is preferable to take a medication right after nursing your baby. For most short-acting drugs, the amount that appears in your milk reaches a peak level one to two hours after taking the medication. The level in milk then starts to decline, so that much of it will be cleared before your baby nurses again.

- Take once-daily medications just prior to your baby's longest sleep period at night. However, most long-acting drugs will maintain a fairly constant level in breastmilk throughout the day.

- As a general rule, a medication that was considered safe to take while you were pregnant will continue to be safe during breastfeeding. Similarly, drugs, such as many antibiotics, that commonly are prescribed for infants are safe for nursing mothers to take.

Common Drugs That Are Compatible with Breastfeeding When Taken in Usual Doses*

Acetaminophen
Anesthetics (local, for dental work, etc.)
Antacids
Antibiotics (most)
Anti-histamines (most)
Anti-seizure medications (many)
Asthma medications (most)
Blood pressure medications (many)
Blood thinners (most)
Corticosteroids
Decongestant nasal spray
Diuretics (most)
Ibuprofen
Insulin
Laxatives (bulk forming and stool softening)
Over-the-counter medications (most)
Prescription pain medications (most)
Thyroid replacement hormone

* This list is not comprehensive.

- Keep in mind that some medications, such as estrogen-containing contraceptives, decongestants, or anti-histamines, may decrease your milk supply.

Baby's Reactions to What You Eat

While true allergy to mother's milk does not occur, some breastfed babies react adversely to certain foods eaten by their mothers. Typically babies become fussy three to six hours after their mother has eaten an offending food. It usually takes one to four hours for allergic components of foods, also known as food antigens, to appear in your milk. Your baby may react within minutes after nursing, although the usual reaction time is two to four hours. The reaction can continue as long

Psychiatric Medications

Psychiatric medications taken by nursing mothers appear in breastmilk and theoretically might affect a baby's developing brain and nervous system. However, a low dose of a single psychiatric medication usually is considered relatively safe during breastfeeding. The risks and benefits should be carefully weighed, and babies should be observed closely for possible adverse effects. (See pages 282.)

as the offending substance remains in your system and continues to enter your milk—a week or longer after eating certain foods (such as dairy products).

COMMON OFFENDERS

The most common foods that provoke allergic reactions include milk and other dairy products, wheat, eggs, peanuts and tree nuts, soy, and fish and shellfish. Often the food (or foods) your baby reacts to is something you eat daily or something you ate frequently during your pregnancy, most commonly milk or eggs.

TYPICAL ALLERGIC SYMPTOMS

Common symptoms of a food allergy that you might see in your breastfed baby include skin rashes, red cheeks, vomiting, diarrhea, runny nose, cough or congestion, wheezing, fussiness, and "colic."

Allergic Colitis

Certain food antigens (food proteins that trigger an allergic reaction) can cause inflammation in your baby's developing gastrointestinal tract during the first few months of life. This sensitivity to the allergic components of foods in your diet is known as allergic colitis. The main symptom is visible specks or streaks of blood mixed with mucus in your otherwise healthy baby's stool, typically when she's around

two months of age. The major triggers are cow's milk, and less commonly soy or eggs. Despite the alarming appearance of blood in the stool, babies remain well, without vomiting, diarrhea, or growth problems. Most often the blood clears when you eliminate all dairy products (cow's milk, cheese, yogurt, and ice cream as well as packaged products containing casein or whey protein) from your diet for at least two weeks, to allow your baby's bowel time to heal. Months later, you can try reintroducing milk into your diet and see if the same symptoms return. Rarely, your baby may need to interrupt breastfeeding for a week or two and drink a special hypoallergenic formula until her irritated gut has healed.

> **Tip**
>
> Because bloody stools can be due to various other medical causes, contact your baby's doctor right away and arrange to have her checked if you ever see any blood in her stools.

Anaphylaxis

Anaphylaxis is a rare but potentially fatal allergic reaction. Symptoms often appear rapidly and may include swelling of the mouth and throat, a drop in blood pressure, hives, stomach cramps, vomiting and diarrhea, difficulty breathing, and unconsciousness. Anaphylaxis is a medical

Other Adverse Food Reactions

Babies can be sensitive to foods in other ways than an allergic reaction. For example, a baby might be extra fussy and irritable if her mother drinks too many caffeinated beverages, or she may become gassy due to broccoli, onions, cabbage, or other cruciferous vegetables in her mother's diet. These unfavorable reactions are not true allergic reactions.

Lactose intolerance is a non-allergic, adverse reaction to dairy products that is commonly misinterpreted as a milk allergy. Lactose is the major sugar in human milk, and lactase is the enzyme that digests lactose in the small intestine. Very rarely, a baby is born with the inability to digest the lactose in breastmilk. Undigested lactose causes watery diarrhea, cramping, gas, and bloating. A baby with congenital lactase deficiency needs to drink lactose-free formula containing a different sugar. More commonly, a temporary deficiency of lactase can develop in healthy infants following a bout of diarrhea, which can strip the small intestine of lactase. However, lactase returns to normal levels within a few weeks, once the intestinal lining has recovered. Many adults have a relative deficiency of lactase because the enzyme gradually decreases after early childhood. These individuals may develop lactose intolerance and need to limit their intake of dairy products to avoid symptoms.

emergency and requires immediate treatment, including injection with epinephrine (adrenaline). Physicians should prescribe an epinephrine auto-injector for individuals with food allergies to carry with them at all times, in case anaphylaxis occurs.

Very rarely, a baby can experience an anaphylactic reaction as the result of drinking her mother's breastmilk—if the mother has eaten a food to which her baby is highly allergic (most often cow milk).

KEEPING A FOOD DIARY

If you think your baby is reacting to something in your diet, discuss it with her doctor. At the same time, start keeping a daily food diary that records what and when you eat, when you nurse your baby, and the time and type of problem behavior or other symptoms you observe in your baby. While you are keeping the log, simplify your meals. Try to eat only three different types of food at each meal. Avoid multiple seasonings and multiple ingredient dishes. By scanning your daily diary, you may be able to track a relationship between your baby's symptoms and specific foods you eat.

ELIMINATING FOODS

Usually only a few foods in your diet cause a problem for your baby. Completely eliminate the one or two most likely offending foods for at least two weeks to get the food entirely out of your own and your baby's systems.

Several studies have found

that in some nursing mothers, consuming dairy is linked with colicky behavior in their babies. If you eliminate dairy products from your diet and your baby's excessive crying and fussiness diminish, you can be fairly certain that dairy products were at the root of the problem. To confirm your suspicions you can later try eating a small amount of dairy again to see if your baby's symptoms reappear. *Do not reintroduce a potentially offensive food to your diet if your baby has had a severe reaction to it previously!* Always discuss your baby's possible food allergies with her doctor. Ask to be referred to a pediatric allergist who can safely perform allergy testing, especially if you have a strong family history of allergic disease.

Tip

If your baby is allergic to a certain food, strict avoidance of the allergen is the best way to prevent a long-term or severe allergy. Fortunately most food allergies are outgrown in early childhood, although peanut allergy is likely to persist lifelong.

Colicky Behavior

Few things are more distressing than the sound of your own baby crying. Mother Nature intended it this way, to guarantee that you respond promptly to your baby's needs. Fortunately by trial and error and good intentions, most parents soon learn to read their baby's cues and manage to keep crying to a minimum. Since human milk is the ideal infant food and is so easily digestible, many breastfeeding mothers assume that their babies automatically will be content most of the time. But babies have a wide range of temperaments and differing needs. Babies cry an average of one and a half hours a day in the first six weeks of life. However, any crying can feel like too much when it exceeds your threshold for coping. (See Chapter 5, pages 115–121.) If your baby cries excessively, have her checked out by her pediatrician and consider the following causes:

- **Hunger**
  Many breastfeeding mothers automatically assume that their baby can't be hungry because "she nurses all the time." But frequent breastfeeding does not always guarantee that your baby is getting all the milk she needs and wants. If your baby cries excessively and you can't

---

Tip

A baby who is crying because she is hungry usually gives I-want-to-be-fed cues—such as sucking on her fingers, fist, or pacifier—and is quickly consoled by feeding.

figure out why, start with a weight check to be sure she is gaining at a normal rate. Don't settle for over-the-telephone advice about your baby's "colicky" behavior unless she's been weighed in the last week. Many breastfed infants presumed to have colic are actually underweight, hungry babies. If your baby is not gaining weight as expected, her crying might be due to hunger. (See pages 226–227.)

• **Your Diet**
Food allergies and other adverse reactions to foods you eat can cause colicky behavior in your breastfed baby. (See pages 218–221.)

• **Overabundant Milk Supply and Overactive Letdown**
Some women are blessed with an overabundant milk supply and a brisk letdown reflex. As soon as the milk ejection reflex is triggered, milk jets from their nipple openings so fast that it is all a baby can do to handle the flow without choking.
As the baby gulps and sputters through a feeding, she may get overwhelmed, or she may pull off the breast and cry in frustration until the milk stops spraying. Other babies keep nursing but end up overeating and swallowing excessive amounts of air. This can cause indigestion and uncomfortable gas and lead to unexplained crying during or after feedings. (See pages 210–211.)

GASTROESOPHAGEAL REFLUX DISEASE (GERD)

Many babies spit up at least once a day during the first three to four months of life. The backward movement of stomach contents into the esophagus (food pipe) and sometimes out the mouth, is known as reflux, or gastroesophageal reflux (GER). The lower esophageal sphincter (LES) is a circular muscle that acts as a valve regulating the passage of food between the esophagus and the stomach. When the LES relaxes at the wrong time, stomach contents can reflux into the esophagus, often reaching the mouth and resulting in regurgitation. Reflux episodes commonly occur when a baby is lying on her back and the pressure in her abdomen is increased, for example during crying, coughing, straining to have a bowel movement, or raising her legs during diaper changes.

Symptoms of GERD

Only a small percentage of babies progress to reflux *disease* when they develop additional symptoms from chronic irritation of the esophagus by stomach acids and digestive juices. Babies with GERD not only spit or vomit after feedings, they suffer acid damage that can produce an uncomfortable burning sensation, leading to irritability, excessive crying, and poor sleeping. When the baby tries to eat, she experiences discomfort and distress rather than pleasure, which results in perplexing feeding behaviors. Under these circumstances, your baby may latch onto your breast and suck briefly, then release the nipple, arch her body, and cry. In addition, a few babies with GERD grow poorly or develop respiratory symptoms due to acid irritation of the airways.

Treatment of Reflux and GERD

Fortunately time usually solves the problem of GER and frequent spitting up. However, dealing with an infant with GERD can be a very stressful experience. Excessive crying and persistent feeding difficulties can put a damper on new parenthood. Simple lifestyle and feeding changes are recommended first to reduce symptoms and prevent complications:

- Hold your baby in a semi-upright position for feedings and avoid overfeeding, which provokes spitting. Burp your baby often during feedings, whenever she pauses. If she spits up, don't offer your breast right away. Wait until the next feeding.

- Many babies with GERD naturally self-regulate their milk intake by grazing—eating just enough to take the edge off their appetite, while avoiding a distended tummy. Others insist on taking a full feeding, which makes regurgitation more likely.

- Keep your baby upright—by holding her, wearing her in a carrier, or propping her in a swing—for at least twenty minutes after feedings.

- In the past, mothers were often advised to place babies in their car seat after feedings to prevent reflux. Now it has been found that young infants, who have little muscle tone, tend to slump or slouch when sitting in a car seat. This position increases the pressure in your baby's abdomen and actually makes reflux worse. Use a car seat only for riding in the car.

- Dress your baby in loose clothing, since a tight diaper or waistband can provoke reflux. Avoid jostling your baby, lying her on her back, or changing her diaper immediately after feedings.

- Since exposure to tobacco smoke is linked with reflux, that's one more good reason to keep your baby away from it.

- While feeding and lifestyle modifications help many babies with GERD, sometimes other measures are required, and you may need to consult a pediatric gastroenterologist. Medication often is prescribed to decrease or neutralize stomach acids.

- Because cow's milk allergy is a common cause of vomiting in infants, you may be asked to eliminate dairy products, including cow's milk, from your baby's diet for a two-week trial period.

Tip

Allergy to cow's milk is more likely in infants who have eczema, chronic congestion, or a family history of allergies.

COLIC

Colic is a vague term that describes excessive crying for no apparent reason in an otherwise healthy infant during the first three months of life. Colic occurs in an estimated 10 to 20 percent of infants, and it is one of the most difficult and frustrating challenges you may face as a new mother. Crying attributed to colic is intermittent and intense, often coming in sudden attacks and lasting an hour or more at a time. There is usually a pattern to the crying, which escalates in the evenings, when you are most likely to be exhausted and least able to cope with stress. What often compounds that stress is the belief that your colicky baby is in pain when she draws up her legs, clenches her fists, and grimaces. She also may stiffen and pass gas during a crying episode. While it's important to try to comfort your baby during these challenging episodes, try to remember that colic is not believed to be caused by pain, and it is not a serious condition.

CAUSES OF COLIC

Perhaps the most difficult aspect of colic is the effect it has on parents, not only in terms of fatigue and

Defining the Indefinable

Although healthy babies display a wide range of crying patterns, physicians use the following criteria to make the diagnosis of "colic":

- Crying exceeds three hours a day for more than three days a week for at least three weeks.

- Excessive crying typically begins when a baby is two to three weeks old, reaches a peak at six to eight weeks, and resolves by three to four months of age.

Tip

The diagnosis of colic should not be made until your baby's doctor has first confirmed that no medical problem exists.

frustration, but guilt—the belief that you have done something wrong to cause your baby so much distress. Try to remember that you are not at fault for your baby's crying! There are colicky babies in every culture, race, and class, and it affects breastfed babies as often as babies who are fed formula. No definite cause has been identified for this common babyhood condition, although numerous theories have been proposed, including sensitive temperament, immature digestive system, excessive intestinal gas, formula intolerance (in formula-fed babies), overfeeding, immaturity of the newborn brain, maternal anxiety, or a reaction to specific foods in the nursing mother's diet. Ironically—and despite the toll colic takes on new parents—most colicky babies are well fed and healthy, appear alert, active, and content between crying spells, and show no long-term effects of colic. Mercifully the condition is outgrown around three months of age. (See Chapter 5, pages 115–121.)

Illness

Anytime your baby seems extra fussy, consider whether she might be ill. Both extremes of behavior—lethargy or increased irritability—are common signs of illness in young babies. Other possible indicators of infant illness include fever, feeding less often or less vigorously, cough or difficulty breathing, poor skin color (pale, dusky, grayish), vomiting, diarrhea, or rash. The younger the baby, the more concerned you should be. Never hesitate to call your baby's doctor and describe any change in behavior that might mean your baby is ill.

Insufficient Milk Supply and Inadequate Infant Weight Gain

While your worries about not having enough milk for your baby often are unfounded, you are not alone if you have concerns about

Other Causes of Insufficient Milk

Other causes of low milk supply may be unrelated to breastfeeding practices. For example, you might have difficulty producing enough milk if you have or had:

• Breast surgery

• Breast radiation that has damaged milk glands and ducts

• Inadequate stores of body fat

• Postpartum complications, such as hemorrage, anemia, high blood pressure, an infection, or other illness

• Extreme fatigue or emotional distress

• A decreased number of milk glands (sometimes due to older age)

• Underdeveloped breasts

• Hormonal problems, including thyroid disorders or Polycystic Ovary Syndrome

• A history of taking certain medications, such as decongestants

your milk supply. In fact, the belief that a mother doesn't have enough milk or that breastmilk alone doesn't satisfy her baby are the top reasons women give for discontinuing breastfeeding during their baby's first year. In many cases, a mother's suspicion that her baby isn't getting enough milk proves to be valid. Your baby may be taking insufficient milk, either because your supply is low or she is unable to nurse effectively. Either way, she will not gain adequate weight unless she is able to take more with breastfeeding or is fed supplemental milk. In most instances, a low milk supply results from breastfeeding problems that lead to infrequent or ineffective milk drainage. Fortunately many nursing moms are able to boost their production by improving their breastfeeding technique, helping their babies nurse more effectively, or using an electric breast pump to drain their breasts more efficiently. (See pages 228–230.)

SIGNS THAT YOUR BABY MAY NOT BE GETTING ENOUGH MILK

If you suspect that your milk supply is low or that your baby is not taking enough milk, there are reliable ways to confirm whether this is true. Your baby's current weight and her pattern of growth provide important clues, as outlined here, to help you and her doctor know whether she is getting enough milk:

- **Losing too much weight after birth.**
  If your baby continues to lose weight beyond four days of age or loses 8 to 10 percent or more of her original birth weight, this is considered abnormal and usually signals that your baby is not getting enough milk.

- **Remaining below birth weight by ten to fourteen days of age.**
  If your baby is still under her birth weight by two weeks of age, it is likely that she is not drinking enough breastmilk.

- **Gaining less than one ounce each day during the first several months of life.**
  When your breastfed infant is not gaining approximately an ounce each day between her check-ups (five to seven ounces per week or one and a half to two pounds a month), your baby may not be getting as much milk as she needs or wants.

- **Weight percentile is much lower than height percentile.**
  In general, a baby's length and weight tend to be proportionate in early infancy, with the head circumference following its own curve independent of length and weight. If your baby is not getting enough calories, the rate at which she gains weight declines first, followed by a slowing of the rate at which she increases in length. Head circumference is affected last, because limited nutrients are used preferentially for brain

growth. If your baby's height is at the seventy-fifth percentile, while her weight is only at the fifteenth percentile, she is most likely not receiving enough calories and will appear thin. Ask to see your baby's growth curve at each pediatric visit; your baby's doctor can interpret and help you understand her growth pattern at each check-up.

- **Steady decline in rate of weight gain.**
Every baby grows along her own unique curve or percentile on infant growth charts. An unexplained fall in your baby's weight percentile, however, could signal that she is not getting enough milk.

- **Not gaining or losing weight between doctor visits.**
Babies grow rapidly in the first year of life. At each visit to her pediatrician, your baby should weigh more than she did at the last visit. Not gaining any weight, and certainly losing weight, between two office visits should raise a red flag.

- **Frequently acting hungry.**
If your baby often acts hungry after nursing, fusses and cries excessively, frequently requires a pacifier to be consoled, or nurses more frequently than usual, she may be trying to convey that she is not getting all the milk she needs and wants. Contact your baby's doctor and arrange to have your baby weighed to see whether she is gaining weight as expected.

MEASURING HOW MUCH MILK YOU MAKE—AND HOW MUCH YOUR BABY TAKES

If your baby is not gaining weight as expected, or you suspect your milk supply is low, there are two convenient techniques that are easy to use and provide very helpful information about how much milk you're making and how much milk your baby is taking.

Pumped Milk Volumes

This sounds technical, but all you need is a high-quality, double electric breast pump, such as a hospital-grade pump available at your lactation consultant's office. Simply by pumping your milk at your baby's usual feeding time, you can get an accurate picture of the quantity of milk that is available to your baby at a typical feeding. After the first two weeks, your baby will probably drink about twenty-six to twenty-eight ounces of milk each day. This averages out to a little more than one ounce per hour for every twenty-four hours. Thus, you should be able to pump at least one ounce for each hour that has passed since you last finished breastfeeding or pumping. (See Chapter 6, pages 144, 148–149.)

Infant Feeding Test Weights

This is a simple, accurate method of measuring your baby's milk intake during a breastfeeding. The test-weighing procedure can be preformed by your lactation consultant or your baby's doctor. Or, you can rent an accurate scale (see Resources) and perform the procedure yourself at home. Begin by weighing your baby before you start breastfeeding. Write down the weight (some scales remember the weight for you). Next, breastfeed your baby. Then, reweigh your baby, making sure she is wearing exactly the same diaper and clothes. Finally, subtract your baby's pre-feeding weight from her post-feeding weight. The difference between the two weights equals the volume of milk your baby drank while breastfeeding. Some infant scales are specially designed for performing test weights and will automatically calculate the weight change. If you want, you can weigh your baby after feeding from each breast to measure the amount of milk she takes from each side.

Tip

Do not change your baby's diaper until you have completed the test-weighing procedure, or the results will be inaccurate.

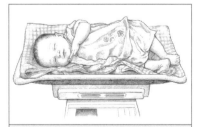

Weighing your baby on an accurate electronic scale before and after she nurses allows you to measure how much milk she drinks while breastfeeding.

Tip

A simple rule of thumb for how much breastmilk your baby drinks between approximately two weeks to five or six months of age is: about one ounce of milk per hour.

Both pumped milk volumes and test-weighing results must always be interpreted by your baby's physician or your lactation consultant together with other information about your baby, such as her weight naked and her rate of weight gain between visits. No firm conclusions should be made about your milk supply based on a single test weight result!

HOW TO INCREASE YOUR MILK SUPPLY

Most commonly, a low milk supply is the result of breastfeeding problems that have interfered with effective milk drainage. The sooner you recognize there's a problem and get help from a lactation consultant, the better your chances for increasing your production. The following strategies should help you get back into the flow and help your baby take more milk when breastfeeding:

- **Well-drained breasts**
  Make sure your breasts are effectively and frequently drained—by your baby using good nursing technique (see Chapters 3 and 4) and/or with

the use of an efficient breast pump (see Chapter 6). Try to nurse more often—at least every two to three hours from the beginning of one feeding to the beginning of the next—and limit breastfeeding to twenty to thirty minutes. (Longer feedings yield little additional milk and can be exhausting for both you and your baby.)

• **Breast compressions**
Use breast compressions when your baby's sucking slows down during feedings. To do this, support your breast with your fingers below and thumb above your areola (the area surrounding your nipple). Compress (squeeze) firmly, but gently, to squirt a spray of milk into your baby's mouth to keep her drinking milk. You either can hold the compression (the gentle breast squeeze) as long as your baby keeps sucking actively, or you can compress and release your breast at intervals. (See Chapter 4, page 96.)

• **Switch nursing**
Try "switch nursing" to help your baby keep sucking and take more milk. When your baby's sucking and swallowing slow down—even when you're using breast compressions—remove her from the first breast. Try to bring her to a more wakeful state, and offer her the second side, where the milk flow is usually faster. Keep using breast compressions and switch sides each time your baby stops sucking at one breast.

• **Breast pumping**
Use a hospital-grade or an effective daily-use double electric breast pump for ten to fifteen minutes immediately after breastfeeding to provide additional breast stimulation and remove any extra milk. The remaining milk you express will be calorie-rich, high-fat hindmilk and can be used to supplement your infant. (See When Supplemental Milk Is Necessary). In most instances, pumping does not add to the total time you spend on feeding because, if you have a low milk supply, you are probably used to nursing for very long periods to try to satisfy your baby. The combined time for nursing, supplementing, and pumping should not exceed fifty to sixty minutes. (See page 236.)

• **Healthy habits**
Focus on good nutrition and adequate hydration for your overall well-being—and to help you make more milk, especially if you've been skipping meals or forgetting to drink adequate fluids.

• **Decompress from the stress**
Evaluate the stress in your life. Try to relax and adopt a positive, optimistic attitude, and create a calm, relaxed environment in your home. Cut back on your commitments and activities and do only the bare necessities for the next two weeks. If supplemental milk has been prescribed because your baby is underweight, you may experience a huge sense of relief

just knowing that she is now receiving enough calories. As a bonus, your reduced anxiety may actually translate into increased milk production.

- **Doctor visits**
  Get treatment for any medical condition that might adversely affect your milk supply. Your body may cut back on producing milk if you're stressed by physical discomfort from sore nipples or a medical illness, such as a breast infection, abscessed tooth, high blood pressure, anemia, or emotional stress.

Tip

If you are completely exhausted or very anxious, consider consulting with your doctor about sleep aids or anti-anxiety medication to help you relax and get the sleep you need to help increase milk production.

Galactogogues (Food Supplements and Other Milk-Boosting Prescriptions)

It seems that every culture has special food supplements (known as galactogogues) that are popularly believed to enhance milk production. In addition, certain medications prescribed for other purposes have a side effect of raising prolactin levels and increasing a mother's milk supply. While studies have not confirmed that insufficient milk can effectively be treated with specific supplements or medications, some breastfeeding experts recommend them for women with a low milk supply. Your lactation consultant, together with your physician, can help you weigh the pros and cons of trying a galactogogue to boost your milk supply.

Fenugreek, an annual herb cultivated in India and areas of the Mediterranean, is the most commonly recommended herbal galactagogue. Fenugreek seeds have long been used as a traditional medicine and as a food spice to flavor artificial maple syrup and curry. Many lactation consultants recommend ground fenugreek seeds, available at health food stores in capsule form and as a tea, to increase milk production. The usual dose is two to three capsules taken three times daily. At higher doses, your perspiration may smell like maple syrup. Many mothers feel that their milk supply increases within a few days of beginning to take the herb. However, no research confirms the effectiveness of fenugreek as a galactogogue. Although widely considered to be harmless and effective, herbal products are not regulated by the FDA or tested for safety, effectiveness, or contaminants. Allergic reactions to fenugreek can occur, especially if you are allergic to other legumes, like peanuts or chickpeas. If you decide to take fenugreek, inform your baby's doctor, and take a well-known brand with fenugreek as the sole ingredient, rather than a combination product.

Metoclopramide is the most widely used prescription

medication in the United States to try to increase milk production. This medication is usually prescribed for heartburn, nausea, and other gastrointestinal complaints. Its use as a galactogogue is considered "off label." Generally you can expect your milk supply to double while taking a seven- to fourteen-day course of metoclopramide. The drug is not a panacea, however, as milk production tends to decline after the medication is stopped. Some physicians will taper the medication slowly and continue a low dose for a longer time to try to maintain your production. Possible side effects include sedation, headache, depression and drug-induced movement disorders. In March 2009, the FDA issued a "black box" warning (their strongest warning), highlighting the risk of involuntary and repetitive movements of the body and face, associated with long-term (usually longer than three months) or high-dose use of metoclopramide. The abnormal movements persist even after the drug is discontinued.

Domperidone is another medication used to treat stomach disorders that has a side effect of raising blood prolactin levels and boosting breastmilk production. It is commonly used as a galactagogue in countries outside the United States. In the United States, however, the FDA has not approved domperidone for any use, citing safety concerns. Although domperidone is widely believed to have fewer adverse side effects than metoclopramide, it has been linked to serious heart rhythm abnormalities.

WHEN SUPPLEMENTAL MILK IS NECESSARY

In an ideal world, insufficient milk could be prevented or remedied, and every mother could be helped to reach her personal breastfeeding goals. In reality some women—through no fault of their own—do not produce enough milk to meet their baby's essential need for calories and nutrients. Without receiving supplemental milk, their babies are at risk of becoming malnourished and developing complications of inadequate nutrition. If you are not able to breastfeed exclusively, do not feel as if you have failed in some way. By feeding your baby essential supplemental milk, you are giving her exactly what she needs to be healthy and happy. Contrary to popular belief, supplementing will not ruin your chances of long-term breastfeeding. In fact, supplementing is compatible with continuing to nurse and offers your baby a number of advantages:

- When your unhappy, hungry baby starts getting enough to eat, she undergoes a striking personality change. She sleeps soundly between feedings, cries far less, and appears (and *is*) much more content. You'll quickly gain confidence and a sense of competence at being able to meet your baby's needs. Your once-hungry infant—whom you'd perceived as "colicky" or "high needs"—is quickly transformed into a "delightful" and "easy" baby.

- Once a supplement is started, your baby will likely gain weight at a remarkable rate. Newborns may gain two to three ounces a day for the first couple days, followed by a steady gain of about an ounce each day. Gaining a pound of catch-up weight the first week is not uncommon. Seeing your baby gain rapidly provides enormous reassurance about her well-being and eliminates the need for expensive diagnostic tests to evaluate her health.

- Your baby may nurse more vigorously once she is getting enough to eat. An underweight infant usually does not nurse effectively and is unable to increase her mother's milk supply by her own efforts. Breaking the cycle of underfeeding is always the best advice.

Tip

When your baby is thriving, your entire outlook on life improves—and this in turn can make you and your partner feel much more relaxed as parents. And there's one more bonus: A healthier nursing baby and a less-anxious mother often lead to a spontaneous increase in milk production.

Options for Supplemental Milk

There are several options for providing supplemental milk when your own supply does not meet all your baby's nutritional needs. If your baby is four months or older, you may introduce solid foods. (See pages 180–181.) The extra calories provided by solids may eventually reduce the amount of supplemental milk your baby requires.

- **Donated breastmilk**
  Pasteurized donor human milk from a Mothers' Milk Bank is an ideal supplement for newborns and premature infants, those who have an adverse reaction to commercial formulas, and infants with certain digestive or immune problems or other medical conditions that make human milk essential. (See Resources.) Although far more expensive than infant formula, medical insurance usually pays for donor milk in cases where a baby cannot tolerate commercial formulas.

Tip

Using milk donated from a well-meaning friend or relative is not considered medically safe, since unpasteurized milk could transmit viruses (including HIV) and other disease-causing microorganisms.

- **Milk-based formula**
  Most breastfed babies who require supplemental milk receive iron-fortified infant formulas. They are available in ready-to-feed, concentrated, and powdered preparations.

- **Soy-based formula**
Soy-based infant formulas, although commonly used, have no advantage over cow's milk–based formula for breastfed babies. Soy formula often is promoted as desirable for infants who are at increased risk for allergic disease; however, it has no proven value in preventing allergies. In fact, many babies who are allergic to cow's milk also are allergic to soy.

Tip

If a close family member (parent or sibling) has allergic disease (food allergy, eczema, asthma, or hayfever), a hypoallergenic formula should be considered. However, these are more expensive than standard formulas.

A Perfectly Good Choice

Some mothers have a negative opinion of infant formulas because of the commercial industry formulas represent. The truth is, infant formulas have been in wide use for more than eighty years. While less desirable than human milk, iron-fortified infant formulas represent the safest, most nutritious alternative to mother's milk.

Options for Feeding Supplemental Milk

There are many methods of feeding necessary supplement to babies, each of which carries its own advantages and disadvantages. (See Chapter 3, pages 68–71.) Whichever method you use, your baby should not spend more than twenty to thirty minutes taking her required extra milk after nursing. Also, be sure to include your baby's health-care provider in any decision about how you give supplemental milk to your baby.

Bottle feeding is the most common method of giving extra milk to breastfed infants. In most instances, the bottle proves to be the fastest way to feed a hungry baby. The greatest and most publicized disadvantage of feeding a breastfed infant by bottle is the risk that your baby will develop a preference for bottle feeding. Many babies switch back and forth between breast and bottle with relative ease, using the correct sucking technique for each feeding method. Some babies clearly prefer the breast, despite receiving bottles on a daily basis, while others may quickly show a preference for bottle feeding and begin to lose interest in nursing. Bottle preference is most likely to occur when your milk supply remains very low and your baby discovers that she can get milk much more readily from a bottle. If this starts to happen, try using a slower flow nipple, and consider switching to an SNS (see following page) system for giving your baby her supplement, at least for a few feedings each day.

The *Supplemental Nursing System (SNS)*, which allows a baby to take supplemental milk while simultaneously breastfeeding, is an ideal way to supplement a breastfed baby. The milk supplement is placed in a plastic bottle, which is connected to a thin, silicone tube that is laid next to the mother's nipple. The baby takes both the breast and the tubing into her mouth when she latches on to nurse. Using the SNS actually enhances a baby's breastfeeding technique by providing the nursing infant with a prompt flow of milk while she is breastfeeding. Yet despite this significant advantage, the SNS has some drawbacks. For one thing, SNS is not as widely available as bottle-and-nipple units, though it is carried by electric breast pump rental sites, lactation consultants, hospital breastfeeding boutiques, breastfeeding clinics, and La Leche League. (See Resources.) Furthermore, the device is harder to use and clean than a bottle.

If your baby is significantly underweight, supplementing with a bottle is recommended until she achieves critical catch-up growth. At that point, you can try using the slower SNS device and phase out

the use of bottles, if desired. The SNS works best for young infants, as babies over three or four months of age are more likely to resist its use or pull at the tubing while the SNS is in place.

Cup feeding provides necessary supplement to breastfed newborns and avoids exposing an infant to artificial nipples that could interfere with learning to nurse. Several cup-like devices have been developed for the specific purpose of supplementing young breastfed infants. (See Resources.) In the first two days of life, the amount of supplement that your baby might require is quite small (often a half ounce) and is easily given by cup.

Older babies (beginning around six months) can learn to drink their supplemental milk from a spouted cup. Sipping from a cup takes longer at first, but most babies master the skill very quickly.

Some lactation consultants recommend giving supplements to newborns by *spoon or dropper*. This is a reasonable method for the first few days of life, when

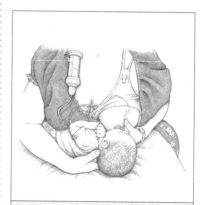

Using the SNS allows your baby to drink necessary supplemental milk simultaneously while breastfeeding.

> **Tip**
>
> Use the SNS system only with the guidance of a lactation consultant who has demonstrated its correct use and who will closely monitor your baby's weight.

> **Tip**
>
> After hospital discharge, cup feeding is not recommended for the long term. First, frequent sucking is important for normal oral development in young infants. Second, it is generally slower to cup-feed the larger amount of milk a baby requires after hospital discharge than to give the supplement by bottle.

the amount of supplement a baby might need is relatively small and parents may want to avoid artificial nipples while their baby is learning to nurse. These methods are not suitable beyond the hospital period, however, since they tend to be slow and ineffective in delivering an adequate amount of the supplement to a baby.

Still another method of supplementing breastfed infants—particularly newborns—is *finger feeding*. Finger feeding involves using the SNS or a similar feeding device by placing the tubing along the palm (pad) side of the parent's index finger. The baby suckles the adult finger and tubing simultaneously to obtain supplemental milk from the attached reservoir bottle. Those who advocate this method feel that it is less likely to confuse a baby than bottle feeding, that a parent's finger is more "natural" than a silicone nipple, that finger feeding is easier for parents than

using the SNS in its traditional manner, and that the method allows parents to evaluate how well their baby sucks. Despite its popularity with many lactation consultants, no scientific data support this method of feeding over other alternatives.

Triple Feeding

Continuing to breastfeed while providing milk supplements to your baby, and attempting to increase your milk supply involves an elaborate and time-consuming regimen, often referred to as "triple feeding." First, the mother nurses her baby. Then she uses a hospital-grade or an effective daily-use double electric breast pump to remove any remaining milk and provide additional breast stimulation. Finally, she offers her baby adequate quantities of expressed breastmilk and/or formula (usually by bottle) to complete the feeding. If another caretaker is on hand to help, he or she can feed the supplemental milk to the baby while the mother is pumping, saving valuable time and allowing a longer interval between feeding sessions. When no helper is available, however, the mother may choose to feed the extra milk (expressed milk collected earlier or formula) immediately after nursing if her baby is fussy and demanding. Or, if her baby is content for a few minutes, she may prefer to pump her breasts first and then offer the milk she has expressed and/or previously pumped milk (plus formula, if necessary). Whew!

Note: Triple feeding is an enormous commitment of time and effort. Fortunately, it is usually a short-term strategy until your milk supply increases and your baby is able to nurse effectively. To allow a reasonable break until the next feeding, set time constraints on triple feeding. Marathon feeding sessions can be distressing and even self-defeating. Generally your baby should nurse approximately ten minutes at each breast. Double pumping should be accomplished in about fifteen minutes, and your baby should drink all her supplemental milk within twenty minutes. You should have about two hours before starting the process all over again. If the entire feeding program takes longer than one hour, you need to talk with your baby's doctor or your lactation consultant about modifying your feeding plan.

Comfort Nursing

Breastfeeding is much more than a feeding option. It also is a style of mothering and a method of comforting your baby. It is fortunate that we have two different words to describe the process—"breastfeeding" and "nursing"—to remind us of the dual feeding and nurturing aspects of breastfeeding. If your baby starts to lose interest in breastfeeding because she is frantically hungry, you may have better success offering her some supplement first and then nursing "for dessert." Many mothers explain that their babies derive such comfort from nursing that they routinely return to the breast to fall asleep after taking their fill from the bottle. Using breastfeeding as a pacifier is one of the best ways to keep your baby interested in nursing, despite a low milk supply.

Working and Breastfeeding

9

oday more than half of mothers with babies under one year old are employed. Countless new moms have attempted to combine work and breastfeeding, and many enjoy remarkable success. Others, however, experience frustration and disappointment due to lack of support, pumping facilities, time, energy, and eventually, lack of milk. While continued breastfeeding is certainly possible for women who work, it is by no means easy. However, even women who face daunting obstacles working as health-care professionals, educators, corporate executives, flight attendants, factory and field workers, and performers have managed to find feasible solutions. If you're considering combining breastfeeding and working, it helps to have an encouraging partner, employer and co-worker support, adequate child care, an effective pump and a place to use it, a sense of humor, and determination. This chapter will help you explore options for continuing to nurse your baby while working away from home.

Advantages of Breastfeeding at Work

Considering how harried most working mothers feel, you might wonder if it is really worth the effort to continue nursing after going back to work. Only you can make that decision for yourself and your baby, but for many women, the answer has been an unqualified yes! Here are some specific advantages to consider.

YOUR BABY STAYS HEALTHY

The longer you breastfeed, the longer your baby receives ideal infant nutrition. In addition, the immune properties in your milk help your baby resist disease and reduce the chances that he will become ill. This benefit is even more important if your baby will be in day care, where children are generally exposed to more infections than at home.

YOU MISS LESS WORK

Working mothers who are able to continue nursing enjoy an added benefit that accompanies a healthier baby—less absenteeism. Most employed mothers drag themselves to work, even when they're feeling crummy, so they can use their sick days when their baby gets an illness. Breastfeeding helps decrease the likelihood that they'll have to miss work because their baby is sick.

EVERYONE FEELS BETTER!

Continuing to breastfeed after you go back to work or school allows you to reap all the health benefits of nursing. If you're breastfeeding, in all likelihood you'll return to your pre-pregnant weight sooner; lose less blood after giving birth; delay your menstrual periods; and have a lower risk of breast cancer, ovarian cancer, diabetes, heart disease, and stroke. By having a healthier baby, you'll have fewer health-care costs and fewer stressful debates over who takes off work to care for a sick infant. Your employer will feel better, too (see below).

YOU ENJOY A GREATER CONNECTION WITH YOUR BABY

Pumping your milk during your workday can help you feel closer and more connected to your baby while the two of you are separated. As your breasts swell with milk during the passing hours, you experience a powerful physical reminder of your bond to your baby. The ambivalence most women feel when they leave their baby with a substitute caretaker can be reduced by leaving a part of yourself—your expressed breastmilk—with your baby each day.

YOUR OUTLOOK ON LIFE IS RESTORED

For eight hours or more at your workplace each day, your universe tends to shrink down to the walls of your office or cubicle. Taking a lactation break helps to refocus your attention on your larger world—your precious child and family and your "lifework" as a parent.

YOU CAN STILL NURSE YOUR BABY

By maintaining your milk supply during the workday, you have the option of resuming breastfeeding each time you are reunited with your baby. The special intimacy of the nursing relationship makes mother-baby reunions extra meaningful after a separation.

Getting Ready

Successfully combining breastfeeding and working actually should begin long before your first day back on the job. There are many things you can do during your maternity leave that will improve your chances of being able to continue breastfeeding after returning to work. Naturally, the more prepared you are, the more confident you will be.

GET OFF TO A GREAT START

Many mothers who anticipate returning to work after delivery assume that breastfeeding will go smoothly during their maternity leave and all they need to learn is how to use a breast pump at work. The truth is that early breastfeeding problems plague working women at least as often as other mothers. It is much more difficult to combine breastfeeding and working if you are dealing with unresolved breastfeeding problems, such as sore nipples or a low milk supply. Don't be discouraged, however; with the right preparation chances are good that your breastfeeding routine will be well established before you return to work.

- Get as much information as possible before you deliver. Attend a prenatal class that covers breastfeeding basics and offers specific information about pumping and storing expressed breastmilk.

- Use your hospital stay to get the best possible start with breastfeeding. (See Chapter 3.) Ideally you will be able to hold your baby skin-to-skin immediately after birth, begin nursing right away, and room-in with your baby. Request hands-on help to establish correct breastfeeding technique. Feed your baby on demand, including throughout the night, and avoid giving him a pacifier for at least the first several weeks.

- Ensure that your baby is seen by his doctor within forty-eight hours of discharge. If you are having any breastfeeding problems, request to be referred to a lactation consultant for additional help. Early follow-up and timely assistance helps

ensure that breastfeeding goes well during the next several weeks.

DELAY YOUR RETURN TO WORK

If you are already employed and plan to return to work after your baby is born, take the longest possible maternity leave and delay going back until you are physically and emotionally prepared. Avoid making a firm commitment in advance about when you will return to work. It is safer to request more time than you think you will need or ask for a range of time (for example, sixteen to twenty weeks). A longer maternity leave increases your chances of long-term success. Even a few extra weeks can help. Don't be afraid to ask for special concessions. Remember, you are a valued employee. Inquire about the possibility of flexible scheduling when you return to work. For example, consider whether you could job-share or telecommute several days a week to decrease the time you are away from your baby.

LEARNING HOW TO EXPRESS YOUR MILK

In much earlier times, breastfed babies and their mothers were inseparable. Women simply took their babies to their place of work and nursed on demand as they went about their daily responsibilities. Babies were "worn" in slings and carriers on their mother's body, and breastfeeding was so natural and so accepted that a nursing baby was not viewed as disruptive to a woman's work.

Today working mothers may be separated from their babies during regular work hours, plus the additional time required for commuting between work and home. Relatively few working mothers in the United States have on-site child-care arrangements that allow them to nurse their babies throughout the workday. Instead, most working nursing mothers must maintain their milk supply by using a breast pump to express their milk at regular intervals during their absence from home. Additional pumping tips for working mothers include:

• Learn about pumping options as early as possible, preferably before your baby is born. Begin pumping and storing milk during your maternity leave so you will be thoroughly comfortable with milk expression before you return to work. By practicing in advance, you can condition your milk ejection reflex (letdown) to be triggered with pumping, so you can pump efficiently during a time-restricted break.

• Use a hospital-grade or daily-use double electric breast pump. Some women are blessed with an abundant milk supply and quick letdown that makes it easy for them to use any pump, or even their hand, to express milk. For most women, however, an effective, fully automatic double electric pump will be the most comfortable and efficient way to drain your breasts during a short

break at work. The faster and easier you can express, the more likely you will be able to pump as often as necessary.

• Learn alternate methods. Even if you don't have access to a pump, you can still drain your breasts using hand expression.

COLLECTING AND FREEZING MILK

Chapter 6 provides a detailed discussion of milk expression and the storage and handling of breastmilk. Knowing that you have ample stores of frozen breastmilk for your baby will give you extra peace of mind when you return to work. Many women begin stockpiling milk as soon as their breasts become engorged after delivery. By maximizing your milk production in the early weeks after you give birth, you can help ensure that you have a generous supply when you return to work. Most women have more milk in the morning, after they have slept at night, than they do later in the day. When your breasts are quite full, your baby may fill up on the first breast and take less from the second. Pumping the milk left behind after one or two morning feedings allows you to collect several extra ounces of high-fat, calorie-rich hindmilk each day. In this way, you will be able to accumulate a stockpile of frozen milk before you return to work.

Remember, however, that your extra stores of milk should be used only for emergencies. Once you start working, don't assume that you can rely on your frozen stores. If you don't pump regularly when separated from your baby, or if you use stored milk in place of breastfeeding, your milk supply could decline, and you may rapidly deplete your once-generous stockpile. While you are at work each day, try to pump at least as much milk as your baby drinks while you are gone.

You will need to communicate closely with your child-care provider about how much milk your baby drinks during the workday. In general, if you can pump at least one ounce of milk for each hour that has passed since your breasts were last drained, you should have sufficient milk to meet your baby's needs. For example, if three hours have passed since you last finished pumping or nursing, you should expect to get about three ounces of milk when you pump. You may be able to pump much more. It is always preferable to have too much milk than too little. Keeping your supply generous also helps ensure that your baby will not develop a preference for bottle-feeding. You may be able to pump and store so much milk that your baby can continue to drink expressed milk for weeks or months after he has stopped breastfeeding.

INTRODUCING YOUR BABY TO BOTTLE-FEEDING

Most likely your baby will drink your expressed milk from a bottle while you are at work. Young babies (under about seven months of age) require liberal sucking, both for emotional gratification and for proper oral development. Once breastfeeding is going well—usually by three to four weeks—you should begin to introduce your baby to bottle-feeding if you intend to work away from home. (See Chapter 6, pages 156–158.) Some breastfed babies accept a bottle easily, while others are very resistant to a new method of feeding. The following suggestions may be helpful in encouraging your baby to accept a bottle:

- **Plan a time when you can devote ten to fifteen uninterrupted minutes to bottle-feeding.**
  Your baby will feel pressured if you are rushed. Choose a time when your baby is alert and slightly hungry so he will be motivated to learn a new way to receive milk. Avoid offering a bottle when your baby is ravenous. An upset, frantically hungry baby will be in no mood to try something new.

- **Offer your freshly expressed milk, so the taste will be familiar to him.**
  Sometimes expressed milk acquires an unpleasant taste

during freezing. (See Chapter 6, page 155.) If your milk has been refrigerated, warm the bottle first, taking care not to overheat the milk.

- **There is no particular bottle-nipple combo that works best for every baby.**
Generally a slow-flow nipple is preferred so that your baby does not guzzle his milk. If he uses a pacifier, he might prefer a nipple with a similar shape. Stick with one type of nipple for several days. Trying numerous different nipples may just confuse your baby.

- **Consider alternate caregivers.**
Your baby may accept a bottle more readily if your partner offers it to him. If you try to give your baby the bottle, he may protest and turn toward your breast to nurse. On the other hand, he may actually accept the bottle more willingly when he is in your arms and is reassured by your voice.

- **Remember to stay calm when offering a bottle to your baby.**
At first he may resist somewhat by turning away, grimacing or making a face, or pushing the nipple away with his tongue. Don't force the bottle at any time and discontinue your efforts if your baby starts to get upset.

- **Go slowly and gently, first touching your baby's lips with the nipple and watching his reaction.**
Do not force the nipple past his lips. Instead, let him draw the nipple into his mouth at his own pace.

- **Drip a little milk from the nipple onto your baby's lips or tongue.**
Remove the nipple before he protests. Keep a smile on your face and keep talking in a reassuring tone the whole time. Babies are keen observers of their mothers' and caretakers' facial expressions and take their cues from them.

- **Patiently wait for your baby to explore or draw the nipple into his mouth.**
Keep smiling and offer reassuring words in a calming voice.

- **If your baby starts to get upset, try to calm him by talking in a soothing voice.**
Wait until he starts to settle before you remove the nipple from his lips. Avoid letting him get very upset and then immediately taking the nipple away. This will teach him that

> **Tip**
>
> Most important, don't be discouraged. You can take comfort in knowing that countless women have managed to entice their breastfed babies to accept a bottle. While the same techniques are not necessarily effective for every mother and baby, something always works. You will find a solution, too.

if he protests enough, you will remove the nipple. It is better to withdraw the nipple before he becomes upset or to try to calm him with your voice before you remove the nipple.

- **Don't spend more than about ten minutes on this process and stop sooner if you or your baby becomes frustrated.** It is better to end the session on a positive note and try again tomorrow.

MAKING CHILD-CARE ARRANGEMENTS

Long before you begin work, you will want to finalize your child-care arrangements and enlist the support of your baby's caretaker in your breastfeeding plans. Think about whether to choose a caregiver who lives near your home or close to your workplace. If your child-care provider is near your work, you may be able to visit your baby during the day or nurse him at lunch. Or you may be able to "top him off" when you arrive in the morning and nurse him immediately at the end of your workday. Young babies do best when they have a close, nurturing relationship with a single caretaker or just a few consistent caregivers.

Once you are certain that your child will be physically safe and that his emotional and intellectual development will

---

Tip

Make sure the caretaker or center is licensed, and always check references. Voluntary national accreditation by an agency such as the National Association for the Education of Young Children (NAEYC) or the National Association for Family Child Care (NAFCC) is a higher standard than licensure and provides additional assurance that you are dealing with a quality program. If something does not seem right to you, trust your intuition, and remove your child from the setting.

Tip

Arrange to leave your baby with your child-care provider for several hours on one occasion or more before you return to work. Show her how to quiet and comfort your baby when he is upset. Ask her to feed your baby while you are gone. These trial sessions give your baby and the caretaker the opportunity to get to know one another. The assurance that your child-care provider can feed your infant successfully will reduce your anxiety and give you peace of mind.

be optimized in the setting you have selected, you can turn your attention to your breastfeeding plans. Your child-care provider not only is responsible for your baby's welfare, she also needs to be your unwavering ally in your efforts to continue breastfeeding. Ask whether the caretaker has breastfed her own children or cared for other breastfed babies. How does she feel about handling your expressed milk or coping with a baby who may not take a bottle readily? If other babies in this setting also receive their mothers' milk, what precautions are taken to avoid feeding the wrong milk to a baby? Clarify for the babysitter what to do if you are late picking up your baby and whom to call in an emergency. You should expect her to review your baby's eating, sleeping, elimination, and behavior patterns with you at the end of the day.

ENLISTING SUPPORT

You are more likely to be able to continue breastfeeding after returning to work if you have plenty of support from people who can nurture and encourage you. For most women, the support of their husband or partner has the greatest impact on their efforts. Maybe your mother or mother-in-law will be your champion, or perhaps you have a coworker who has breastfed and who can encourage you. In some large workplaces, several breastfeeding women may be pumping at one time and can support one another.

The Importance of Keeping a Generous Milk Supply

Working nursing moms often wait until their breasts are uncomfortably full before they take time to pump. Workplace distractions are so prevalent, and work-related demands so pressing, you may be tempted to postpone pumping sessions as long as possible. However, you should not wait until your breasts are painfully hard before expressing your milk. This is an all-too-common scenario that inevitably leads to diminished milk supply. It is not surprising that low milk is the leading complaint among working breastfeeding mothers. Remember, milk production slows down when your breasts remain overfull.

Faithfully adhering to your pumping schedule may be the most important thing you can do to keep a generous milk supply. How frequently you need to pump will depend on the age of your baby and your breast storage capacity. (See Chapter 6, pages 144, 148–149.) Because young babies nurse more often than older babies, the sooner you begin working after giving birth, the more often you will need to pump. If you start working when your baby is four weeks old, you will need to pump more often than if you return when your baby is four months old. Before returning to work, count the number of times your baby typically nurses in twenty-four hours. This will be your target number for how often you need to pump and/or nurse each day once you are back at work. Try to nurse twice each morning before arriving at work.

> **Tip**
>
> Conscientious employees often put the needs of others above their own. They let the "urgent" phone call, staff meeting, or special project take precedence over pumping. To succeed at breastfeeding, you need to be appropriately selfish. Outline a realistic pumping schedule and resolve to stick to it. If you cannot do this for yourself, insist on doing it for your baby. Most work-related priorities can wait ten or fifteen minutes until you finish pumping.

Options for Combining Breastfeeding and Working

Every woman's circumstances are unique, and thankfully there is a wide range of options for combining working and nursing—and each has its own pros and cons. After reviewing the following options, you can choose a plan that fits your individual circumstances, resources, lifestyle, and motivation.

NURSING YOUR BABY AT WORK

Work is least likely to interfere with breastfeeding if you and your baby can remain in contact or if your baby can be brought to you for feedings. A few lucky women are able to make arrangements to bring their baby to work, perhaps keeping their baby with them in a bassinet or having him cared for at an on-site child-care facility. These arrangements work best if you have a flexible schedule that allows you to nurse your baby on demand or to go to the child-care center when your baby requires feedings. Some self-employed women pay a caregiver to tend to their baby's needs, perhaps in her own office or in an adjacent room. The nanny cares for your infant while you perform your work duties. When your baby needs to be fed you can take a work break to nurse him. Or, an off-site child-care provider or relative may be able to bring your baby to your workplace for some, if not all, feedings. Having contact with your baby throughout the workday is especially important if you must return to work within a few weeks postpartum, when your baby may be nursing every two to three hours. A recent study of breastfeeding mothers who returned to work found that being able to feed directly from the breast during the workday—or to breastfeed and pump—was linked with a longer duration of breastfeeding than pumping only.

WORKING PART-TIME

Working part-time rather than full-time increases your chances of breastfeeding longer. Part-time work is less disruptive of breastfeeding because it allows you to have more time with your baby. You might work fewer hours every day or fewer days each week. With fewer hours away from your baby (and more opportunities to nurse), your milk supply is less likely to dwindle and your baby will miss fewer nursings. If you

Tip

If a part-time position is not feasible in the long-term, you might try to negotiate the possibility of temporarily working part-time when you return from maternity leave. Even a few weeks of part-time employment will ease your transition back to work and your baby's transition into his day-care setting. You can begin to incorporate milk expression into your workday before resuming a full-time position. If none of these options is possible, try to return to work on a Wednesday or Thursday, to shorten your first workweek.

work fewer hours each day, you may need to pump only once during your workday, or perhaps not at all, if your baby is older than about four months. If you are a part-time employee who works a full day but who puts in fewer days each week, you will need to pump several times during your workday. However, you might have four or five days each week to breastfeed exclusively after having worked a couple of days.

PUMP AND SAVE

The most common strategy used by working nursing moms who are separated from their baby is to pump their breasts when they would typically nurse. Highly efficient daily-use double electric breast pumps that drain both breasts in ten to fifteen minutes are especially popular among working mothers. You can keep your expressed milk at work in a refrigerator or an insulated bag or cooler with a frozen cold pack. If you are able to effectively drain

A highly efficient daily-use double electric breast pump is a popular option for working mothers.

your breasts at frequent intervals during the workday, you have the best chance of keeping up a generous milk supply. As long as your milk production is abundant, your baby is likely to nurse eagerly when the two of you are together and to go back and forth easily between breast and bottle. (Chapter 6 includes a detailed discussion of pumping, storing, and handling breastmilk.)

PUMP AND DUMP

A few working mothers have no options for safely storing their expressed milk. However, regular expression of milk is still desirable even if your milk can't be saved and used, because emptying your breasts is critical to preserving a generous milk supply and will reduce your risk of mastitis. If you have collected a stockpile of frozen milk during your maternity leave and continue to pump and store extra milk while at home, you may have enough expressed milk for your baby's feedings during the workday. Or, your baby can be fed infant formula while you are separated, if expressed milk is not available.

OTHER OPTIONS

If you are unwilling or unable to pump at all during the workday, partial breastfeeding is still possible. You can nurse your baby in the mornings and evenings, while he is fed formula during the workday. You might also choose to breastfeed more at night. (Bear in mind that employed women who neither pump nor breastfeed during the workday tend to discontinue breastfeeding sooner.)

Some women report that their breasts adjust to making more milk during the times they are with their babies and less milk when they are away. Others find that their milk supply diminishes significantly if milk is not removed from their breasts regularly during the workday. Women who can store more milk in their breasts will maintain their supply better than women with a smaller storage capacity.

Planning for Pumping at Work

Before going back to work, make arrangements for when and where you will express milk. Inform your employer of your intentions to pump your milk during the workday. Be prepared to cite the advantages of improved mother-baby health and reduced absenteeism. Explain that you will be using your breaks as "lactation breaks," and that you also will pump while you eat lunch.

Try to find a suitable place at work that is close to your office or work station, so that you won't have to waste precious minutes getting there. You will want a quiet, private location where you can relax and pump your breasts without fear that you will be interrupted by a co-worker. If you don't have a private office, your company may provide a formal employee lactation lounge or other suitable area. Or, you may be able to use a portable privacy screen to create a suitable pumping niche.

Ideally the place you select should have an electrical outlet to allow you to use an electric pump. If no wall outlet is available, however, you still can use an electric pump if it comes with a battery pack. When fully charged overnight, these pumps will run by battery for about an hour. Your pumping place should also have a sink and running water so you can wash your hands and clean your equipment. If soap and water are not available, you can conveniently clean your pump parts with Medela's Quick Clean wipes. (See Resources.) Take the time while you're pumping to read and relax—and calling your caregiver to check in on your baby may help trigger your milk letdown. Looking at a photograph of your baby as you prepare to pump may also help start your milk flowing. The main thing is to feel relaxed, comfortable, and unrushed.

Corporate Support for Breastfeeding Moms

These days, more companies are providing a private, comfortable work-site location for pumping breastmilk, where employees are allowed flexible use of their break times to express their milk. The most elaborate programs provide

access to a lactation consultant who can give expert breastfeeding advice for any problems that arise. (Lucky you, if you work for one of these companies!) The growth of programs like these is based on the discovery that supporting breastfeeding makes good business sense. In addition, your employer saves in the following ways: Worker absenteeism is higher among parents of formula-fed babies over breastfed babies. Companies with a breastfeeding support program enjoy higher employee morale and less turnover. By returning to work, you save your employer the costs

Note: Ask whether your company offers any lactation support services. The more women who ask about breastfeeding accommodations, the more companies will consider providing pumping facilities, on-site child care, and lactation consultant support. More than twenty states have already enacted legislation encouraging employers to recognize the benefits of breastfeeding and to provide unpaid break time and appropriate space for employees to breastfeed or express milk. To check whether your state has a law related to breastfeeding in the workplace, visit the Web site of the National Conference of State Legislatures at www.ncsl.org/programs/health/breast50.htm. National legislation has been drafted, and one day may be enacted, that will protect a woman's right to breastfeed or pump milk in the workplace.

What Will My Co-workers Think?

Many new mothers feel guilty about taking a maternity leave, and fear that their co-workers resent their absence. Consequently you may feel reluctant to ask for any concessions to continue breastfeeding at work. In fact, your willingness to expend extra effort for your baby's welfare is highly praiseworthy and commendable. An enlightened employer (and would that we all worked for one) should recognize the labor of love involved in pumping milk to reflect your dedication and commitment, sense of priorities, time-management skills, and strong work ethic. This may sound a bit idealistic, but working moms have to start somewhere.

You may need to be politely firm at times. A co-worker or supervisor who has never pumped her breasts may not understand why it can't be put off for an hour or so. Humor and quick wit go a long way toward getting your needs met, but jokes about pumping, innuendos, and snickering on the part of co-workers are all inappropriate and shouldn't be tolerated. Although many women put up with this kind of behavior, you absolutely do not need to.

associated with hiring and training your replacement. These points translate to a better bottom line for your employer and a better working environment for everyone.

Helpful Hints for Working and Breastfeeding

• **Wear clothing that is convenient for pumping and nursing.**
Select blouses that open in the front and pull up. Choose clothes that will not show stains from leaking milk (avoid silk!). Keep an extra neutral-colored blouse and a sweater at work in case milk leaks onto your outer clothing. If you leak easily, wear breast pads to avoid wet spots on your clothing or try using non-absorbent, soft silicone nursing pads that prevent leaking by adhering tightly to your breast. (See Resources.)

• **Use a hands-free pumping bra.**
Purchase a "hands-free" pumping bra to free up your hands while you pump, so you can read, talk on the phone, or eat your lunch. (See Chapter 6 and Resources.) These specialized bras are highly convenient and popular.

• **Drink extra fluids at work.**
At home, you are more likely to practice normal breastfeeding routines, such having a tall glass of water or a warm cup of tea each time you nurse. At work, however, it is all too easy to get distracted and unintentionally limit your fluid intake.

A hands-free pumping bra allows you to multi-task while expressing your milk.

Tip

Don't wait until you're thirsty to drink something; thirst is an indicator that you are already dehydrated. Keep a sports bottle at work and water and juice on hand.

Constipation can signal that you need extra liquids.

- **Set your alarm half an hour earlier each morning to enjoy a leisurely nursing session before your hectic day begins.** A few extra minutes of sleep can be traded for the quiet, relaxing joy of having a contented baby at your breast. Although the rest of your day may be governed by time constraints, you don't have to start the day feeling hurried.

- **Communicate with your child-care provider so your baby is ready to nurse as soon as you're together.** Your provider can make sure that your baby has not just finished a bottle when you walk through the door with full breasts. Nursing your baby at the end of a hectic day can be the most peaceful reunion of all.

- **Keep your focus on the nursing relationship, not the amount of milk you produce.** When you pump and measure your milk on a daily basis, it is easy to become preoccupied with the amount of milk you produce. Focusing too heavily on the quantity of milk can create anxiety and interfere with milk letdown, which only compounds the problem.

Tip

Some working mothers pump abundant milk with relative ease, while others get less through no fault of their own. No matter how much milk you are able to pump, focus on being able to nurse your baby when the two of you are reunited each day. Even if you need to use some supplemental formula, a satisfying nursing relationship can continue as long as you and your baby desire.

- **Try to breastfeed exclusively on weekends and days off, to build up your milk supply**

and restore your nursing relationship.
Both you and your baby can enjoy the emotional rewards of a few days of exclusive breastfeeding after making it through another week of work. This is a big commitment, considering that most women usually spend their days off buying groceries, running errands, doing laundry, cleaning, preparing meals, and the like. However, keeping your baby close by on weekends and allowing unrestricted breastfeeding can help boost your milk supply before the start of a new work week.

• **Consider practicing reverse-cycle nursing—that is, nursing more in the evenings and at night when you are available to your baby.**
This strategy works well for some working mothers, but it's not for everyone, especially for those who consider adequate nighttime sleep to be essential if they must work full-time.

A Working Mom's Survival Guide

The good news is that despite all the challenges of working away from home—and being separated from your baby for hours at a time—most difficulties can be prevented or remedied, and none has to mean the end of breastfeeding.

FATIGUE AND DISCOURAGEMENT

New motherhood is challenging, whether or not you breastfeed and whether or not you work outside the home. Fatigue plagues all new parents from time to time. Certainly, many women enjoy their jobs and derive fulfillment from their work. Some manage to juggle home and office without getting ruffled. Most, however, admit that wearing multiple hats occasionally pushes them into role overload. Caring for a young baby is hard enough without adding the demands of outside employment, a daily commute, unrelenting time pressures, regular milk expression, and running a home. Don't assume there is something wrong with you if you sometimes get tired and discouraged! Examine your situation to see if there is anything you can do to simplify your life for a few months. Ask your friends and relatives for help. If you can afford it, hire someone to do chores you don't have time for right now. Drop some of your commitments, lower your house cleaning standards, turn off the TV, and go to bed earlier. It'll make a huge difference in your energy and outlook.

DECREASED MILK SUPPLY

Perhaps the most common concern voiced by working moms who breastfeed is decreased milk supply. The problem usually results from being unable to pump frequently enough during the workday. When your breasts don't get drained as well by pumping as they would by nursing, your milk supply can diminish. Several other factors can contribute to the problem of low milk supply, including physical exhaustion, inhibited milk letdown, stress, not eating or drinking enough or a baby who does not nurse well when you are available for feedings. You can tell if your milk supply has decreased if: you are expressing less milk at pumping sessions than previously; you are unable to pump as much milk as your baby wants to drink in your absence; you are no longer able to satisfy your baby by breastfeeding when you are together; or your baby stops gaining adequate weight.

Maintaining a generous milk supply from the start is easier than trying to increase your milk once it has dwindled. But if your milk has diminished, there are several things you can do to try to increase your supply: Pump more often at work, preferably with a hospital-grade or a highly efficient, daily use, double electric pump. Pump at least ten minutes, even if your milk stops flowing sooner. Nurse your baby at least every two to three hours when the two of you are together. (For additional strategies, see Chapter 8, pages 228–231.)

If your baby sleeps longer than six hours at night, consider pumping your breasts just before you go to bed and after nursing your baby in the morning. Eat a balanced diet and healthy snacks, drink enough fluids, rest as much as possible, and try to get help with household duties.

INHIBITED MILK EJECTION REFLEX

A mother nursing her hungry baby in the privacy and comfort of her home usually has little trouble getting her milk to flow. Your milk ejection reflex may be triggered as soon as you pick up your baby or begin familiar nursing routines, like sipping a glass of juice or settling into a cozy recliner with your baby. Certainly the work environment is less conducive to conditioning your letdown response. Milk flow can be inhibited when you have to pump under time constraints or wonder if your privacy will be interrupted or whether your coworkers resent your absence. Inhibited letdown can prolong pumping sessions or lead to poor milk drainage and diminished milk supply. For strategies to trigger your milk ejection reflex, see Chapter 6, pages 141–142.

PLUGGED DUCTS

A clogged duct often results from an irregular pumping schedule that prevents your breasts from getting well drained. The best treatment of a clogged duct is nursing more frequently on the affected breast, nursing in different positions, and applying heat and gentle massage to the clogged area. These therapies are difficult, if not impossible, to perform during the workday. Certainly you should attempt to nurse (if feasible) or pump more often while at work if you have a clogged duct. Pumping your breasts singly sometimes helps because you can use your free hand to massage or apply gentle pressure to the clogged area. Don't overdo any breast manipulation, however, because such "trauma" can increase your risk of mastitis (a breast infection). For additional strategies to relieve a clogged duct, see Chapter 8, pages 204–206.

MASTITIS

Working mothers are particularly susceptible to a breast infection (mastitis) if they go too long without pumping. Other risk factors for mastitis include cracked nipples, clogged ducts, and extreme fatigue. A breast pump that generates excessive suction or a breast flange that is too tight can injure your nipples and make you more prone to a breast infection. Breast trauma leading to mastitis also can occur from overly vigorous massage or improper hand expression.

For information about the symptoms and treatment of mastitis, see Chapter 8, pages 206–209. To minimize your risks of getting mastitis, try to express your milk regularly, using a comfortable, efficient pump, get treated for nipple sores or cracks, and do your best to get enough rest. If you develop a fever or body aches, feel like you are getting the flu, or notice a firm, painful area in one of your breasts, contact your doctor promptly. He or she can diagnose mastitis and prescribe an antibiotic.

YOUR BABY LOSES INTEREST IN NURSING

Some babies increase their desire to nurse because they link breastfeeding with their mother's presence. Others gradually lose interest in nursing as they grow more accustomed to bottle feeding during the workday, especially if the mother's milk supply starts to dwindle. (See more about "nursing strikes" in Chapter 8, pages 213–215.) Although some babies will nurse enthusiastically even when the flow of milk is less than they desire, most babies quickly become frustrated with breastfeeding if milk does not flow as readily from the breast as it does from the bottle.

> **Tip**
>
> To prevent your baby from losing interest in nursing, try to keep your milk supply generous with regular pumping. When you are with your baby, nurse him as often as he desires, preferably before he gets too hungry.

If your baby starts to show a loss of interest in nursing, take the following steps to try to correct the problem:

If your milk supply is low, try to pump more often at work. Use the most efficient pump you can obtain. For more information on additional ways to increase your supply, see Chapter 8, pages 228–231.

Offer your breast frequently to comfort, settle, or pacify your baby. This will help remind him that breastfeeding is more than nutrition—it is a unique source of security and emotional satisfaction. If your baby still seems uninterested, try nursing him when he is drowsy or asleep. Nighttime nursings usually go well and can help entice your baby back to the breast. When your baby does cooperate by nursing, don't rush him or make him come off the breast before he's ready. Instead, focus your attention on your baby and allow him to continue as long as desired in a quiet, relaxed environment.

You might need to pump after nursing your baby to ensure that your breasts receive adequate stimulation and drainage.

Note: Often, a nursing mother who complains about being tired and discouraged will be advised to stop breastfeeding. But weaning seldom improves the situation: You still have a baby to feed, diaper, bathe, and care for. Nursing moms usually describe breastfeeding as one of their few relaxing daily interludes. Besides, when you consider the number of years you spend caring for your child, breastfeeding is only a small portion of it. Are you sure you want to cut this experience even shorter? Weaning might free up some time at work that you would have spent pumping, but the price you pay is the lost opportunity to enjoy leisurely nursing your baby in the mornings, evenings, and on weekends.

Breastfeeding

in Special

Situations

Perhaps you are thinking about breastfeeding but worry that it might be too difficult to pursue, especially if you have a premature or high-risk infant or twins. Or maybe you have had previous breast surgery or would like to nurse an adopted baby. This chapter is dedicated to your special needs. You may be surprised and relieved to learn that breastfeeding is still an option for you, despite your unique challenges. Fortunately there are a number of organizations and support groups that are geared to your particular needs.

Breastfeeding Premature or Other High-Risk Babies

No matter how unprepared you may feel when your baby arrives early, you are not alone! Countless mothers of high-risk infants have faced the same kinds of questions, challenges, and concerns you may be experiencing. In fact, breastfeeding is not only possible for premature infants and babies with medical problems, it is strongly recommended. Breastmilk offers your baby valuable immediate and long-term health benefits. The beauty of breastmilk is that it can still be a precious gift to your baby whether you breastfeed or express your milk partially or fully. Both you and your baby have nothing to lose and a great deal to gain.

WHY BREASTMILK IS SO BENEFICIAL TO YOUR PREMATURE OR HIGH-RISK BABY

There are many advantages to nursing your baby or expressing breastmilk for her if she is born premature or has special medical needs.

Colostrum, the first milk your breasts produce, is rich in immunities and is easily digested—the perfect first food for premature infants who often have trouble tolerating early milk feedings. Minimal amounts of breastmilk help "prime" your baby's gut, promote the growth of friendly bacteria in the intestinal tract, and improve the rate at which your premature baby advances to full nutritional feedings. Babies who tolerate feedings better are often able to go home sooner.

The composition of human milk is ideally suited for premature infants. Your milk is digested more easily than formula, so your baby's stomach empties faster. The many growth factors in breastmilk help your baby's intestinal tract to mature and absorb nutrients. The proteins in your milk are digested easily, and the fats are absorbed especially well by premature infants.

> **Tip**
>
> If you have delivered a premature baby, the milk you produce for the first month is actually *higher* in several essential nutrients than the milk from mothers of full-term babies.

Colostrum and breastmilk contain white blood cells, antibodies, and valuable immune properties to help your baby resist infection. Babies born early have a weakened immune system that leaves them more susceptible to infectious diseases than full-term infants. Numerous studies have shown that feeding breastmilk to premature infants helps protect against a variety of infections, decreases the incidence of chronic lung disease, and reduces respiratory illnesses in the first year of life.

Breastmilk helps improve the neurological (brain) development of premature infants. Follow-up studies of extremely premature infants show that those who were fed their own mother's milk later scored significantly higher on developmental and behavioral tests compared to those who were fed premature-infant formula.

Many mothers deeply appreciate being able to contribute to their baby's well-being in a uniquely personal way by providing their own breastmilk. Expressing your milk helps you feel more connected to your baby and involved in her care and is something no health professional can do for her. By starting to express your milk, you are offering your baby and yourself the chance to benefit from all the advantages of long-term breastfeeding. With expert help and support, you may be able to nurse your baby as long as you had planned.

IF YOUR BABY IS IN A NEONATAL INTENSIVE CARE UNIT (NICU)

Having a baby in a Neonatal Intensive Care Unit (NICU) or a Special-Care Nursery (SCN) can be an overwhelming experience. If you delivered prematurely, you may feel unprepared for motherhood, unfamiliar with routine baby care, and intimidated by the highly specialized equipment in a NICU. You may not have had the opportunity to prepare for routine breastfeeding, let alone learn the details of pumping and storing milk—and your baby may be cared for at a regional center some distance from your home, preventing you from being present in the nursery as often as you wish. Notwithstanding all these obstacles, the health team at your hospital, including your baby's neonatologist—a physician who specializes in the care of premature and high-risk infants—no doubt will urge you to pump milk for your baby's feedings. Colostrum and breastmilk are so beneficial to premature infants that they are considered to be as much a "medicine" as food. Fortunately lactation consultants are part of the health-care team in virtually all NICUs in the United States—which means you will be given the specialized information and support you need so that you can begin expressing and storing your milk. (See Chapter 6, pages 142–145, 151–156.) Your baby's nurses and lactation consultant will help you start breastfeeding as soon as your baby is able, and can offer ongoing guidance to help you make the transition to full breastfeeding after your baby is discharged.

BRINGING IN AND KEEPING AN ABUNDANT MILK SUPPLY

The key to bringing in an abundant milk supply for your baby is to begin expressing your milk early and to pump frequently. For more details about bringing in and maintaining your milk supply when your newborn is too sick or too premature to nurse, see Chapter 6, pages 137–145. Here, too, are a few tips to get your milk flowing and your baby well supplied:

- **Use a hospital-grade, rental-quality electric breast pump with a double collection system.**
  After the first several weeks, when your milk supply has been well established, you may be able to maintain your production over the long-term by using an effective, daily-use double electric pump.

- **Begin regular milk expression as early as possible, preferably within the first six to twelve hours after birth.**

- **To express the maximum amount of milk, use breast massage and hand expression prior to pumping, and continue using breast massage while you pump.**
  This technique of "hands-on pumping" has been shown to increase the amount of milk you are able to express. (See Chapter 6, pages 137–138.)

- **Pump a minimum of seven times every twenty-four hours (approximately every three hours, with one longer interval of up to five hours at night).**
  If possible, pump every two to three hours, or eight to ten times each day for the first two weeks. This is the critical period during which you are "placing your order" for your long-term milk production.

- **Pump for a minimum of ten minutes at each pumping session.**
  If your milk is still flowing, continue for a total of fifteen minutes.

- **Record the amount of milk you express from each breast**

at each session in a daily pumping log.
Your lactation consultant can provide these forms. Tally your twenty-four-hour total each day to easily track your progress and spot any downward trends.

- **Use techniques to help trigger your milk ejection reflex (letdown) to ensure that your breasts get well drained.**
(See Chapter 6, pages 141–142.)

- **By the end of the first week, expect to express nineteen to twenty-four ounces every twenty-four hours.**
By two weeks, you might produce more than thirty ounces each day.

- **Eat a healthy diet, drink plenty of fluids, and rest whenever you can.**
If your milk supply starts to dwindle, meet with your lactation consultant and review your pumping routines to see what might be improved, such as the type of pump you are using, your flange size, breast massage and hand expression, how frequently you express, the effectiveness of your milk ejection reflex (letdown), or the environment where you are pumping. If your supply still remains low after troubleshooting with the lactation consultant, ask your doctor about trying a galactagogue to increase your milk production. (See Chapter 8, pages 230–231.) Now is the time to enlist help from your partner, family, and friends who are ready and willing to help give you the support you need. Meanwhile, rest assured that your baby will benefit from any amount of milk you are able to produce. You may find that your supply increases when your baby is able to begin breastfeeding.

Tip

If your supply falls short of your baby's requirement for milk, ask whether your baby can receive screened, pasteurized donor milk from a Mothers' Milk Bank. (See Chapter 8, page 232, and Resources.) Your medical insurance is likely to cover the processing fee for donor breastmilk.

FORTIFYING YOUR EXPRESSED MILK

At first, your baby will likely be fed small amounts of your colostrum and early milk through a feeding tube. As your baby is able to digest larger volumes, extra nutrients and calories may be added to your expressed milk. If your baby is born very premature (weighing less than about three and a half pounds), fortifying your breastmilk assures that she gets all the extra nutrients she needs to thrive.

THE AMAZING BENEFITS OF KANGAROO CARE

Most NICUs now practice "kangaroo care" as a convenient way to provide premature infants with essential skin-to-skin contact with their mothers. (See Chapter 3, page 43.) Similar to a kangaroo mother, whose baby enjoys the nurturing benefits of close proximity in her pouch, you'll be able to cuddle your premature baby snugly between your breasts. In the NICU, you'll be offered a special chair that tilts back, allowing you to hold your baby upright and tummy down—relaxed against your bare chest and covered with a loose blouse and a blanket. Even the smallest infants—hooked up to all kinds of essential tubes—can benefit from carefully monitored kangaroo care.

> **Note:** Recent studies show that kangaroo care of premature babies helps regulate their heartbeat, breathing, and temperature. Your body is the optimal and most stabilizing environment for your preterm baby. Infants who receive kangaroo care also tend to cry less, sleep more soundly, start breastfeeding earlier, and gain weight faster. In addition, kangaroo care increases your milk production, helps prolong the duration of breastfeeding, increases your confidence, and strengthens your bond with your baby. Is there any wonder the practice of kangaroo care has increased dramatically in NICUs around the world?

Kangaroo care has a significant positive impact on premature babies and their parents.

BEGINNING BREASTFEEDING

There is no specific age or weight at which premature infants can start to nurse—it all depends on your baby's general condition and her ability to coordinate sucking, swallowing, and breathing. Most premature infants are able to begin breastfeeding by thirty-four weeks of gestation. Your baby may be ready earlier if she has had numerous opportunities to practice rooting and latching.

In the past, neonatologists believed that premature infants first needed to be able to bottle feed well before learning to breastfeed. Now it has been shown that breastfeeding is less stressful for premature babies than feeding by bottle. Preterm infants take less milk during their first attempts at breastfeeding compared to bottle feeding, and the slower flow of milk when breastfeeding makes it easier for your baby to coordinate sucking and swallowing. Today most

Pacifiers and Premature Infants

Although pacifiers are not recommended for full-term, breastfed newborns until breastfeeding is well established, sucking on a pacifier during tube feeding is believed to be beneficial for premature infants. This "non-nutritive sucking" has been shown to calm and soothe premature babies, improve digestion, and increase weight gain. Your breast can act as a "pacifier," too. Pump immediately before your baby's feeding so she can use your nearly empty breast as a pacifier while she is being tube-fed.

NICUs make an effort to introduce breastfeeding before an infant is fed by bottle. Early "practice sessions" latching on to your empty breast during tube feedings make it easier for your baby to learn to nurse. The following strategies will help your baby make a smoother transition to breastfeeding:

- As you begin breastfeeding your premature infant, try to be available in the nursery for several hours each day so you can attempt to breastfeed her when she is in an optimal alert and responsive state. Think of these early attempts as learning sessions, not meant to provide much nutrition. At first your baby will breastfeed only once a day and will continue to receive feedings by tube. Your baby's nurse will help you judge when she is ready to increase the number of daily breastfeeding sessions. Communicate closely with the nurse so you can be available to breastfeed when your baby is ready to learn.

- As you prepare to nurse your baby, ask for a portable screen if you need privacy. Fortunately many NICUs now have individual rooms for most infants, giving you the privacy you need to relax and take your time to nurse your baby. Get comfortable, preferably in a chair with both back and arm support. Place a pillow on your lap and another under your arm to support your baby. Use a footstool to decrease the distance between your lap and your breast, and ask your baby's nurse to help you position your baby, who may be connected to multiple wires and tubes.

- Your premature baby will need extra support for her weak neck muscles and relatively heavy head. The football hold and the cross-cradle hold work best for most premature infants. Both of these positions provide good support for your baby's head and give a clear view of her mouth on your breast.

- The small size of your baby's mouth may make it difficult for her to grasp your entire nipple and a sufficient amount of the surrounding areola. (See Chapter 3, pages 48–57, for tips on helping your baby attach correctly.) Her weak muscle tone will make it harder for her to keep your breast in her mouth.

You will need to support your heavy breast throughout the feeding.

- If your baby has trouble grasping your breast correctly, try pumping just before nursing to help pull your nipple out and to start some milk flowing. After many weeks of expressing your milk, your letdown should be easily triggered by the pump.

- If your baby has trouble latching or staying attached to your breast or if she falls asleep shortly after latching on, ask your baby's nurse or lactation consultant about using an ultra-thin silicone nipple shield to help your baby breastfeed more effectively. (See Chapter 3, page 64.) Use breast compressions to help your baby drink more milk after her sucking slows down. (See Chapter 4, page 96.)

Tip

In the past, nipple shields were considered ineffective. However, newly designed ultra-thin silicone nipple shields have been shown to help premature infants keep the breast in their mouth and take more milk when breastfeeding. Your baby may need to use a nipple shield until she reaches her due date. (See Chapter 3, page 64.)

Even after you start breastfeeding, your baby will most likely continue to receive some feedings by bottle or tube. She may also require additional milk after breastfeeding if the amount she takes when nursing is not enough. Fortunately most premature babies readily go back and forth between feeding methods, especially when they have regular opportunities to breastfeed.

The Importance of Pumping After Nursing

Because your baby's early breastfeeding attempts will not remove much milk, it is essential that you pump after each nursing to drain your breasts well. If you do not pump after nursing your baby, your milk supply will decline. Keeping your supply generous will help your baby get milk more easily when breastfeeding. You will probably need to pump after feedings until your baby reaches her due date, or longer.

HOW MUCH MILK IS YOUR BABY GETTING?

Many NICUs routinely use highly accurate, electronic infant scales to measure how much milk babies take when they breastfeed. Attempts to guess how well a baby has breastfed by observing her sucking pattern or how often she swallows can be highly inaccurate. Such estimates don't provide the necessary information to give at-risk babies the best care. Weighing your baby before and after feeding is a simple and accurate method of measuring the amount of milk your baby drinks while breastfeeding. (See Chapter 8, pages 227–228.)

This is how it works: Your baby is weighed (wearing the same clothes) before and after breastfeeding. The difference in her pre-feed and post-feed weights equals the amount of milk she drank. (It is important not to change your baby's diaper while performing the test-weighing procedure because this will affect the outcome and give you an inaccurate read.) Before and after feeding weights can help you follow your baby's progress with breastfeeding. The results help you know whether or not your baby needs to be supplemented after nursing.

Tip

Don't be alarmed if the before and after feeding weights show that your baby has taken only small amounts of milk with her first breastfeeding attempts. This is entirely normal for premature babies who are just learning to nurse. With practice, and as your baby matures, she will soon learn to take more milk when she breastfeeds.

COMING HOME

As your baby's discharge date approaches, she will probably be breastfeeding several times a day, in addition to drinking expressed milk and/or premature-infant formula by bottle. Deciding how often and how long to breastfeed, how much additional milk to offer your baby, how closely to monitor your baby's weight, how to wean from a nipple shield, and how to taper off pumping can make the transition to full breastfeeding feel quite daunting. Fortunately your lactation consultant and pediatrician can help you navigate this passage, and using an accurate, in-home scale can reassure you about your baby's weight gain as you gradually move toward full breastfeeding at home. Plan to room-in at the hospital with your baby, breastfeed on demand, and provide most of her care for a day or two before you take her home.

Making the Transition to Full Breastfeeding

Many mothers choose to rent accurate, user-friendly, electronic infant scales (see Chapter 3, page 74; Chapter 4, page 90; Chapter 8, pages 227–228; and Resources) so they can track their baby's daily weight at home and periodically perform infant feeding test weights. Being able to tell how much milk your baby takes while nursing and following her weight gain closely can give you peace of mind and help you monitor her breastfeeding progress. The following suggestions can guide you—together with your baby's doctor and your lactation consultant—as you make the transition to fully breastfeeding your premature baby:

- If the amount of milk you pump every twenty-four hours exceeds the amount your baby drinks each day, you can expect to provide all the milk she needs. However, you can't assume that your baby will take enough milk by breastfeeding alone during the first weeks home from the hospital. Most likely, she will need to drink additional expressed milk after some breastfeeding sessions. Your baby's doctor may advise you to add a small amount of powdered post-discharge "enriched" formula to your expressed breastmilk or prescribe extra feedings of enriched post-discharge formula to provide the additional nutrients needed by premature infants for at least six months. Supplemental vitamins and iron also will be prescribed for your baby.

- During the first weeks at home, you can expect your premature infant to continue to show some immature feeding behaviors, such as not waking to feed, difficulty latching on, falling asleep early in the feeding, and irregular sleep patterns. Breastfeeding will continue to require extra effort and patience. Gradually, as your baby matures and gains weight, she will learn to nurse more efficiently. However, it will take additional time before she is able to get all

her nutrition from breastfeeding alone.

- Your baby will need to feed at least eight times every twenty-four hours. Don't expect her to nurse at exactly three-hour intervals, however. How often she nurses and how much she takes may vary from feeding to feeding. She should have a wet diaper with every feeding and at least one bowel movement each day (several each day if she is less than one month old).

- Your baby will probably drink more milk nursing from both breasts at a feeding than from one side. Switch sides when her sucking and swallowing slow down (usually after about ten to fifteen minutes), and let her nurse as long as desired on the second side. Some babies do better nursing from a single breast at each feeding, however. The entire nursing session should not exceed about thirty minutes.

- Don't let your baby waste valuable energy by frequently sucking a pacifier until you are confident that she is obtaining enough milk by nursing. Sucking on a pacifier could limit how well and how often she breastfeeds.

- Ideally you will have a generous milk supply and produce at least 50 percent more milk than your baby needs to drink each day. This surplus will help your baby get milk more easily when she nurses. Although you will be eager to discontinue the inconvenience of pumping, it is crucial that you keep expressing your extra milk after most nursings. Your electric breast pump will remove milk from your breasts more efficiently than your premature baby. If your breasts do not get well drained regularly, your milk supply will diminish and your baby will have to work harder to remove milk when breastfeeding. You can gradually taper your pumping once your baby is gaining weight well with breastfeeding alone.

Following Up at Your Pediatrician's Office

You will need to stay in close contact with your baby's doctor as you make the transition from partial to full breastfeeding in the first weeks after hospital discharge. Your baby should be weighed and examined a few days after going home and twice weekly as long as you are making feeding changes. In the first several months, your baby should gain about an ounce a day if she is drinking plenty of milk.

Breastfeeding Twins and Triplets

The number of multiple births in the United States has increased 70 percent since 1980, with one multiple in every thirty-four babies. New fertility treatments are the main explanation for the increase in multiple births. Another reason is that more women are having babies at an older age, when more eggs are released during the menstrual cycle.

Breastfeeding is far more challenging for mothers of twins and higher multiples than for mothers of single infants. However, nursing twins is certainly possible and can be very rewarding. Breastfeeding triplets also can be accomplished—and a few women have even nursed higher multiples, at least for several months. To succeed at breastfeeding more than one baby, you need to be highly motivated and have a strong support system, since one of the greatest obstacles in the early weeks is sheer exhaustion.

Tip

In the long run, breastfeeding twins can be more convenient than using formula because your babies can be fed simultaneously without any preparation and with less disruption at night. Getting off to a successful start is no easy matter, however. Statistics show that mothers of twins are less likely to start or to continue nursing their babies compared to mothers of single babies.

THE CHALLENGES OF NURSING MULTIPLES

Breastfeeding twins and triplets is a great deal more challenging than nursing a single infant for many reasons. For example, there is an increased risk that the babies will be born smaller and earlier than usual. At least half of all twins and 90 percent of all triplets are born early. Often delivery occurs before you have had a chance to attend a prenatal class on breastfeeding, so you may lack knowledge about even routine aspects of breastfeeding. If you are the mother of twins you may have pregnancy complications and will probably have a cesarean birth. Your babies may need special care that delays the start of breastfeeding or require supplemental feedings for low blood sugar or other medical concerns. You will need extra help in guiding each of your babies to learn to nurse correctly. This is especially important because if both infants do not nurse vigorously and regularly, you may not establish a milk supply sufficient to nourish them.

It really does take "a village" to get your babies off to a healthy start, even under the best of circumstances, so now is the time to muster the troops. Helpers can bring your babies to you for nursing and assist with positioning, burping, and changing. Breastfeeding can be extremely time-consuming during the early weeks when your babies are learning to nurse effectively and may need to be fed individually. Fortunate is the woman whose partner, extended family, and friends are committed to helping her babies glean all the health benefits of breastfeeding. Remember too that most hospital wards and NICUs are well equipped to help you get started breastfeeding, even if you have limited outside assistance.

PRODUCING ENOUGH MILK FOR YOUR BABIES

There is no doubt that some women are capable of producing sufficient milk to nourish two, three, and even four infants. On the other hand, some women who attempt to nurse multiples will not have enough milk. Fortunately you can take steps in the early days after delivery to establish a generous supply and avoid the frustrating problem of low milk.

Because feeding problems are so common among babies born early or small, mothers of multiples are advised to begin "prevention pumping" with a hospital-grade electric pump. (See Chapter 6, page 145–146.) The extra milk you express can be used to supplement your babies until they are nursing well. The goal is to establish and maintain a generous milk supply from the start, even if your babies do not yet nurse effectively or take all the milk you make. As your babies grow, mature, and drink more breastmilk, you can gradually taper your use of the breast pump until you no longer need to express extra milk. You will want to work with a lactation consultant, who can tailor your breastfeeding plan to meet your babies' unique needs.

TIPS FOR NURSING TWINS

Because twin infants often nurse from one breast at each feeding, twins can be expected to breastfeed at closer intervals than single babies (at least nine times daily). When first learning to nurse your twins, you will probably need several pillows to make yourself comfortable and to position your babies properly. A well-cushioned sofa, wide overstuffed chair, or bed will allow you ample room to practice different holds. (Never sleep with your babies on a sofa or chair, as this greatly increases their risk of SIDS! See Chapter 5.) Several pillows specially designed for nursing twins are available in stores and online. (See Resources.)

You might wonder whether you should assign each baby the same breast at each feeding. Although same-breast nursing might reduce the risk of one infant spreading germs to the other, it is virtually futile to try to keep twins from sharing the same germs. Actually, it is advantageous to alternate breasts when nursing twins to ensure that each breast receives balanced stimulation from both babies. If one baby breastfeeds less effectively than the other, it is especially important for the vigorous baby to nurse on both sides throughout the day to keep your milk supply balanced.

Twins can be nursed simultaneously or separately. In the beginning, you will probably find that it takes both hands just to get one twin latched on correctly. Nursing the babies

separately allows you to get to know and form a unique bond with each one. As soon as both babies are breastfeeding well, you will inevitably nurse your babies simultaneously at times, either out of necessity or convenience. At first you will need help from another person to handle and position both infants to nurse them at the same time. You may prefer to nurse your babies separately during the day to interact with them individually, and nurse them simultaneously at night to save time.

Separate Cue-Based Feedings

Nursing each of your babies individually, based on each of their feeding cues—signs they give you that they're hungry and ready to be nursed (see Chapter 3, pages 57, 66)—has the important advantage of allowing you to give each baby your full attention during feedings. Besides, a baby who is ready to eat is likely to nurse better than one who has been awakened for feeding. In addition, you'll have both hands free to position your baby and can focus on the unique personality and feeding style of one baby at a time. Although individual cue-based feedings are more time-consuming, feeding each baby separately is an excellent way to form a unique attachment with each infant.

Modified Cue-Based Feedings

For many mothers, the most practical way to feed multiples is to nurse the first baby who gives feeding cues. Immediately afterward, the second twin is gently awakened to nurse. Feeding your babies consecutively will buy you a little more time between feedings in which to get rest and restore your energies. The main drawback to this method, however, is that your second baby may be difficult to wake up and may not nurse as well as the first twin.

Simultaneous Nursing

Nursing your babies at the same time has the benefit of saving time and allowing the more vigorous baby to trigger the letdown reflex for the smaller twin. In addition, nursing twins simultaneously may actually stimulate increased milk production. On the other hand, some mothers feel that nursing their twins at the same time doesn't allow them to give each of their babies enough individual attention. (It is also hard to simultaneously nurse two babies discreetly in public.)

With simultaneous nursing, the hungrier baby sets the pace. When one baby is ready to eat, the second twin is awakened to nurse. You can try a variety of positions for nursing simultaneously, including a football or cradle hold, or a football-cradle combination. (See Chapter 3, pages 49–50, for details about each of these nursing positions.)

Doing What Works

In many instances, mothers of twins find they are unable to nurse both babies exclusively. If your supply is low, you may choose to alternately nurse one baby and feed formula to the other. Or, if your babies have persistent difficulty latching-on or breastfeeding effectively, you may decide to predominantly express your milk and feed it by bottle. Each mother's circumstances and challenges are unique, and you can personalize your breastfeeding experience to meet your own and your babies' needs. A lactation consultant may be able to help you increase your milk supply or improve your babies' breastfeeding effectiveness.

BREASTFEEDING TRIPLETS

Although it is far more difficult than breastfeeding twins, some women have nursed triplets successfully, and a few have produced enough milk to nourish four or more babies for several months. In addition to the obvious challenges of near-continuous feedings and phenomenal milk requirements, breastfeeding of higher multiples is further complicated by the fact that

Nursing twins simultaneously using the football and cradle hold

the babies are usually born prematurely and are hospitalized with special health needs. If you have triplets, you can nurse two of your babies simultaneously, then allow your third to breastfeed from both sides. Rotate which baby nurses last, to make sure that he or she gains the benefits of nursing from your breasts when they are their fullest. In reality, most mothers of three or more infants end up working out a combination of breast- and bottle feeding. For quadruplets, two infants can be breastfed while the other two are fed by bottle. The infant(s) who receive bottles are rotated so each baby breastfeeds the same number of times daily. As a practical matter, mothers who have three or more babies simply breastfeed as often as they are able and bottle-feed as often as necessary. Mothers who use a breast pump to drain any remaining milk after nursing can use the expressed milk for some of the bottle feedings.

Breastfeeding Babies with Chronic Medical Problems

Some infants have medical conditions that impact their ability to breastfeed. Like premature babies and multiples, these infants require a special feeding plan and close monitoring of their growth.

CLEFT LIP AND/OR CLEFT PALATE

Cleft lip and cleft palate (roof of the mouth) are common birth defects that can cause multiple complications, including significant feeding difficulties, frequent ear infections with possible hearing loss, dental abnormalities, and speech and language problems. A cleft defect results very early in fetal development when the tissues of the face or mouth do not close together normally. Cleft lip and cleft palate (oral-facial clefts) can occur separately or in combination and can be present on one or both sides of the face. A cleft lip can range from a small notch in the upper lip on one side to a complete gap, involving the upper gum and lip and extending into the bottom of the nose. Cleft palate can involve only the soft palate at the back of the roof of the mouth, or the gap can extend forward to include the hard palate, thus affecting the entire length of the roof of the mouth. In most cases, an oral-facial cleft is an isolated birth defect. In some instances, however, other birth defects are also present. Consequently all babies with oral-facial clefts must be screened carefully for the presence of other abnormalities.

Medical Problems Associated with Cleft Lip and/or Cleft Palate

Children with cleft lip and/or cleft palate require an extensive program of care involving many medical experts who work together as a team, including specialists in pediatrics; plastic surgery; dentistry; speech and language development; hearing; as well as ear, nose, and throat specialists. A cleft palate support group can be the source of enormous information and support if you are the parent of a child with cleft lip or palate. (See Resources.)

The most immediate problem for a baby with a cleft defect is difficulty feeding. You may be able to find a lactation consultant with special knowledge and expertise working with these babies. An infant with only a cleft lip may be able to nurse effectively since your breast tissue can fill the gap and allow your baby to create a seal with her mouth on your breast. Special positioning techniques may increase breastfeeding effectiveness. Because infants with a cleft palate cannot compress their mother's breast against the roof of their mouth or create an adequate seal to generate suction, these babies rarely are able to breastfeed effectively. Even feeding with a bottle is difficult and the babies choke and gag easily. Most babies do well using a soft squeeze bottle and long cross-cut nipple.

Feeding a Baby with Cleft Palate

A small plastic palatal plate, also called an obturator, is a made-to-fit oral prosthesis for infants with cleft palate. The obturator creates an artificial palate, separating your baby's mouth from her nose passages. With the palatal obturator in place, feeding by breast or bottle may be easier for a baby with cleft palate, and in some cases, effective breastfeeding may eventually be possible. However, the plate must be cleaned regularly and re-fitted often as your baby grows. Although an obturator may help your baby breastfeed, you will probably need to give supplemental milk by bottle.

Early "practice sessions" at the breast provide important comfort and skin-to-skin contact and may help your baby eventually learn to take some milk with breastfeeding. The most accurate way to tell whether your baby with cleft lip or cleft palate is able to take any milk by breastfeeding is to weigh her before and after a breastfeeding session, a procedure known as test weighing. (For more information about test weights, see Chapter 8, page 227–228.) Because feeding can be so difficult for babies with cleft defects, you would be wise to rent an electronic infant scale to closely monitor your baby's weight at home or measure how much she drinks during breastfeeding attempts. (See Chapter 3, page 74; Chapter 8, pages 227–228; and Resources.) Weighing your baby between medical visits can help you know whether she is getting enough to eat. Proper nutrition is especially important during the early months of life, when babies typically gain weight most rapidly.

Providing Breastmilk for Babies with Cleft Palate

If your baby has cleft palate, she will not be able to nurse well enough to keep your milk supply abundant. Yet your breastmilk is the best possible food for her and may help protect her from chronic ear infections. To provide milk for her feedings, you'll want to use a hospital-grade double electric pump to establish a generous milk supply. Fortunately the pump rental fee is usually covered by medical insurance with a physician prescription. Once your supply is well-established, you may be able to maintain your milk production using a highly effective, daily-use double electric pump. Using a special bottle that your baby "milks" with her tongue and jaws instead of sucking can help her to get milk more effectively and ensure that she grows properly. (See Resources.) With an abundant milk supply and a thriving baby, you can start working with a lactation consultant to explore

Note: Corrective surgery for cleft lip can be performed within weeks of your baby's birth, and usually by three months of age. Cleft palate repair may be delayed at least six months, or as long as eighteen months. Ordinarily breastfeeding can begin immediately after cleft lip repair and within one day following cleft palate repair. Some babies will need other procedures over time. The commitment to express milk for your baby, who may never be able to breastfeed effectively, represents a true labor of love. Some mothers pump so much milk that they are able to continue feeding expressed breastmilk to their baby for months after they stop pumping.

special breastfeeding positions and techniques that might enable your baby to take some milk with breastfeeding.

DOWN SYNDROME

Down syndrome is one of the most common genetic birth defects. It is caused by extra genetic material from chromosome 21. The condition is also known as Trisomy 21 because people who are born with Down syndrome have three number 21 chromosomes. Although the incidence of Down syndrome increases with the age of the mother, most babies with Down syndrome are born to mothers under the age of thirty-five, because younger women have more babies. Children with Down syndrome have varying degrees of delayed development, short stature, a characteristic facial appearance, and low muscle tone. Many babies with Down syndrome are also born with a heart defect or serious abnormality of the intestinal tract or develop vision and hearing loss or low thyroid.

Because babies with Down syndrome are highly prone to infections, the protective effects of breastmilk can be especially important for them. The intimacy and tranquillity of breastfeeding may help you form a special bond with your exceptional baby. Breastfeeding also helps tone and strengthen your baby's facial muscles and improves her mouth and tongue coordination. Just like every other baby, your baby with Down syndrome will benefit from the skin-to-skin contact and social stimulation that breastfeeding provides.

Because babies with Down syndrome have low muscle tone and tire easily with feedings, breastfeeding can be challenging for both you and your little one. She may be placid and need to be roused for feedings; in that case, frequent, shorter feedings are often more effective. To help your baby get milk with less effort, you can use breast massage and hand expression to trigger your letdown before latching her on and perform breast compressions while she nurses. (See Chapter 4, page 96.) Many infants with Down syndrome have a small mouth and lower jaw, making it difficult for them to grasp the breast correctly. Your baby may benefit from using a nipple shield initially. (See Chapter 3, page 64.) Sucking pressures and patterns are less efficient in babies with Down syndrome than in other infants. Your baby may have trouble coordinating sucking, swallowing, and breathing while feeding. A lactation consultant can suggest special positioning techniques to help elevate your baby's head during feedings to reduce gagging and to compensate for her low muscle tone. By supporting her body well and providing extra chin and jaw support, your baby can conserve energy and breastfeed more effectively.

To establish an abundant milk supply, begin prevention pumping with a hospital-grade electric breast pump shortly after delivery. (See Chapter 6, pages 145–146.) Fortunately the cost of renting a super-efficient hospital-grade pump may be covered by medical insurance. Keeping your milk supply generous will help your baby get milk more easily during nursing sessions. If necessary, your expressed milk can be used to supplement your baby's intake until she learns to nurse effectively. You may want to rent an electronic scale to monitor your baby's weight at home until she is feeding and gaining well. (See Resources.) From time to time, you can also perform infant feeding test weights to evaluate your baby's progress with breastfeeding. (See Chapter 3, page 74, and Chapter 8, pages 227–228.) Of course, a scale is not a substitute for close follow-up and monitoring by your baby's physician, so do make sure that she sees her doctor regularly.

Tip

Over time, with practice and patience, many babies with Down syndrome are able to breastfeed effectively. As a parent, you can benefit enormously from the empowering information and strengthening support available through the National Down Syndrome Congress and National Down Syndrome Society. For more information, see Resources.

Breastfeeding When You or Your Baby Is Unwell

Because routine breastfeeding can span many months and even years, you can expect that you and your baby will have several illnesses while you are breastfeeding. While some illnesses may require special breastfeeding management, it is unlikely that you will ever have a medical condition that is incompatible with breastfeeding. However, if you have a significant illness such as a breast abscess or tuberculosis, your doctor as well as your baby's physician need to be aware of the problem and collaborate on breastfeeding recommendations. In some instances, you can obtain expert advice by contacting individual medical specialists, such as infectious disease experts, or the Centers for Disease Control and Prevention or La Leche League International Center for Breastfeeding Information. (See Resources.)

IF YOUR BABY HAS A MINOR ILLNESS

Although it is well known that your breastmilk helps protect your baby from many illnesses, she may still suffer from occasional colds, ear infections, diarrhea, vomiting, and other minor illnesses. Breastmilk is an ideal food for a sick baby. It provides essential fluids and is easily digested. In addition, the breastfeeding relationship is a valuable source of comfort and solace for a sick, uncomfortable baby.

In the past, doctors commonly recommended discontinuing milk feedings and giving babies only clear liquids during bouts of vomiting and diarrhea. Today, mothers of infants with stomach or intestinal illness are encouraged to continue breastfeeding because breastmilk is well absorbed and does not aggravate diarrhea. With vomiting, babies should drink small amounts often. With diarrhea, babies can usually handle larger feedings. If an oral rehydration solution is required to treat your baby's dehydration, it can be offered in addition to nursing.

Your baby's normal breastfeeding routines may be disrupted during a minor illness. For example, she may nurse more often than usual, preferring to be comforted at the breast for prolonged periods. A fussy baby or sleepy baby with an ear infection may nurse less vigorously or less frequently than normal. If you suspect that your baby is not draining your breasts well, you should express milk remaining after nursing to prevent breast engorgement and a decline in your milk supply.

WHEN YOUR BABY IS IN THE HOSPITAL

Your baby may require hospitalization for a variety of reasons, such as a serious infection, accident, minor or major surgery, or other treatment. Fortunately most pediatric wards allow parents to remain with their children at all times. Rooms may have sofas or pull-down beds to accommodate you overnight. Continued breastfeeding not only provides your baby with easily digested nutrients, it also provides pain relief when blood must be drawn and serves to calm and comfort her after necessary procedures. Breastfeeding also provides a sense of security and reassurance in unfamiliar surroundings.

If your baby's food intake is restricted, you might ask whether you could "comfort nurse" her after first expressing your milk with a breast pump. She will likely get only a trickle of milk when she nurses after you've pumped. If your baby is having surgery, find out when you need to discontinue breastfeeding prior to surgery and how soon she can nurse afterward. Whenever your baby is not able to breastfeed routinely, plan to express your milk to maintain a generous supply.

One of the most distressing aspects of your baby's hospitalization is the uncomfortable sense of near-total dependence on the care and expertise of others. Being able to nourish and comfort your baby by breastfeeding allows you to provide for your infant in a way no nurse or doctor possibly can.

BREASTFEEDING WHEN YOU HAVE A MINOR ILLNESS

You can continue to breastfeed while experiencing common illnesses like colds, sore throats, sinus infections, bronchitis,

> **Tip**
>
> Don't skip meals or neglect to drink enough fluids while you stay with your baby at the hospital. Ask the nurses if you can arrange to receive meal trays, fruit juice, or snacks. Most pediatric wards have family kitchens with a communal refrigerator or microwave where you can store and prepare some convenient meals.

> **Tip**
>
> If you take any prescribed or over-the-counter medications to treat your illness, ask your doctor about their transfer into your breastmilk and whether they pose any risk to your nursing baby. (For more information about the transfer of medications into breastmilk, see Chapter 8, pages 215-218. Be aware that some nursing mothers have reported a decrease in their milk supply when they take pseudoephedrine.)

diarrhea, or urinary tract infections. In most cases, by the time you develop symptoms, your baby has already been exposed to the germ that's caused your illness. Interrupting breastfeeding at this point is counterproductive since antibodies to the germ causing your illness will appear in your milk and help protect your baby from getting sick. With any illness, it is important to wash your hands thoroughly before handling your breasts or your baby.

If you are not feeling well, be sure to get extra rest and drink plenty of liquids, especially when your fluid requirements are increased because of fever, diarrhea, vomiting, or runny nose. For a few days, make your top priorities breastfeeding and resting; other responsibilities can wait until you are feeling better. Although your milk supply might temporarily decline during your illness, it should increase again once you recover, especially with frequent nursing. If you have reserves of frozen breastmilk, you can temporarily supplement your baby with your expressed milk, if needed.

SERIOUS INFECTIOUS DISEASES

Occasionally a serious infection in a breastfeeding mother can pose a threat to her nursing baby. In some cases, such as human immunodeficiency virus (HIV), the infecting organism is present in breastmilk and can be passed to your baby through breastfeeding. In other instances, such as active tuberculosis, infection is spread by close physical contact between you and your baby and is not passed in breastmilk. Unfortunately health professionals often have insufficient information about the transmission of infections by breastfeeding. The Committee on Infectious Diseases of the American Academy of Pediatrics publishes and updates a thick red paperback reference for their members, known as the *Red Book*. This valuable physicians' resource answers many questions about more than one hundred infectious diseases and often includes information about whether breastfeeding is recommended. The Infectious Diseases department at your local children's hospital is another excellent source of up-to-date information about the risk of transmitting infectious diseases through breastmilk.

HIV

The most serious and well-publicized infection that poses a risk to nursing babies is human immunodeficiency virus (HIV). HIV has been detected in the breastmilk of infected women, and cases have been documented throughout the world in which HIV has been transmitted from mother to baby through breastfeeding. But in certain parts of the developing world, the risk of infant death from malnutrition and infectious diseases as a result of *not* breastfeeding may outweigh the risk of acquiring HIV through breastfeeding. In these cases, breastfeeding by an HIV-infected mother is currently recommended by the World Health Organization. In the United States, however, infectious diseases and malnutrition are not major causes of infant death, and feeding infant formula is a safe alternative to breastfeeding. The American Academy of Pediatrics and the Centers for Disease Control and Prevention do *not* recommend that women in the United States breastfeed or provide expressed milk for their infants if they are infected with HIV. With routine HIV testing every woman can know her HIV status and receive counseling about whether to breastfeed, and about methods to prevent acquiring and transmitting HIV.

> **Tip**
>
> If you are pregnant and test positive for HIV, you can receive new antiretroviral medicines that greatly reduce the risk of passing the infection to your newborn baby and will help you stay healthier longer.

Tuberculosis

Tuberculosis (TB) is a chronic bacterial infection that usually affects the lungs. Women with active TB are highly contagious to their babies. Although the disease is passed by respiratory droplets and not by breastmilk, infected mothers should not breastfeed (or even be around their infants) until they have been treated and are no longer contagious (usually a few

weeks after treatment is started). Meanwhile, an infected mother can pump and collect her milk for her baby's feedings until the two of them can safely be reunited. The drugs used to treat TB are excreted into breastmilk, but most are compatible with breastfeeding. Babies of infected mothers also need treatment. Breastfeeding is permissible for women with a previously positive tuberculin skin test, but without evidence of the disease.

> **Tip**
>
> If you previously had a negative tuberculin skin test, but recently tested positive, you should be evaluated for active disease before you begin or continue breastfeeding.

Hepatitis

Hepatitis is a viral infection of the liver that can cause fever, jaundice, loss of appetite, nausea, and fatigue. The three major types—there are a total of five—of hepatitis are known as hepatitis A virus (HAV), hepatitis B virus (HBV), and hepatitis C virus (HCV). You should inform your baby's doctor if you have been diagnosed with acute hepatitis or if a blood test confirms that you are a carrier of chronic hepatitis. In most cases, however, a mom who is a chronic carrier can still breastfeed.

HAV. Hepatitis A usually causes a mild illness and does not become chronic. The virus is shed in human feces and is easily passed from person to person due to poor hand-washing habits. Food-borne and water-borne epidemics occur commonly, and the disease spreads easily from young children (who usually have few symptoms) to adult workers in child-care centers, especially when diapered children are present. A mother with HAV may continue breastfeeding. However, her baby should receive a shot of gamma globulin (to boost her immunity temporarily) and the hepatitis A vaccine. Routine vaccination of all infants with hepatitis A vaccine is recommended between twelve and twenty-three months of age.

HBV. Hepatitis B can cause illness ranging from minimal symptoms to chronic liver disease or death. HBV is passed through blood or body fluids, for example, by sexual activity or a contaminated needle. Transmission by a blood transfusion is now rare in the United States due to current screening and handling procedures. Although HBV has been found in human milk, infants born to mothers who test positive for HBV are permitted to breastfeed as long as specific precautions are taken: All infants born to mothers infected with HBV should receive hepatitis B–specific immune globulin and their first vaccination against HBV immediately after birth. Two additional vaccine doses (at one to two months and again at six months) are necessary to complete the vaccine series and protect the baby. She should be tested at nine to eighteen months of age to see if the vaccine worked and make sure she was not infected with HBV during the birth process.

HCV. Hepatitis C tends to cause mild disease, but persistent infection is common. Up to half of patients with HCV will develop chronic liver disease, and some will get liver cancer. The virus is passed by blood, and transmission by sexual activity occurs rarely. Little data is available on which to base a recommendation about breastfeeding when a mother has chronic HCV. At this writing, breastmilk has not been proven to transmit HCV, and according to the Centers for Disease Control and Prevention, breastfeeding is permissible for mothers infected with HCV. However, if blood (for example, from a cracked nipple) is present in breastmilk, the mother should temporarily pump and discard her milk. She can resume breastfeeding when her nipples have healed and blood is no longer present. Consult your doctor and your baby's doctor to decide whether breastfeeding is recommended in your individual case.

Herpes

Herpes simplex virus (HSV) causes oral cold sores (sores in your mouth) and genital herpes infections. If you have an active herpes infection, either oral or genital, you can pass the herpes virus to your baby if she comes into direct contact with the sores. Young babies can become very seriously ill from herpes infections. To protect your baby, wash your hands thoroughly, before and after caring for her, and keep sores covered so that they do not come into contact with your baby. You may breastfeed her, so long as there are no herpes sores on your breasts and all sores elsewhere on your body are covered. If you or any of your baby's caretakers has active oral cold sores, you should not kiss or nuzzle your baby until all sores are crusted and dried. If you have herpes sores on your breasts you should not breastfeed on the affected side until the infection has cleared completely. Keep active sores covered to prevent your baby from contracting the virus. Pumping and discarding your milk from the affected breast will allow you to keep your supply up until your sores have healed.

CHRONIC ILLNESSES

If you have a chronic illness and are concerned about whether you can breastfeed your baby, you should discuss your plans with your baby's pediatrician, your obstetrician, and any other physicians and specialists who care for you. Be encouraged to know, however, that women with a wide variety of medical conditions— including diabetes, kidney transplant, heart disease, epilepsy, cystic fibrosis, inflammatory bowel disease, arthritis, lupus, multiple sclerosis, and physical limitations including blindness, deafness, and paraplegia—have breastfed successfully. In each instance, special guidance may be necessary to accommodate breastfeeding, such as a review of your medications, appropriate dietary changes, practical advice about breastfeeding issues, or assistance with nursing technique.

PSYCHIATRIC ILLNESSES

Women who suffer from mental health problems, such as depression, anxiety, bipolar illness, and schizophrenia, are often able to breastfeed successfully—while under the care of a psychiatrist or other mental health worker of course. Although psychotropic medications appear in breastmilk, many are present in only minimal amounts, and some are considered safer than others. The decision to take a psychiatric medication while breastfeeding should be made with your doctor, weighing the considerable benefits against the relative risks, and using the lowest effective dose while closely monitoring your baby.

Major depression is the most common psychiatric illness in new mothers—a condition that warrants the close care of mental health providers. Two common factors that play into women's depression are social isolation and limited sources of support. Generally new mothers who are depressed are less able to read their baby's cues and interpret their baby's needs, and they tend to breastfeed for a shorter period of time. Depressed mothers show less emotion, speak less, and play less when they interact with their baby. Young infants are incredibly sensitive to the emotions of their caregivers, and having a depressed mother can affect a baby's growth and development. (See Chapter 5, pages 121–124, for more information about postpartum depression.)

While depressed mothers should receive treatment, both for their own welfare and the sake of their baby, little information is available about the effects of antidepressants on infants of breastfeeding mothers. Commonly prescribed antidepressants and other psychiatric medications appear in breastmilk and are passed to the infant, and it is possible that daily exposure to these drugs might affect your newborn's behavior and development. On the other hand, the newest antidepressants, known as selective serotonin reuptake inhibitors (SSRIs), are remarkably effective, and some are considered relatively safe for breastfeeding. For example, only minimal amounts of sertraline (Zoloft) appear in breastmilk, and no untoward effects have been observed in breastfed infants of mothers taking sertraline. Blood levels in the small number of infants that have been studied are minimal or below the levels of detection. If you are depressed, talk with your doctor about taking an SSRI at the lowest effective dose, in addition to getting counseling and other support. Your baby's doctor can monitor your baby for any adverse effects and order a test to see if any medication is detected in her blood. (To learn about physician resources for information about medications and mothers' milk, see Chapter 8, page 217.)

HOSPITALIZATIONS

If you need to be hospitalized—whether for a medical problem, elective or emergency surgery, or because of an injury—you may be worried and stressed about how your baby is going to be fed and comforted in your absence. Fortunately many hospitals allow your baby to stay with you in your hospital room as long as an adult family member or support person stays with your baby at all times to attend to her needs. Ask your doctor whether the medications you are taking are safe for your breastfed baby. Fortunately only minimal amounts of general anesthetics pass into breastmilk. It is safe to breastfeed as soon as you are awake enough after surgery to do so. Most pain medications and antibiotics are compatible with breastfeeding. (See Chapter 8, pages 218.)

Even if you can't breastfeed your baby while you're hospitalized for a few days, you can resume breastfeeding when you get home. Meanwhile, your baby can drink any reserves of breastmilk you may have in the freezer (along with supplemental formula, if need be). Be sure to express your milk

Note: If you have scheduled an elective hospital procedure, you can begin days or weeks in advance to express, store, and stockpile milk so that your baby will have an ample supply, if the two of you are separated or if you must take a medication that temporarily prevents you from breastfeeding. A scheduled hospital stay also gives your baby time to learn to drink from a bottle or cup so that feedings don't turn into a crisis when she's separated from you.

regularly, however, to avoid breast engorgement and to maintain your supply. You can store your expressed milk for your baby's use later on, so long as the medications you take are compatible with breastfeeding.

Breastfeeding After a Breast Surgery

If you had cosmetic breast surgery in the past, you may have been unconcerned about breastfeeding at the time. Years later, however, you might have questions about the possible impact of breast surgery on your ability to breastfeed. If possible, contact your breast surgeon to learn the specific procedure that was performed, and ask whether your surgery is likely to interfere with breastfeeding.

BREAST AUGMENTATION

Generally women who get breast implants are advised that the surgery will not affect their ability to breastfeed. Certainly many women breastfeed successfully after breast augmentation. However, research confirms that breastfeeding women who have had augmentation surgery have an increased risk of insufficient milk compared with women who have not had implants. Here are some of the ways augmentation surgery may adversely impact breastfeeding:

Disruption of Milk Ducts

Breast augmentation can be performed through several types of surgical incisions. The most common sites are slightly above the crease where the breast attaches to the chest wall, along the margin of the areola, and in the armpit. The location of the incision is usually based on the surgeon's preference and experience, as well as your desires. During the operation, the surgeon attempts to avoid injury to the milk ducts. However, when the incision is made at the edge of the areola, damage to the ducts easily occurs. Cutting or damaging milk ducts can prevent milk flow from certain lobes (or sections) of the breast. This will decrease your chances of providing a full milk supply to your baby. A few days after giving birth, the milk glands in your breasts will fill with milk. However, milk production continues only in the lobes of your breasts that are well drained. Within a matter of days, milk glands that cannot drain start to dry up.

Nerve Damage

The nerve supply to the nipple not only allows normal sensation to the nipple area, it also plays an important role in triggering the hormone responses involved in breastfeeding. (See Chapter 4, pages 79–81.) Many women have a change in nipple sensitivity following breast surgery. You may have diminished or absent nipple sensitivity, or in some cases, the nipples become overly sensitive. Changes in nipple sensitivity following surgery suggest that the nerve supply to the nipple has been damaged. However, it is not known how such nerve damage affects the normal prolactin and oxytocin responses to breastfeeding. Although regrowth of nerves can occur, the process may be slow. Sometimes nerve regrowth causes hypersensitivity of the nipples that makes breastfeeding very uncomfortable.

Severe Postpartum Breast Engorgement

The presence of implants can cause increased breast "tightness" when your milk comes in and an

> **Note:** Many women worry that using a breast pump could rupture an implant. This is unlikely, since the pressure generated by a good quality daily-use or hospital-grade electric breast pump does not exceed the vacuum created by your baby when she nurses. Still, it makes sense to use your pump at the lowest vacuum level and gradually increase the amount of suction without causing discomfort.

exaggeration of normal breast engorgement symptoms. Early regular use of an effective double electric breast pump to express some of the milk remaining in your breasts after feedings will help get your milk to flow, soften your breasts, and stimulate a generous milk supply. Once excessive pressure is reduced and engorgement subsides, your baby should be able to remove milk easily by breastfeeding. Pumping after nursing gradually can be discontinued after a week or so.

BREAST REDUCTION SURGERY

Excessively large, heavy breasts can be physically and psychologically disabling for a woman. The condition tends to run in families, with rapid breast growth often beginning during the teenage years. Disproportionately large breasts can cause you to feel self-conscious, limit your physical activity or athletic participation, and make it difficult to find clothing that fits well. In addition, large breasts often cause physical complaints, such as muscle strain

Underdeveloped Tubular Breasts

Sometimes women choose to have breast augmentation surgery because of a problem with breast development, such as tubular-shaped breasts. Tubular breasts are less full and rounded and have a more elongated shape. (See Chapter 2, pages 29–30.) They may have fewer milk glands, which are concentrated beneath the nipple and areola. Some women with tubular-shaped breasts have difficulty producing enough milk for their baby. Before attributing breastfeeding problems to breast implant surgery, consider whether breast augmentation was performed to correct a breast variation that might have impacted breastfeeding.

and neck and upper-back pain, bra strap pressure marks, breast pain, and irritation of the skin where the lower breast attaches to the chest.

Many women with excessively large breasts choose to have a breast reduction procedure to achieve smaller, more comfortable, shapelier breasts that are more proportionate to the rest of their body. During the surgery, excessive breast tissue and skin are removed, the breasts are reshaped, and the nipples are repositioned at a higher level. Sometimes the nipples are removed and reattached during the procedure. In most cases, the nipples are repositioned without being removed.

Breast reduction surgery is more disruptive than augmentation procedures and carries an increased likelihood of nerve or

Tips for Breastfeeding After Breast Surgery

•Get the best possible start breastfeeding your baby in the hospital. (See Chapter 3, page 44-46.) Hold her skin-to-skin often and offer your breast frequently.

•Inform the hospital lactation consultant and your baby's doctor about your breast surgery and arrange to have your infant's weight monitored closely after hospital discharge. Consider renting an electronic infant scale to use at home until feedings are going well and your baby is gaining weight steadily.

•Begin "prevention pumping" after your baby nurses to help maximize your milk supply during the first postpartum weeks. (See Chapter 6, page 145-146.) The milk you express can be used to supplement your baby, if necessary.

•Observe your baby's feeding behaviors for signs that she is drinking milk. (See Chapter 4, pages 84-89.) Keep a daily record of your baby's feedings, bowel movements, and wet diapers. Notice when your milk comes in and whether both breasts soften after your baby nurses.

•Schedule an appointment with a lactation consultant (or your baby's doctor) when your baby is approximately four days old and your milk has come in. The lactation consultant can evaluate your breastfeeding technique and your breast changes with feeding. She can assess your infant's weight and perform a test-weighing procedure to tell how much milk your baby is able to drink when she breastfeeds. By four days of age, your full-term baby should be able to take about two ounces of milk at a feeding. The lactation consultant can evaluate your milk production in each breast and suggest modifications in your breastfeeding routines. The information from this early visit will help you know whether your milk supply is likely to meet your baby's needs or whether supplemental formula will be necessary.

duct damage. (See pages 283–284.) Absent or diminished nipple sensitivity may result, and damage to milk ducts may severely limit the amount of milk that is available to your baby. However, when women are informed before their surgery about their realistic chances of breastfeeding in the future, they usually report that their improved lifestyle, appearance, and comfort are sufficient compensation for their inability to breastfeed exclusively. Fortunately newer modifications in the surgical techniques for reduction breast surgery are giving more favorable results, with some women being able to breastfeed fully. Nevertheless, breast reduction surgery greatly increases your risk of not being able to provide all the milk your baby needs. For more information about breastfeeding after breast and nipple surgeries, visit www.bfar.org.

A PREVIOUS BREAST BIOPSY

On first consideration, a simple breast biopsy to diagnose breast cancer may not seem likely to have an effect on breastfeeding. However, a biopsy incision that is made around the areola may interfere with your ability to breastfeed by cutting through milk ducts, which prevents normal milk drainage. If the milk available from the biopsied breast is very low, your baby may not get enough milk to grow well. In some instances, generous milk production from the other breast will compensate for diminished milk on the biopsied side. Fortunately

newer ultrasound-guided needle biopsy techniques have reduced the need for surgical biopsy.

Breast Surgery While You're Still Nursing

Sometimes a breast biopsy or other breast surgery is necessary while you are still breastfeeding. As breastfeeding rates increase, these surgeries are becoming more common. Because there is so much extra blood flow to the breasts

Note: It is possible to wean from one breast while continuing to nurse on the other side. This is a good option if you are hesitant to give up breastfeeding but must wean from one breast for medical reasons, such as a breast abscess, chronic breast infections, or debilitating pain. Sometimes the "problem breast" produces much less milk than the healthy one, so weaning on that side has little impact on your baby's breastmilk intake. When your baby stops nursing on one side, that breast will begin drying up and gradually stop lactating, even though you continue to breastfeed on the other side. The length of time before milk production ceases can vary, depending on your milk supply and the age of your baby. Usually within a week or two, the unsuckled breast will produce little or no milk.

during pregnancy and lactation, operating on the breast is more difficult. Some physicians will ask you to wean your infant if breast surgery is needed. However, you may be reluctant to discontinue breastfeeding before you'd planned—unless it is absolutely necessary. Postponing required surgery until you've weaned is not an acceptable option, since prompt diagnosis and treatment of breast problems are essential, whether or not you are breastfeeding. Fortunately more surgeons are gaining experience operating on the breast during lactation, usually with good results.

Breastfeeding After Breast Cancer

While not common, pregnancy may occur after treatment for breast cancer. Many women who have lumpectomy and radiation therapy for breast cancer are in their childbearing years. If they later become pregnant, they may wonder whether breastfeeding is possible for them. Radiation therapy for breast cancer causes damage to milk glands and ducts, preventing normal lactation. If you conceive after receiving radiation therapy to your whole breast, the treated breast does not undergo normal pregnancy changes, and milk does not come in abundantly on that side after you deliver your baby. Typically only a few drops of milk are produced from the radiated breast, and your baby will quickly

lose interest in nursing on that side. However, nursing your baby from the breast that was not treated with radiation is still possible. In some cases, your baby may receive enough milk by nursing exclusively from the untreated side. Even if some supplemental formula is required, partial breastfeeding can be highly satisfying for you and beneficial to your baby.

Breastfeeding Through Pregnancy

Now that most women start breastfeeding and more succeed in nursing long term, some women are still breastfeeding when they discover that they are pregnant again. Although breastfeeding offers some protection against conceiving, especially during the first six months postpartum, it is certainly possible to become pregnant while nursing. If you are breastfeeding and learn you are pregnant, you may have questions, such as:

Q & A

Q: Do I have to wean because I am pregnant?

You may assume that it is not possible for your body to provide the considerable nutrient needs of a growing fetus at the same time you are nursing another infant. In fact, pregnancy hormones cause your milk supply to decrease within weeks or months of conceiving. As your milk decreases in volume, it returns to a more colostrum-like composition, making it saltier and less sweet. As the amount of milk decreases and the taste changes, your nursing baby may self-wean. If you're breastfeeding a toddler when you become pregnant, your baby is already eating other foods, drinking from a cup, and can tell you when she is hungry. In all likelihood you will not place your youngster at a significant nutritional risk if she receives less milk when you nurse her. On the other hand, if you conceive while nursing your two-month old, the resulting drop in milk supply could affect her weight gain, unless she receives supplemental formula.

Q: Can I continue to nurse my older baby, even after my new infant is born?

You may choose to nurse both babies after you give birth. Breastfeeding two siblings who are not twins is known as *tandem nursing*. It will require a great deal of understanding and patience on your part to meet the unique needs of nursing two babies at different developmental stages. For example, your older baby may be jealous of the new baby and compete for nursing privileges. While care must be taken to assure that the younger baby has first access to your milk supply, a vigorously nursing older sibling may prove helpful in stimulating generous milk production! Tandem nursing, like nursing twins, can be extremely demanding and a very physical experience, leaving you "touched out" by the end of the day.

Q: Can breastfeeding during pregnancy cause premature labor?

Oxytocin, the hormone that causes milk letdown during breastfeeding, is the same hormone that causes the uterus to contract during labor. In the early months of pregnancy, the uterus does not react to oxytocin, but by mid-pregnancy, oxytocin *does* cause contractions of the uterus. So, yes, it is possible that breastfeeding throughout your pregnancy could trigger premature labor due to frequent oxytocin release. This risk should be of particular concern to you if you have had a high-risk pregnancy before—if you have had a previous premature birth, for example, or are carrying multiples. Although no studies confirm this link, it would be wise for you to stop nursing by mid-pregnancy if you are at risk for an early delivery.

Q: Will my developing baby be harmed if I continue to breastfeed?

So long as nursing through your pregnancy doesn't trigger premature labor, your unborn baby will not be harmed. The amount of milk you produce decreases dramatically early in pregnancy, and the small amount you continue to produce should not keep your developing baby from getting all the nutrients she needs. Of course you should eat a healthy diet, and your doctor will closely monitor your weight to ensure that you gain a normal amount during your pregnancy.

Q: If I decide to nurse through my pregnancy, will my new baby still get colostrum?

Yes, your newborn will receive all the special health benefits of colostrum during the first few days after you deliver. Your milk will then "come in" again, within three days after giving birth, and surge in amount, as it gradually changes to plentiful mature milk.

BREAST CHANGES WHEN YOU'RE PREGNANT AND BREASTFEEDING

If you become pregnant while breastfeeding you may discover that your nipples, long accustomed to nursing, become extremely sensitive. This new onset of nipple tenderness is believed to be due to pregnancy hormones. Some women describe nursing during pregnancy as somewhat unpleasant or off-putting, and as their pregnancy progresses, they discover that it can also be tricky to find a comfortable nursing position. For some, these physical challenges prompt them to wean their older babies during their pregnancy. Weaning is usually not difficult, since your baby's interest in nursing often wanes as your milk gradually diminishes and tastes less sweet.

Relactation and Induced Lactation

Some women are able to start producing milk again after having weaned their children.

Re-establishing breastfeeding after an interruption is known as *relactation*. In developing societies, one often hears amazing stories of post-menopausal grandmothers who were able to nurse a grandchild after the infant's mother died in childbirth. Women have also been known to start producing milk again for an adopted infant, sometimes months or even years after having breastfed a biological child.

You may choose to relactate for a variety of reasons. For example, you may have weaned your baby and later regretted the decision. Perhaps you've discovered that your baby doesn't tolerate infant formula. Or, as the mother of a hospitalized premature infant, your milk supply may have dwindled following weeks of pumping, and now falls short of your baby's nutritional needs. In any case, you'll undoubtedly want to know if it is possible to "get your milk back." The short answer is yes, you may be able to relactate successfully and ultimately produce a full, or at least a partial, milk supply.

The production of breastmilk by a woman who has never been pregnant or has never previously nursed a baby is called *induced lactation*. Today many adoptive mothers have heard about induced lactation and are eager to know if they can produce milk and nurse a baby without having been pregnant.

Although relactation and induced lactation certainly are possible, it is difficult to predict how much milk you might produce. Relactation is generally more successful than attempts to induce lactation. Without ever having been pregnant, it is highly unlikely you will be able to produce a full milk supply, despite heroic efforts. However, if your breasts have experienced the hormonal influences of pregnancy, and particularly if you've previously breastfed, you can expect to produce more milk if you try to relactate than another woman who is attempting to induce lactation. Relactation is also more successful if you are still nursing your child, or have recently weaned, than if you have not breastfed for many months or years.

If you have never been pregnant and want to breastfeed your adopted baby, however, keep your focus on your new relationship rather than on how much milk you produce. Any breastmilk you are able to provide for your baby should be viewed as a bonus.

TIPS TO RELACTATE OR INDUCE MILK PRODUCTION

The amount of milk produced varies widely among mothers who have tried relactation or induced lactation. Even under the best of circumstances, your baby probably will require supplemental formula in addition to the milk you produce. The emphasis should be on forging a close, enduring bond with your baby through your nursing relationship. Your baby should be closely monitored to make sure she is getting enough nutrition and gaining a healthy amount of weight. Infant feeding test weights will show you how much milk your baby

actually takes while breastfeeding. You can also measure the amount you are able to pump to get an idea how much your baby might drink when she nurses. (See Chapter 8, page 227–228.) This information can provide a guide for how much supplemental milk your baby may need. Meanwhile, try some of these tips to help stimulate milk production:

- **Use a breast pump.**
  The most important requirement for relactation or induced lactation is regular breast stimulation. For adoptive mothers, this can be achieved by using a hospital-grade double electric breast pump for ten to fifteen minutes every four hours or so for several weeks to several months before your baby arrives.

- **Breastfeed your baby.**
  Not only is breastfeeding more rewarding than pumping, it helps trigger additional milk production. However, your baby may have little interest in breastfeeding unless her efforts are rewarded by a flow of milk. An ideal way to encourage your baby to suckle when little milk is produced is to use the Supplemental Nursing System (SNS). (See Chapter 3, page 71; and Chapter 8, page 234.) The SNS device allows a baby to breastfeed while simultaneously receiving supplemental formula. Using the SNS enables you and your baby to experience the intimate breastfeeding relationship no matter how much milk you produce.

• **Use medications to raise your prolactin level.**
At present, no drugs are FDA-approved for the specific purpose of promoting relactation or inducing lactation, but several medications have a side effect of raising prolactin levels. Some of these drugs have been prescribed, with variable success, to stimulate milk production. In the United States, the most widely used medication to aid with relactation or induced lactation is metoclopramide, a drug commonly prescribed to treat reflux or combat nausea. (For more information, see Chapter 8, page 231.) Several studies have shown that metoclopramide raises prolactin levels and can increase milk production while you're taking it. Some prospective adoptive mothers take the medication for weeks before adoption is anticipated while pumping their breasts four or more times a day. However, the FDA recently issued a strong warning highlighting the risk of involuntary, repetitive movements of the body and face associated with long-term (usually longer than three months) or high-dose use of metoclopramide. (See Chapter 8, page 231.)

• **Use hormones to stimulate breast development.**
A few physicians temporarily prescribe combination birth control pills (containing both estrogen and progestin) to adoptive mothers waiting for a baby. These hormones, which are high during pregnancy, stimulate development of the milk glands and ducts. However, no research has confirmed the safety and effectiveness of hormonal therapies to try to induce milk production. Once your adopted baby arrives, the estrogen and progestin are stopped, to mimic the sudden decrease in pregnancy hormones after delivery. Meanwhile, you may continue to use a breast pump and take metoclopramide for several weeks, while your baby breastfeeds using the SNS device.

Resources

Breastfeeding Aids and Accessories

BabyChecker Scale

This lightweight, portable rental electronic infant scale is ideal for the accurate in-home monitoring of an infant's or toddler's weight. Not meant for measuring breastmilk intake. www.medela.com

BabyWeigh Scale

This lightweight, portable rental electronic infant scale is used to weigh a baby before and after breastfeeding to accurately measure breastmilk intake to 0.1 ounce. The scale weighs in grams or pounds and ounces. Ideal for both professional and home use. www.medela.com

Breast Pads (Hydrogel)

Soft hydrogel pads provide a moist healing environment and cool, soothing relief for severe sore nipples. The pads fit discreetly under a nursing bra and may be used from one to several days, depending on the brand. www.ameda.com; www.medela.com; www.soothies.com

Breast Pads (Non-absorbent)

Reusable LilyPadz are an innovative alternative to traditional nursing pads. Made of soft, flexible, and non-absorbent material, these pads conform to your breast, prevent leaking, and are virtually invisible under your clothing. Order online or use the Web site to locate a retailer near you. www.lilypadz.com

Breast Shells

Wearing breast shells can help draw out flat or inverted nipples or protect sore nipples. www.ameda.com; www.medela.com

Lanolin

Ameda's Lasinoh is a medical-grade, 100 percent ultra-pure lanolin that soothes and helps heal sore nipples. www.ameda.com

Medela's Tendercare Lanolin is a special, easy-to-apply, blended medical-grade lanolin that soothes and helps heal sore nipples.

Motherwear

Motherwear publishes a catalog exclusively for nursing mothers, and the Web site offers quality nursing clothing and products, as well as breastfeeding information. www.motherwear.com

Nipple Shields

Using an ultra-thin, flexible silicone nipple shield can help a newborn overcome latch-on difficulties. A nipple shield occasionally is used to cushion a sore nipple. www.medela.com; www.ameda.com

Nursing Pillows

The popular Boppy feeding and infant-support pillow provides essential support while breastfeeding to reduce strain on your arms, shoulders, and neck. The pillow also can be used to prop your baby on her back during tummy time or as she practices sitting. www.boppy.com

Double Blessings is a supplier of twin specialty products, including the EZ-2-Nurse Twins nursing pillow designed for nursing multiples. www.doubleblessings.com

SpecialNeeds Feeder

This feeding system is designed for babies with facial or oral problems that impair their ability to maintain adequate suction for feeding. The special feeder adjusts milk flow to match the baby's needs. www.medela.com

Supplemental Nursing System (SNS)

The SNS is a unique breastfeeding assistance kit that allows a mother to give necessary supplemental milk while the baby simultaneously breastfeeds. It is used for special breastfeeding challenges, such as low milk supply or infant suck problems. An economic Starter SNS is designed for short-term use. www.medela.com

Breastmilk Expression and Storage Supplies

Breastmilk Storage Bags

These durable breastmilk storage bags allow for the convenient and hygienic collection and storage of expressed breastmilk and maximize freezer space. www.lansinoh.com; www.medela.com; www.ameda.com

Disinfecting Products

Medela's quick-clean micro-steam bags allow you to disinfect your breast pump accessories, bottles, caps, nipples, and pacifiers in less than three minutes. The microwave steam cleaning process kills 99.9 percent of most harmful bacteria and germs. www.medela.com

Medela's quick-clean disinfectant wipes allow easy and convenient cleaning of breastshields, valves, and membranes without soap and water. www.medela.com

Easy Expression (Bustier or Halter) Hands-Free Pumping Bra

This patented hands-free pumping bra, worn while you pump, allows you conveniently to read, write, talk on the phone, or use a computer while pumping. Order online or use the Web site to locate a retailer near you. www.easyexpressionproducts.com

Breastfeeding Information and Peer Support

La Leche League International (LLLI)

LLLI is an international, nonprofit organization whose mission is to help mothers worldwide to breastfeed through mother-to-mother support, encouragement, information, and education. The Web site allows you to find a local LLL group or leader, read about a variety of breastfeeding topics, or submit your own question using an online help form. www.llli.org

National Conference of State Legislatures

Check whether your state has a law protecting public breastfeeding. www.ncsl.org/programs/health/breast50.htm

Nursing Mothers Counsel (NMC)

NMC is a nonprofit organization dedicated to helping mothers have a relaxed and happy feeding relationship with their babies by providing breastfeeding information and support. The Web site offers breastfeeding information and links to other resources. www.nursingmothers.org

Special Supplemental Nutrition Program for Women, Infants, and Children (WIC)

All pregnant women in the WIC Nutrition Program are educated about breastfeeding as the best way to feed their baby. Women who choose to breastfeed are provided counseling and support to ensure their success, and receive additional foods if they breastfeed exclusively. The Web site includes information about how to apply for WIC and provides breastfeeding promotional materials from WIC's Loving Support Makes Breastfeeding Work national breastfeeding campaign. Breastfeeding mothers enrolled in WIC can receive breast pumps, breast shells, or nursing supplements to help them overcome breastfeeding challenges and continue nursing. Many WIC agencies have peer counselor programs. www.fns.usda.gov/wic/

Hospital-Grade Breast Pumps

Medela

Medela manufactures hospital-grade, rental-quality electric breast pumps in addition to a variety of personal-use breast pumps and breastfeeding accessories to meet the unique needs of breastfeeding mothers. Order online or find local retailers of Medela products. The Web site has a wealth of breastfeeding information on a wide variety of topics. www.medela.com

Ameda

Ameda manufactures hospital-grade, rental-quality electric breast pumps in addition to a variety of personal-use breast pumps and breastfeeding accessories to meet the unique needs of breastfeeding mothers. Order online or find local retailers of Ameda products. The Web site has a wealth of breastfeeding information on a wide variety of topics. www.ameda.com

Lactation Consultants

Ameda

The Web site allows you to search for local retailers who sell Ameda pumps and products and also offers lactation consulting services. www.ameda.com

The Breastfeeding National Network (BNN)

BNN will help you locate Medela breast pumps and products and breastfeeding specialists in your area. http://medela.findlocation.com

International Lactation Consultant Association (ILCA)

ILCA is the professional association for International Board Certified Lactation Consultants (IBCLCs) and other health-care professionals who care for breastfeeding families. The Web site offers a list of lactation consultants with the IBCLC credential in your area. www.ilca.org

Medical and Health Organizations

The American Academy of Pediatrics (AAP)

The AAP is a sixty-thousand-member professional organization of U.S. pediatricians committed to the optimal physical, mental, and social health and well-being of infants, children, adolescents, and young adults. The AAP strongly recommends breastfeeding and educates its members about the benefits of human milk and best breastfeeding practices. The Web site includes information for parents on a variety of topics, including breastfeeding and human milk. www.aap.org

Baby-Friendly USA

The Baby-Friendly Hospital Initiative (BFHI) is a global program to encourage and recognize hospitals and birthing centers that offer an optimal level of care for breastfeeding mothers. Baby-Friendly USA is the nonprofit organization that implements the BFHI in the United States. www.babyfriendlyusa.org

Food Allergy and Anaphylaxis Network (FAAN)

FAAN is an excellent source of information, advocacy, and support for parents of children with food allergies. www.foodallergy.org

Human Milk Banking Association of North America (HMBANA)

HMBANA is the professional member association that sets the standards and guidelines for donor human milk banks in the United States, Canada, and Mexico. The Web site provides information about how to contact a milk bank to donate milk or order screened, processed donor human milk. www.hmbana.org

International Lactation Consultant Association (ILCA)

ILCA is the professional association for International Board Certified Lactation Consultants (IBCLCs) and other health-care professionals who care for breastfeeding families. ILCA has 4000 members from 50 nations. The Web site allows you to identify lactation consultants with the IBCLC credential in your area. www.ilca.org

World Health Organization (WHO)

In 2006, WHO published new international growth charts based solely on healthy breastfed babies. www.who.int/childgrowth/

Government Organizations

Centers for Disease Control and Prevention (CDC)

The CDC is committed to improving the public's health by increasing breastfeeding rates throughout the United States. The Web site provides information about national and state breastfeeding rates, answers frequently asked questions, and provides links to other breastfeeding resources. www.cdc.gov

Department of Health and Human Services Office on Women's Health (DHHS OWH)

DHHS OWH is the federal source for women's health information. The Web site offers online breastfeeding information, a breastfeeding helpline

staffed by peer counselors, and answers to common breastfeeding questions in both English and Spanish. www.4women.gov

Environmental Protection Agency (EPA)

The EPA Web site contains local advisories about the safety of eating seafood from your local lakes, rivers, and coastal areas. www.epa.gov/ost/fish

Special Supplemental Nutrition Program for Women, Infants, and Children (WIC)

WIC provides Federal grants to states for supplemental foods, health-care referrals, and nutrition education for low-income pregnant, breastfeeding, and non-breastfeeding postpartum women, and to infants and children up to age five. The Web site includes information about how to apply for WIC and offers breastfeeding promotional materials from WIC's Loving Support Makes Breastfeeding Work national breastfeeding campaign. Breastfeeding mothers enrolled in WIC can receive breast pumps, breast shells, or nursing supplementers to help them overcome breastfeeding challenges and continue nursing. www.fns.usda.gov/wic/

U.S. Department of Agriculture (USDA)

The U.S. Department of Agriculture offers tips and resources on the food pyramid, vegetarian diets, and more. www.mypyramid.gov; www. mypyramid.gov/tips_resources/ vegetarian_diets.html

Other Sources of Information and Support

Cleft Palate Foundation (CPF)

CPF is a nonprofit organization dedicated to optimizing the quality of life for individuals affected by facial birth defects. www.cleftline.org

Doulas of North America International (DONA)

DONA provides information and research to mothers and families about birth and postpartum doulas, childbirth, and the postpartum experience. DONA also provides quality training and meaningful certification for doulas. www.dona.org

Dunstan Baby Language

Pricilla Dunstan, an Australian mother with a rare photographic memory for sound, has identified specific crying sounds that represent a universal baby language. www.dunstanbaby.com

LactMed

LactMed (part of the National Library of Medicine's Toxicology Data Network) is a free online database with information on drugs and lactation. www.toxnet.nlm.nih.gov

Medications and Mothers' Milk

Dr. Thomas Hale's comprehensive reference has information on the impact of more than eight hundred drugs, vitamins, herbs, and vaccines on breastfeeding mothers and infants.

www.ibreastfeeding.com. Information for health professionals is available. http://neonatal.ttuhsc.edu/lact

National Down Syndrome Congress (NDSC)

NDSC is a nonprofit national organization whose purpose is to promote the interests of people with Down syndrome and their families through advocacy, public awareness, and information on all aspects of Down syndrome. www.ndsccenter.org

National Down Syndrome Society (NDSS)

NDSS is a nonprofit organization whose mission is to benefit people with Down syndrome and their families through national leadership in education, research, and advocacy. www.ndss.org

National Organization of Mothers of Twins Clubs (NOMOTC)

NOMOTC is a nonprofit organization representing more than 450 local clubs that provide mutual support for parents of twins and higher-order multiples through education, research, and networking. www.nomotc.org

Postpartum Support International (PSI)

PSI is a non profit organization whose mission is to increase awareness among public and professional communities about the emotional changes women experience during pregnancy and postpartum. PSI disseminates information and resources through state volunteers, the Web site, and an annual conference. www.postpartum.net

Web Sites Devoted to Breastfeeding Information and Support

Breastfeeding.com

This comprehensive site for breastfeeding information and support includes blogs, groups, forums, and more. www.breastfeeding.com

Breastfeeding After Breast or Nipple Surgery (BFAR)

This Web site provides information and support to mothers who wish to breastfeed after breast or nipple surgery. www.bfar.org. The sister Web site, www.lowmilksupply.org

is a resource for information about assessing and increasing milk production and supplementing in ways that are supportive of breastfeeding.

Kellymom

This comprehensive Web site provides evidence-based information on breastfeeding, sleep, and parenting. It offers free handouts in pdf format for individual use. www.kellymom.com

Your State or County Breastfeeding Coalition

Check out the Web site for your state or county breastfeeding coalition for updates about statewide initiatives, local events, breastfeeding legislation, and general information.

Index

preparing to nurse, 48–51
reading feeding cues, 57–59
removing baby from breast, 55
self-consciousness and, 51–52
supporting breast, 50–51
unrestricted breastfeeding, 46
Breastfeeding National Network (BNN), 296
Breastfeeding problems, 193–236. *See also specific problems*
common early problems/concerns, 62, 94–105
indicating illness, 103–104
mothers and babies who need extra help, 72, 73
when to get help, 84–94
where to get help, 104–105
Breastmilk
benefits of. *See* Benefits of breastfeeding
collecting. *See* Breast pumps; Expressing milk
coming in, 62, 79, 89, 91, 284
compared to formula, 6–9
containers for, 151–152
donated, 232
feeding, breastfeeding vs., 158
foremilk, 83, 211
hindmilk, 83–84, 146, 211, 229, 242
how it is made and released, 79–82
increasing supply of, 146, 228–231, 253–254. *See also* Low milk supply
meant for babies, 5–6
nutritional content, 7–8
as perfect food, 7–8, 9
storing. *See* Storing milk
thawed, reusing, 154–155
thawing frozen, 154
transitional and mature, 79
transporting, 154
unpleasant smelling/tasting, 155
Breast pads, 24, 81, 92, 103, 168, 198–199, 203, 209–210, 251, 293
Breast pumps, 24, 138–140. *See also* Expressing milk
availability/effectiveness, 135, 158, 248–249

basic parts of, 137
cleaning, 150–151
condensation in tubing, 150
cost of, 35
daily-use double, 139
double, 138–140
hospital-grade, 82–83, 139–140, 295–296
insurance covering rental cost, 140, 274, 275
maintaining, 150–151
occasional-use, 138
recommended frequency of use, 142–148
rental models, 24, 35, 82–83, 138–140, 143, 295
resources for, 295–296
rubber bulb ("bicycle horn"), 139
single, 138
as single-user devices, 139
sources for, 295–296
time required at work, 248
types of, 138–140, 250
WIC providing, 22–23, 105, 295, 296
Breasts. *See also Nipple references*
alternating (switch nursing), 84–85, 95–96, 101, 229
changes when pregnant and breastfeeding, 289
infection of (mastitis), 206–208, 249, 255
internal structures, illustrated, 27
intimacy connection, sex and, 130–132
leaking, 24, 209–210, 251
lumps or masses in, 33
partner appreciating, 13–14
plugged milk ducts, 203, 204–206, 254–255
prenatal changes, 26–28
prenatal enlargement, 29
radiation therapy of, 30, 225, 287
sagging, 33
shape of, 29–30
size of, 29
storage capacity, 144, 149, 246
surgery on. *See* Breast surgery
symmetry of, 30

H

Habits, personal, 166–167
Head circumference, 173–174, 226–227
Help. *See* Support
Hepatitis, 279–280
Herbal products, 166, 230
Herpes, 131, 280–281
History of breastfeeding, 17–18
HIV, 232, 278–279
Hormones
  in breastmilk, 8
  for contraception, 170–171
  disorders affecting milk production,
    225
  involved in milk production and
    release, 12, 27, 80–81. *See also*
    Oxytocin; Prolactin
  postpartum depression and, 121–124
  pregnancy, decline in, triggering milk
    production, 99
  pregnancy, and breastfeeding, 287–288
  pregnancy, stimulating development of
    glands and ducts, 26, 291
Hospital
  Apgar score, 42
  baby in, for illness, 276–277
  baby's second night in, 60–61
  breastfeeding practice standards,
    36–37
  choosing, 37–38
  early skin-to-skin (STS) contact, 41–44
  follow-up after leaving, 74
  getting most from experience in, 59–60
  lactation consultants in, 15, 71, 74,
    104–105
  policies promoting breastfeeding,
    36–37, 44–47
  rooming-in, 45
  starting breastfeeding in. *See*
    Breastfeeding (getting started)
  unrestricted breastfeeding in, 46
  visitors, 60–61
  you in, for illness, 282–283
Human milk. *See* Breastmilk
Human Milk Banking Association of
  North America (HMBANA), 296

Husband. *See* Dads (partners)
Hydrating yourself, 58–59
Hygiene, 168
Hypoglycemia, 67

I

Illness. *See also specific illnesses*
  breastfeeding baby with, 276–277
  breastfeeding when you have, 277–278
  feeding problems indicating, 103–104
  hospitalization for, 276–277, 282–283
  protection against, 8. *See also* Immune
    properties, of breastmilk
  psychiatric, 281–282
  serious infectious diseases, 278–281
Immune properties, of breastmilk
  benefits, 5, 6, 7, 8, 9, 44, 48, 152, 239, 259
  donated breastmilk and, 232
  heating breastmilk and, 156
  premature/high-risk babies and,
    259–260
Immunodeficiency virus (HIV), 167, 232,
  278–279
Induced lactation, 289–291
Inflammatory bowel disease, 8, 281
Insurance
  covering breastfeeding services, 15
  covering donor milk cost, 232
  covering pump rental cost, 140, 274,
    275
Insurance pumping. *See* Prevention
  (insurance) pumping
International Lactation Consultant
  Association (ILCA), 296
Iron, 11, 175, 181, 182
Inverted nipples. *See* Nipples, inverted

J

Jaundice
  in newborns, 97–98, 99
  as a symptom of hepatitis, 279

K

Kangaroo care of premature infants, 43,
  145, 263. *See also* Skin-to-skin (STS)
  contact